From Protest to President

From Protest to President

A Social Justice Journey through the

Emergence of Adult Education and

the Birth of Distance Learning

GEORGE A. PRUITT WITH
MELISSA A. MASZCZAK

RUTGERS UNIVERSITY PRESS
NEW BRUNSWICK, CAMDEN, AND NEWARK,
NEW JERSEY, AND LONDON

Library of Congress Cataloging-in-Publication Data

Names: Pruitt, George A., 1946- author.
Title: From protest to president : a social justice journey through the
emergence of adult education and the birth of distance learning /
George A. Pruitt ; with Melissa A. Maszczak.
Description: New Brunswick, New Jersey : Rutgers University Press, 2023. |
Includes bibliographical references and index.
Identifiers: LCCN 2022010236 | ISBN 9781978829749 (cloth) |
ISBN 9781978829756 (epub) | ISBN 9781978829763 (pdf)
Subjects: LCSH: Pruitt, George A., 1946- | African American college
administrators—Biography. | African American college presidents—
Biography. | African Americans—Education (Higher). | Thomas Edison
State University—Presidents—Biography.
Classification: LCC LA2317.P78 A3 2023 | DDC 378.0092 [B]—dc23/eng/20220419
LC record available at https://lccn.loc.gov/2022010236

A British Cataloging-in-Publication record for this book is available from the British
Library.

References to internet websites (URLs) were accurate at the time of writing. Neither
the author nor Rutgers University Press is responsible for URLs that may have expired
or changed since the manuscript was prepared.

♾ The paper used in this publication meets the requirements of the American National
Standard for Information Sciences—Permanence of Paper for Printed Library Materials, ANSI Z39.48-1992.

www.rutgersuniversitypress.org

Manufactured in the United States of America

Contents

From Protest to President

Chapter One

It's not the cards you're dealt, it's how you play the hand.

—Randy Pausch

On October 7, 2017, I sat in a crowded but elegant ballroom at The Palace at Somerset Park, New Jersey, and listened as former governor Tom Kean provided remarks in my honor. The occasion was a gala to celebrate my retirement from the presidency of Thomas Edison State University after thirty-five years in office. As I gazed across the ballroom filled with colleagues, friends, and family and listened to the generous words echoing from the stage, I couldn't help but marvel about what a long way this was from my grandparents' home in Canton, Mississippi, where I was born, or the South Side of Chicago, where I grew up. I never thought about a career in higher education. For as long as I could remember, I was set on becoming a medical doctor, but I played the hand I was dealt and never looked back.

My father, Joseph H. Pruitt, lived in Chicago and worked for the Illinois Central Railroad, where he met my mother, who was a passenger on his train. After a brief long-distance courtship, they were married in my grandparents' living room in Canton in July 1940 and caught a train to Chicago that afternoon to begin their lives together.

My mother's brother, George Albert Carmichael, my "Uncle Doc," graduated from Meharry Medical College, class of 1933. When he finished his internship and residency, he returned to Canton, where he practiced medicine for fifty-five years. For much of that time, he was the only Black physician in town. For the Black residents of Canton, Uncle Doc was a one-man "Affordable Care Act." He performed surgery, delivered babies, set broken bones, acted as his own radiologist, and was generally responsible for the health care of Black folks in Canton and the surrounding countryside. He treated everyone who needed him, whether they could pay or not. He accepted homegrown vegetables, fruit, and chickens for payment. He paid for medication out of his own pocket when his patients couldn't afford it. He was affiliated with the Afro-American Sons and Daughters Hospital in nearby Yazoo City, Mississippi, the only hospital for Black people in the area. An extraordinary staff of Black physicians, nurses, and health care professionals managed it.

When my mother was expecting my brother, she left Chicago and returned to my grandparents' home to give birth. Uncle Doc delivered my brother, Joseph Henry Pruitt Jr., on May 29, 1941. My mother always joked that the local gossips were counting the days to see if nine months had elapsed from the time my parents got married until Joe was born. It had, but it was close.

In September 1941, my mother's older sister Daisy also gave birth to her son, Percy Abram, in what was becoming the "Carmichael Family Nursery," also known as our grandparent's bed. Five years later in 1946, my mother returned to Canton, and under Uncle Doc's care, she delivered another healthy baby boy. She was so sure she was having a girl that she only had one name chosen: Andrea Pearl Pruitt. That didn't work out for her, and she ended up with me instead. My brother was named after our father, and I was named after Uncle Doc. My identification with my uncle turned out to extend far beyond our shared name. He was one of the greatest influences of my life.

The Carmichael Family Nursery under Uncle Doc's medical supervision continued its legacy with the birth of my cousins. In January 1948, my mother's younger sister, Evie, gave birth to my cousin Evie Helene Wilson. In November 1952, Evie's other daughter, Janice Amelia Wilson, was born.

Mississippi and Chicago were two of the most segregated, oppressive, and violent places in the United States. For many years, my brother and I, along with Janice and Helene, would spend holidays and many long, hot summers in Mississippi. Our father stayed in Chicago, and Janice and Helene's father stayed in Philadelphia for work, but in Canton, we all had Uncle Doc and his wife, Aunt Bert.

In the '40s, '50s, and '60s, Chicago was the second largest city in the United States and the most segregated, with the largest concentration of Black people in the country. The Great Migration brought millions of Black people north to escape the segregation, violence, and oppression of the South and to seek economic opportunity in the cities. New York had over three times the population of Chicago, but with around the same number of African Americans, who were scattered among the city's five boroughs. In Chicago, they were segregated in the city's sprawling South Side.

While my father worked on the railroad, he put himself through the Worsham College of Mortuary Science at night and became a licensed funeral director and mortician the year I was born. Dad ran on the railroad between Chicago and New Orleans and conducted funerals when he was in town.

Though my mother, aunts, uncle, and cousins were all born in Canton, my aunt Daisy would lose her life there. Daisy Carmichael Abram was beautiful and bright with an effervescent personality. About two years after her son, Percy, was born, she was expecting her second child. One day, she was sitting at the kitchen table when, suddenly, she belched up a glob of bright red blood. She called Uncle Doc, and he immediately recognized that she was bleeding internally.

He put her in his car and raced to the hospital in Yazoo City about thirty miles away. He drove straight past the White hospital in Canton because he knew they would not have treated her. When he finally got to the hospital, they didn't have enough of her blood type. The closest blood bank for Black people was in Jackson, about fifty miles away. He left her at the hospital and raced to Jackson. By the time he returned, Aunt Daisy and her unborn child had both died. I don't know what was on the death certificate, but being Black in Mississippi was the real cause of death for my aunt Daisy and cousin. They died three years before I was born, but my family and I have never gotten over the pain of their deaths and its attendant rage.

In 1955, about two weeks after my mother, brother, and I returned to Chicago from our annual summer visit to Mississippi, we heard about Emmett Till. Many Black folks living in Chicago were from Mississippi. Like my family, they migrated straight up the Illinois Central Railroad line and settled on the South Side, returning in the summers to visit their families. Black people returning or visiting from the north were singled out as special targets for harassment. They had to be reminded of "their place" and where they were, which was *not* up in Chicago.

My grandfather George M. Carmichael was a kind, gentle man. The only whipping I ever got from him was for wearing my Cub Scout uniform out in public. When I first got there and he saw it, he looked at "Chicago" printed on the shirt and told me never to wear that out of the house. Several weeks later, I had it on when a friend of my mother's offered to take us to the ice factory for snow cones. I forgot my grandfather's warning as I jumped in the car. When I returned, he saw what I had on, pulled off his belt, and reminded me.

For the record, we did not get spankings; we got whippings, administered by either a switch or a belt. We were generally well behaved, and it was rare, but the deterrent value was unmistakable. Even then, I understood that my grandfather was trying to protect me from the kind of violence, brutality, and horror suffered by Emmett Till.

Emmett Till was taken from his family's home in the middle of the night, beaten to death, mutilated, and thrown in a river. He was fourteen years old, the same age as my brother. We were all outraged. The people who were responsible for this atrocity were arrested but were acquitted by the all-White jury. There was no question about their guilt. Emmett's mother insisted on an open casket, so the whole world could see what they had done to her son.

My father was a friend of Mr. Rayner, the mortician who handled the arrangements. When Emmett's body was brought back to Chicago for the funeral, people lined up around the block to see it. Dad drove me and my brother to the mortuary, where Mr. Rayner let us in the side door to see his body. There are some things you never forget. That was one of them. I was nine years old. I know there are some who would criticize my father for exposing us to that, but I appreciated and respected what he did.

Gruesome pictures of Emmett's body were published in the *Chicago Defender* newspaper as well as *Jet* magazine. My father never wanted us to forget what kind of place we were in when we were in Mississippi. It was the same spirit of protection that my grandfather showed when he disciplined me for taking needless risk, walking around Mississippi with "Chicago" displayed on my shirt.

I never felt safe there. If you were Black in Mississippi, vigilance and trepidation were necessary survival tools. Political campaigns were contests over who could spout the most hateful, racist, and venomous speech in a quest to get votes from the all-White electorate. I had a special contempt for Governor Ross Barnett. Many years later, I returned to Canton to visit Uncle Doc and Aunt Bert. Earlier, the Pearl River had been damned to create a beautiful reservoir for flood control and recreation. Instead of driving directly up the interstate to Canton, I decided to take the scenic route up along the Natchez Trace. I was horrified when I came upon a sign naming this picturesque creation the Ross Barnett Reservoir. I found a suitable private place, got out of my car, unzipped my pants, and paid my respects to the former governor.

"No Place to Be Somebody"
—Charles Gordone

The South Side of Chicago had become the largest ghetto in the United States. When my brother and I were born, my parents lived in a small apartment at 6144 Vernon Avenue. Housing in Chicago was rigidly segregated. With the exception of Hyde Park around the University of Chicago, there were no integrated neighborhoods. There were Black neighborhoods, White neighborhoods, and those in transition, but there were no "diverse" communities. There were Polish, Greek, Italian, Jewish, and Irish neighborhoods, each with its own politics and culture. It was a tribal city.

Richard Daley was the mayor and a master of coalition politics. He was Chicago's undisputed "boss." To those outside Chicago, that was a bad thing. To those living in the city, not so much. During the height of the civil rights movement in the sixties, I spent a lot of my energy opposing the mayor's policies in public education and housing, but I respected and sometimes even admired his leadership skills in running the city. Chicago was known as the "City that Works." It worked largely because of Richard Daley. Public transportation was excellent, and snow removal was quick and efficient. I went to public school from kindergarten through high school, and I never knew that some cities in the rest of the country closed schools because of snow. The city's downtown was beautiful, and the parks and beaches were plentiful, clean, and free.

Daley was a boss, but he knew how to maintain the support and loyalty of Chicagoans. If your apartment didn't have heat in the winter, you didn't call the city to complain; you called your Democratic Party precinct captain. If your uncle had a little too much to drink and you needed help, you didn't call your lawyer; you called your precinct captain, and you got help getting him out of jail. If you really needed a job, you called your precinct captain, and you might get one of the 50,000 patronage jobs available in the city. The precinct captain was local, liked in the community, and hardwired into the Democratic Party, through the channels of city government straight up through the alderman to the mayor. When election time rolled around, those same precinct captains would remind everyone that this whole system worked because of the mayor and his organization. The mayor took care of a lot of people, and a lot of people took care of the mayor.

During the 1968 Democratic National Convention, the nation witnessed the riotous behavior of the Chicago police and the belligerence of an angry mayor. The following election, Mayor Daley was reelected by his biggest plurality. Had he not died in office, he would have been mayor for as long as he wanted.

The Chicago public school system was organized and built around a network of neighborhood schools. The advantage of this was that most Chicago schoolchildren walked to school. The downside was that the schools, like most neighborhoods, were segregated by race. Racially segregated schools are never equal. Public schools in the ghettos of the South Side and the West Side were overcrowded with deteriorating facilities, poor equipment, limited cocurricular activities, and, with some exceptions, less qualified teachers than schools in White neighborhoods.

Another consequence of growing up in a segregated city was the economic and class diversity of the neighborhoods. No matter how well off, a person of color would not be able to buy and live in a White neighborhood. As a result, the 6100 block of Vernon, when we were living there, was an interesting mix of class and professional status. There was at least one physician, several attorneys, teachers, and college-educated Black folks living in the apartment buildings there. Several of them owned the buildings they lived in and received the income from their investment.

The South Side was so large that it created its own economy, which in turn supported a large Black business and professional community. There were Black-owned businesses, banks, insurance companies, cosmetic companies, a newspaper (the *Chicago Defender*), and Johnson Publications, which produced *Jet* and *Ebony* magazines. The best-paying, large institutional employers were the railroads, the steel mills, and the federal government, especially the massive Chicago Post Office. Because the federal employment system made discrimination more difficult, it was a mecca for college-educated African Americans. We used to joke and refer to the large downtown central postal facility as "the University of Chicago," because so many college-educated Black people worked there.

Violence is an unfortunate aspect of southern culture that knows no racial boundaries. Southern hospitality is authentic, but so is southern brutality. Because I followed Uncle Doc around in Canton, I watched, and sometimes helped him, tend to a host of gunshot wounds, stabbings, beatings, and all sorts of mayhem. Having a mortician for a father and a doctor for an uncle, there isn't much that can gross me out.

Chicago was and is violent, too. The first time I remember confronting this personally, I was about six or seven years old. I was riding my bicycle on the sidewalk, and when I reached the corner, I saw a puddle of fresh blood about the size of a saucer. The victim had been removed, as well as all the signs of a crime scene, but no one cleaned up the blood. I found out when I got home that a man had been killed there earlier. No one ever cleaned up that blood. It eventually dried up, but the black stain it left on the sidewalk and in my memory remained.

I started elementary school at A. O. Sexton, which was on the corner of 60th and Evans, about a six-block walk from my home. From first grade on, we all walked to school, came home for lunch, and walked back for afternoon classes. When I entered high school, the violence escalated. A small group of my friends and I had a gun pulled on us at a go-cart track. I had more than a few friends who were jumped on the street, often after parties by people who couldn't get into them. It never happened to me, but I had my share of close calls. It was a good thing I had a lot of friends and knew a lot of people.

At midnight on New Year's Eve, I was calling my girlfriend, and though I don't think I was the target, a bullet pierced the phone booth. One of my closest friends' mother was robbed in the vestibule of her apartment building. The basement of our home was burglarized while we slept upstairs. Four of my classmates were shot and killed. The atmosphere of potential violence was pervasive. You were always vigilant and alert. You lived with that tension, got used to it, and took it for granted. To this day, I look with amazement when I see people leave their cars unlocked and the doors and windows of their homes open. Not me—dead bolt locks and an alarm system.

My parents had been considering moving out of our one-bedroom, one-bath apartment for some time. My brother and I slept in twin beds in what was meant to be a dining room, and as we got older, we outgrew it. I remember my father getting a notice that the rent was increasing to over $90.00 per month. Also, my brother would soon be graduating from eighth grade and heading to high school. My father decided it was time to start looking for a house.

Joe is incredibly smart and was an excellent student. At his graduation, he received every academic award and honor available. Despite the location of the school, he had great teachers who didn't want him to go to the high school he would have to attend in our neighborhood. It was dangerous and academically weak. They encouraged him to apply to attend Emil Hirsch High School. Unfortunately, we didn't live in Hirsch's district, and the school was practically all White. My parents tried to use the address of a relative and claim that Joe lived with him, but that plot was discovered, and his enrollment was blocked. It was then that my parents decided to buy a house in Hirsch's district.

The only available houses were in White neighborhoods. The options in Black neighborhoods were limited to apartments, but as you went farther south, the apartments gave way to single-family homes. Black families had trouble acquiring mortgages for homes in White neighborhoods because the banks denied them loans and some real estate brokers would refuse to show them houses. As Black families began encroaching on White neighborhoods, White residents fled. If Black families managed to overcome all the barriers to become homeowners in these White neighborhoods, they could be subjected to death threats and property damage.

It was in this environment that my parents purchased a three-bedroom, one-bathroom bungalow at 7653 Vernon Avenue, the same street, fifteen blocks farther south. It was a different world. After we closed on the house, we waited to move in. Dad wanted to make repairs, paint, and spruce up the house before we moved in. He also wanted to see if there would be any attempt against the property by our new neighbors. There wasn't; nevertheless, my father kept his pistol on the nightstand by his bed after we moved in.

The stereotype is that when minorities move into a neighborhood, property values go down as well as the maintenance, upkeep, and appearance of the community. In fact, the opposite occurred. The Black families that colonized our neighborhood improved and maintained their homes better than the people who fled the area. For Sale signs began to proliferate, and White flight from the communities was soon in full bloom.

My new school was Martha Ruggles Elementary School. I was in third grade. Again, I walked about four blocks to school. Again, I went home for lunch and returned in the afternoon. This time, instead of concrete and asphalt, I walked past green, manicured lawns in front of modest well-kept homes. Instead of maneuvering around winos and the occasional junkie who had nodded off on the curb, I passed dog walkers. Most of the school was White with only about 20 percent Black students. I developed close friendships with some of my classmates that endure to this day. For me, the transition was easy, and I recall no tension, racial or otherwise.

My brother's transition was not as smooth. He finally got to Hirsch, but the early years were hostile. His experience once he got to school was OK, but getting there could be a problem. Chicago was a city of well-defined boundaries. To Hirsch from our house, you had to cross Cottage Grove and go three blocks farther to Ingleside Avenue. Black kids caught alone east of there were often attacked. To deal with this, my brother and about six of his classmates, boys and girls, would rendezvous at a corner and cross Cottage Grove in a group. At the end of the school day, they would reconvene and reverse the process.

Despite the harassment, my parents' decision to move and secure a better education for my brother proved to be the right one. Hirsch was a

good school. It had competent, well-qualified teachers, adequate cocurricular activities, and his teachers and classmates alike recognized his academic ability. He was admitted to and became the first African American
president of the Hirsch High School chapter of the National Honor
Society.

When he graduated in the winter of 1959, he was admitted to the University of Illinois with two scholarships. In Chicago, the academic year was
divided in two semesters. Depending on your birthday, you could begin
in January or September. My brother began school in September, but
because of his scholastic achievement, he was granted a "double promo-
tion," skipped a grade, and graduated a semester early.

The Black incursion and White flight we were a part of accelerated into
a stampede. When I graduated from Ruggles and went off to Hirsch in
1960, I didn't recognize the school my brother had enrolled in five years
earlier. By then, my neighborhood had become mostly Black, and so had
Hirsch. The school became overcrowded, cocurricular programs were
eliminated, and portable classrooms were brought in to handle the over-
flow. Many inexperienced and uncertified teachers replaced experienced,
well-qualified, and certified teachers who transferred to White high
schools or retired. There were some good teachers left, including the best
teacher I would ever have, Mary Ann Clancy, a math teacher.

When I reported to Hirsch as a freshman, some of us were selected to
participate in honors classes. There were special honors sections for
English, math, and history. The classes were small, and we got the best
teachers. After my sophomore year, they created sections of "high honors" classes for only twelve of us.

While there is often controversy about this kind of merit-based differentiation, and it always raises issues of equity and inclusion, there is no
doubt that those of us selected for this special treatment benefitted enormously. We were pushed and challenged, toughened and stretched. Some
of it was painful, particularly at the hand of three very challenging and
often oppressive English teachers.

We were fortunate to have Miss Clancy for five of our eight semesters of math that included geometry, trigonometry, and advanced algebra. I remember her telling us early on, "The objective of this class is not to teach you mathematics but to teach you how to think, and math is the vehicle to that end." She did teach us math—and how to think. She also taught us how to be independent and critical in our thinking; how to reason and make our own judgments and decisions and not mindlessly follow what we were told; how to challenge and push back against things that were illogical, irrational, and not based on evidence or truth.

She would solve problems on the blackboard and purposely make mistakes. If we didn't catch them and correct her, we'd get extra homework that evening. She told us to always review and correct the mistakes we made on our tests. Occasionally, she would randomly mark a right answer wrong just to see if we would catch it and correct her. If you didn't, she would call you out in public, and you would keep the lower score on your exam. It happened to me once, but never again. She was engaging, demanding, witty, and caring. We liked what she was selling, and we soaked it up with enthusiasm. The problem was that the rest of the faculty hadn't bought into the notion of independent and self-empowering thinking. The three English teachers whom I dubbed "Macbeth's Witches" were the complete opposite of Miss Clancy, and we would engage in combat with them for five of the eight semesters we had to endure.

When I was about seven years old, I got kicked out of Sunday school for questioning my teacher. I didn't like going to Sunday school, especially because it conflicted with my Sunday morning television show, *Flash Gordon*, but my father made me go. I never cared much about Flash Gordon the character, but Doctor Zarkov fascinated me. He was the greatest scientist who ever lived and the predecessor to Mr. Spock on *Star Trek*. No matter what calamity Flash and his colleagues encountered, give Zarkov five minutes in a lab, and he'd find a solution. MacGyver had nothing on him.

This particular Sunday-school lesson was about Jonah and the whale, complete with animated pictures. Like a lot of young people, I have always been fascinated by whales and dinosaurs. I knew it was physically impossible to live in a whale, but I was prepared to go along with the metaphor. My mother's aunt Idella, the most religious, devout Christian I had ever met, was having dinner with our family that afternoon. When she found out I had learned about Jonah and the whale that morning, she smiled, pulled out her Bible, and began reading the related passages. I politely listened, but my attention was captured when she read, "Jonah was taken by a great fish!" Well, I knew immediately that there was a problem here, because a whale is not a fish! For the first time in my life, I couldn't wait to get to Sunday school. As soon as the class started, I raised my hand and informed the teacher that I had found a mistake in last week's lesson and told her the story had to be wrong because a whale is not a fish.

Clearly, she was not a Miss Clancy. She basically told me to sit down and shut up; the story was right, and I was wrong. I informed her that there was a conflict between what the Bible said and what the story said, and I chose to believe the Bible. That made sense to my classmates as well. She evidently didn't see it that way, kicked me out, and sent me home. I was respectful in the way I argued my case, but she was having none of it. Frankly, I was afraid to go home. I didn't know how my father would react. He was not tolerant of misbehavior or disrespect. Although I knew he had had a mischievous streak of his own when he was young, I was nervous when I explained what happened. I was relieved when he smiled and took my side.

He was proud and didn't take any "stuff" from anybody. More than once he told us, "I want you to be successful in whatever you choose to do, but I'd rather see you digging ditches than kissing someone's ass." That must have been in the Black father's handbook, because years later when I was at Tennessee State University, Sterlin Adams, a colleague and good friend, said that his father had told him the same thing. That same spirit got me kicked out of Mrs. Stuckey's English class the first semester of my senior year for standing in solidarity with a classmate who dared to express an independent thought. The stark contrast in cultures from Miss Clancy's class to Mrs. Stuckey's was painful.

You don't get to tell me who I am.
—Malcolm X

Just as I liked to follow Uncle Doc around Canton, I did the same thing with my father in Chicago. That entailed sitting around Miller and Major Funeral Home, near the corner of 63rd and Cottage Grove. One day I walked down to a busy barbershop on 63rd Street. There was a charismatic man holding forth from a barber's chair. It was Malcolm X. Chicago was home to the Nation of Islam's founder, Elijah Muhammad. Malcolm was his most influential spokesperson and spent a lot of time in Chicago even though he lived in New York. At the time, I had never heard of him, and he had not yet burst onto the national scene. He fascinated me. His message of self-reliance, self-determination, and personal empowerment was appealing. He was also masterful in articulating the anger, frustration, and impatience with the oppression everyone in our communities felt.

He liked me because I would spar with him. Members of the Nation of Islam rejected the last names they were given at birth. Their view was that Black folks lost their legitimate names when they were captured, brought to this country, and given "slave names." Members of "the Nation" viewed these slave names as illegitimate. They understood that their "real" names would never be known, so they replaced last names with the letter X. Malcolm's last name was Little. When he converted, he became Malcolm X. When he told me that Pruitt was my slave name, I countered that it wasn't. It was my father's name, and I didn't care who had it before he did. Malcolm shook his head and laughed.

Many mistakenly believed that because he was not "nonviolent," he was violent. That is not true. He taught personal discipline, respectfulness, and courtesy. He and other members of the Nation did not smoke, drink, or use drugs or profanity. He also followed a strict Muslim diet. Malcolm believed that all people had the right to protect themselves from violence. He always abhorred acts of violence committed by White people against

African Americans. He didn't approve of violence and crime against Black people by Black people either.

Martin Luther King's tenets of protest through nonviolent direct action were taken by law enforcement as license to beat and physically abuse protesters without fear of retribution. Malcolm, on the other hand, preached that you had a right to protect yourself by "any means necessary," even against a police officer. Malcolm was famously quoted as saying, "Be peaceful, be courteous, obey the law, respect everyone; but if someone puts his hand on you, send him to the cemetery." White people vilified Malcolm as a violence monger. While Martin Luther King Jr. was the object of hatred on the part of many White people, they were not afraid of him. Many were terrified of Malcolm X, but he was one of the most inspiring and persuasive speakers I had ever heard, exhorting Black people not to feel, think, or behave like victims.

In Kenneth Clark's famous "doll study," which Thurgood Marshall used in his arguments before the Supreme Court in *Brown vs. Board of Education of Topeka*, Black children were given a White doll and a Black doll. The children described the White dolls in positive terms and the Black dolls negatively. It was a powerful demonstration of the brutal effects on personal perspective caused by coerced segregation and discrimination. Low self-esteem leads to self-loathing, which leads to feelings of helplessness and disempowerment.

Malcolm's voice and message had a profound effect on the psyche of African Americans in the country. Malcolm would later leave the Nation of Islam and its extreme views and embrace a more inclusive and broader view of fellowship of all men and women regardless of race. Muhammad Ali is often famously quoted as saying, "You don't get to decide who I am," but those were Malcolm's words.

Miss Clancy wasn't the only good teacher we had at Hirsch. There was Mr. Thomas and Mrs. Katz in history, Miss Otto in chemistry, Mr. O'Hara in band, and then there was Roy Stell. Mr. Stell was an activist and taught Modern World History when we were seniors. By now, the sixties had begun in earnest. I remember someone telling me that I was a product of the sixties; I replied that the sixties were a product of us. The civil rights movement wasn't organized or monolithic. It was a term used to describe thousands of local autonomous micro insurrections occurring in communities across the country.

While Martin Luther King Jr. was the movement's most visible figure and spokesperson, he did not create it or direct it. He served it. The disparity between the all-Black schools and the White schools was striking. Public schools in Chicago were separate and unequal. It wasn't just the schools. Chicago has beautiful beaches along the shores of Lake Michigan. Blacks were allowed on two of them: 55th Street Beach, also known as "The Point," and 63rd Street Beach. The next beach farther south was "Rainbow Beach." It was for Whites only. It was not the law, but it *was* the fact.

In July 1961, an integrated group attempted to use Rainbow Beach. Despite the presence of police, the demonstrators were attacked and beaten. That incident triggered a series of organized demonstrations until the beach was finally integrated. Many Whites left the area and refused to use the beach again.

The unequal conditions in the public schools led to protests, demonstrations, and lawsuits. The administrative hierarchy of the second largest public school system in the country, from the superintendent to the local schools, was all White. At Hirsch, while the honors classes had competent, well-trained teachers, the regular classes often did not. One time I was asked to set up and operate some audiovisual equipment for an English class. While I was operating the equipment, I noticed that the teacher was mispronouncing the name of the River Thames in London. While it is spelled T-h-a-m-e-s, it is pronounced "Tims": I knew that and was appalled that the person hired to teach a class on Shakespeare did not.

Our physics class was taught in a hallway by an uncertified, part-time teacher. We had no laboratory, so he described the experiments using pictures of equipment we didn't have. He also regularly made mistakes in math that the "Miss Clancy–trained" students constantly pointed out. He was frustrated, and we were angry. It wasn't that the teachers, facilities, and equipment weren't available; it was that they were only provided to the White schools. We wanted to do something about it.

Two of our classmates, Alice Best and Beverly Postell, organized a local chapter of the Student Nonviolent Coordinating Committee (SNCC), a new student-led civil rights group. Mr. Stell served as our unofficial adviser. In Chicago, the SNCC was focused on the conditions in the public schools. Black teachers organized as well, and those who supported student activism were at risk for retribution. Mr. Stell gave testimony in several of the investigations and lawsuits brought against the public school system. He was smart, well educated, and committed, and he cared deeply about our welfare and future.

The symbol and object of our protest was Chicago superintendent Benjamin C. Willis. The portable classrooms set up in trailers in the parking lots were nicknamed "Willis Wagons." Calls mounted for Willis's removal. The concept of neighborhood schools was a good idea, but they were administered in a way to perpetuate overcrowding and segregation. It didn't have to be, but it was, and that was a choice, and race was a factor. Plans began to take shape for a boycott of public schools to protest conditions and demand Willis's removal. SNCC groups took the lead in coordinating and planning for a citywide boycott. At Hirsch, Alice Best and Beverly Postell organized and led the preparations. My work at Hirsch supporting Alice, Beverly, and our classmates, with Mr. Stell's encouragement, initiated my personal engagement in the civil rights movement.

On October 2, 1963, Black students in the city of Chicago participated in the first boycott of the Chicago Public Schools. At the White schools it was a nonevent, but on the South Side, which comprised over half of the system's enrollment, participation in the boycott was overwhelming. When we came back to school, students spontaneously began singing civil rights songs in the hallways. Something important had happened, and we were a part of it. I was a part of it, and it felt good. I was in the game, and I would never get out.

I wish I could say that the story had a happy ending. It didn't. Willis did leave, and the system underwent profound change. Some short-term improvements were made in redistributing resources. The administration of the system and the schools increased the diversity of its leadership, but the attention to producing quality outcomes for students went down the drain.

About twenty years later, I would be on a panel at a conference with Bill Bennett, who at the time was serving as secretary of education under President Reagan. We disagreed about many things, but one of the things we did agree on was that the Chicago Public School System had become one of the worst in the country, and while there has been some attempt at managing reforms, its struggle continues to this day.

In my senior year at Hirsch, Mrs. Paulette Katz, a great history teacher, was assigned responsibility for the Program Office, where the class schedules for all students were created. To assist in this, Mrs. Katz assembled a large staff of student workers and asked my friend William Ware and me to serve as student managers. Among the student workers was a cute little sophomore named Pamela Moffett. While Pam was adorable, she was just a sophomore. I was a senior, so she was too young for me to flirt with, but she had an infectious personality and was fun to be around.

We were in the office alone on November 22, 1963, listening to the radio, when the program was interrupted to announce that President Kennedy had been shot in Dallas. I felt like I had just been punched in the stomach. Pam and I looked at each other speechless. Word spread through the school, and everyone was somber. We did not know then the extent of his injuries or even if he was alive. We all went home. I got there, turned on the television, and heard Walter Cronkite announce to the world that President Kennedy was dead. The sixties as a decade of assassinations had begun. I would run into Pam Moffett thirty-four years later, and in 2001, we would share another national tragedy together.

I graduated from Emil Hirsch High School in June 1964. The night of our graduation, my friend Eugene Adams and our girlfriends double-dated at a famous nightclub in Chicago: Mister Kelly's. We had no business being there. The drinking age in Illinois was twenty-one, and the nightclubs in Olde Town wouldn't let you in unless you were twenty-three. We were about a month shy of eighteen. Eugene's mother had a colleague who played in the house band at the club, and he arranged for us not only to get in but to get the best table in the house, right at the foot of the podium where the singer would be performing, and tonight it was no ordinary performer. It was Nancy Wilson. She sang to me all night long, and I fell in love. From that day on, I bought all of her albums and watched her perform whenever I could. On one occasion, I actually got a chance to meet her. I told her about Mister Kelly's, and she laughed. Today, I have a playlist dedicated to her on my phone.

I always knew that I was going to college. It was expected of me, and of course, I was going to be a doctor like Uncle Doc. I laugh today, when I hear my colleagues discussing consultant reports and data about what informs a student's college choice. For me, I was chasing a girl. When I was sixteen, I met Toni Dancy and fell in love. She was fifteen. It was the first time I'd ever felt this way about anyone I'd ever dated, and I was ready to retire from the field. I had met "the one"; we were perfect together, and the world was a wonderful place. Then tragedy struck. Her mother announced that she was moving to Los Angeles, and she was taking my Toni with her. We were both heartbroken.

Her mother asked if I would drive them to the train station when they were leaving town. On January 24, 1963, I shoveled my father's car out of the snow and ice. The temperature was below zero as I put Toni and her mother on a Union Pacific train to Los Angeles. It was something out of a movie. I was on the train platform with tears freezing on my cheeks, and she was at the window weeping as the train pulled away. We were not prepared to accept defeat. We wrote once a week and called when we could. I was on the phone with Toni when that bullet came through the phone booth. Long distance calls were expensive then, and besides, I would go to college in Los Angeles, and we would reunite. We just had to hang in there until then.

While my choice of colleges had a broader purpose, my father was more practical. He said that I could go to any school as long as I got a scholarship. I applied to the University of Illinois at Champaign, where my brother went after he received the Illinois State Scholarship Award and a scholarship from the Pullman Foundation. I also applied to the only two schools in Los Angeles I knew of: the University of California, Los Angeles (UCLA) and the University of Southern California (USC). Unfortunately, UCLA rejected me, the only school to do so. They admitted very few out-of-state students, and USC accepted me but didn't offer any scholarship assistance. I received several other small scholarship offers, but the matter was settled when, ironically, I received the same two scholarships my brother had to the University of Illinois. Though my heart was broken, fate had spoken.

Chapter Two

Being smart is not enough.

—Alan Guarino

In 1964, the University of Illinois was one of the country's great public research universities and the most selective public university in the state. Straddling the borders of the twin cities Champaign and Urbana, it was a city unto itself. With 35,000 students, it had its own public transportation system, police department, hospital, and telephone system. To my knowledge, only one member of the faculty and less than 1 percent of its students were African American.

Although it was only 125 miles from the South Side of Chicago, it might as well have been on the other side of the moon. The campus is in the middle of central Illinois corn country. In fact, the oldest cornfield under continuous cultivation in the United States, named the Morrow Plots after Professor George Morrow, is located on the quadrangle.

The faculty was populated with academic superstars, including more than one Nobel Prize winner. I had a chemistry class in Noyes Lab named after a former chair of the chemistry department, William Albert Noyes. Professor Noyes discovered that the ratio of hydrogen to oxygen atoms in water was two to one (i.e., H_2O).

While the university had students from all over the world, great facilities, state-of-the-art laboratories, and a wonderful cultural life (including its own symphony and opera company), it was not a welcoming place for students of color. We couldn't even get our hair cut on campus. We had to travel to Tommy's, a Black barbershop in Champaign. The university was indifferent. The dilution was so great; we were invisible.

In the four years I spent as an undergraduate, five semesters at the University of Illinois and three semesters at Illinois State University, with one exception, I never shared a class with another student of color, and I never had a class taught by a faculty member or graduate student who wasn't White. While the university was not openly hostile to the few of us who were there, it wasn't hospitable either.

I enrolled in the university as a premed major. Many of my courses involved labs in which you shared your workstation with a partner. When I went to my first labs, everyone averted their eyes when I walked in. It was clear that they were afraid that I might sit next to them. I ignored it and picked a seat that made sense. When I was in the lab, my classmates rarely spoke to me. Other students formed study groups ahead of big exams, but I was never included. Though there were many people in the room, I was alone.

While taking a course in inorganic qualitative analysis, we had to identify and analyze contents of a sample. I had an uncommon aptitude for lab work, but I was totally stumped by my results. I tried every test multiple times, and the results didn't make sense. Frustrated, I went to the instructor, showed her my notes and findings, and asked for help. She reviewed my notes and watched me repeat the analysis. She was puzzled, too. She took the sample, ran the analysis herself, and got the same results I did. Finally, she took my sample and dumped it into a sophisticated machine analyzer. She came back later red-faced and told me that my sample was contaminated. She concluded that while I was away from my station, someone had spit in my sample. Nothing like that ever happened again, but I also began taking better care of my stuff.

I think every freshman who goes away to college, particularly to a big, prestigious state university, wonders if they belong there. Are you prepared? Are you as smart as the other kids? Can you handle it? For a Black kid from a South Side inner-city high school, I had all these thoughts and more.

The university wasn't totally foreign to me. It was demystified when I visited my brother, and we had a lot of fun. I wasn't afraid, and I was reasonably confident that I would do OK. That notion was challenged twice during my first week of classes. In my first zoology class, our instructor posted the "typical" grade distribution he expected at the end of the course. This was a demanding, five-credit-hour science course specifically for students in premed, biology, and zoology. There were about two hundred students in a large, lecture hall. He indicated that he did not grade on a curve, and if experience held up, he expected that a majority of the class would receive D's and F's. At the end of the semester, that was true.

Self-doubt crept in during my first general chemistry class as well. We were asked to retrieve and calibrate our Mettler balances from the storage locker. I had never seen nor heard of a Mettler balance. I watched my classmates go to a cabinet, pick up these contraptions, and bring them back to their stations. I did the same, but then I had no idea what to do with it. I quietly got the attention of my instructor and told him I didn't know what to do. He was surprised but gracious and showed me how to calibrate and use the equipment. When the course started, I was relieved. Good old Miss Otto, my high school chemistry teacher, had prepared me well, and I could hold my own after that first hurdle.

My last semester English teacher in high school, Mrs. Price, asked if I was going to college. I told her I was going to the University of Illinois at Champaign-Urbana. She laughed and asked if I had a backup plan because, given my writing, I would never pass the university's freshman rhetoric requirement. With her dire prediction lingering in the back of my mind, I began freshman rhetoric. We had to write a theme each week. I got a B on every theme and a B in the course. I thought about sending my grade report back to her, but I decided to take the high road and move on. To be honest, I don't think I've ever moved on or forgotten what she said. She told me I was going to fail, but I was determined not to.

At the time, there were only about 250 Black students in the entire university. We were the only support system we had, so by necessity, we all

knew each other. The only Black student organizations on campus consisted of three fraternities and two sororities. These Greek organizations
were the primary source of our social life. There weren't enough of us to
have more than one party at a time, which was usually sponsored by one
of these organizations. For most of the time I was there, Kappa Alpha Psi
was the only one that owned a house. When I visited my brother, I stayed
with him there. It was a lot more polished and sophisticated than "Ani-
mal House," but the general idea was the same.

I had great respect for the other Black students at the university. The
entire community—students, faculty, and staff—were a collection of capable people. You had to be, to be there in the first place, but there was a
special bond and camaraderie among the African American students. We
all knew what it was like to try to survive in places that could make you
feel alienated and irrelevant.

Even though the admissions process was rigorous, the attrition rate was
horrendous. It seemed to follow some perverse form of survival of the fit-
test. Thousands of intelligent students came to this university to experience failure for the first time. The suicide hotline number was printed on
the front page of the *Daily Illini* university newspaper.

My old friend William Ware went to the University of Chicago. His
experience was in sharp contrast to mine. There, if you were good enough
to be admitted, you were good enough to be successful, and they welcomed
you into a community committed to making that happen. There was no
sense of community at the University of Illinois. Just thousands of names
and numbers sorted through a process of natural selection. The university seemed to take pride in the famous people who couldn't make it to
graduation there. At the end of the semester, we didn't ask our classmates
how they did; we asked if they would be back. I knew of an entire residence hall floor who flunked out after one semester.

The attrition rate for African American students was much higher than
for the general student body. The Black students who didn't survive were
just as smart, with the same grades and test scores upon admission as the

other students, but the additional strain of navigating such an uninviting place was crushing. It wasn't the smartest who survived but the ones who persisted despite the alienation. The second semester of my freshman year, nine of us pledged Kappa Alpha Psi fraternity. At the end of the semester, only three of us achieved the grade point average required for initiation. Remember, we were all "the smart kids."

On February 21, 1965, Malcolm X was assassinated in New York City. Millions of African Americans across the country received the news in shock and disbelief. I remembered how I'd felt when President Kennedy was shot. This was worse, much worse. This was deep and personal. I was grief stricken and outraged at the same time. The sense of both personal and collective loss was profound.

Time magazine published a story about Malcolm's death using a mug shot from before his conversion. It was completely dismissive of the enormous contribution and impact that this extraordinary man had on uplifting and empowering the lives of millions of people all over the world. I was infuriated. I had to write my weekly theme for the second semester of my freshman rhetoric class. I wrote about the loss of Malcolm and the injustice of the *Time* magazine article. As in my first semester, but with a different instructor, I'd continued my streak of a B grade every week. This time I got my one and only A in the course.

While there were not many of us at the campus, by 1965 we had become increasingly dissatisfied with the exclusion of Black students, faculty, and staff. Remaining invisible was no longer acceptable. We brought a spirit of activism and sense of engagement spawned by the civil rights movement from our home communities to the university. We began to discuss organizing not around fraternities, sororities, and social life but around civil rights, equity, opportunity, and inclusion. We were angry, and we felt moved to change things.

Black students began to talk about developing a different kind of organization focused on social justice. The conversations evolved into organized meetings. Widespread discussions led to proposals about bylaws, organizational structures, mission, membership, and leadership selection. A pervasive sense of social consciousness had changed the nature of our conversations. Instead of grades, sports, and parties, we talked about politics, civil rights, protest, strategy and how to support direct action that was taking place throughout the country. We had taken responsibility for our self-education and participation in the civil rights movement. The organization we created was the University of Illinois Black Student Union (BSU).

Elections were held, and my good friend from Chicago Dan Dixon was elected as the BSU's first president. We engaged in negotiations with the university administration and issued demands calling for the creation of a program to recruit five hundred new African American students. The initiative was called Project 500. An engaging African American educator, Clarence Shelley, was recruited from Wayne State University as dean of students, to manage the initiative. While the hiring of Dean Shelley and the commitment to provide financial aid and housing for these students represented a serious investment by the university, the first semester of Project 500 began with a massive failure.

The new students arrived on campus only to find out that the promised residence hall space and financial aid had not been provided. Everyone was incensed. In a display of defiance, students took over the Student Union Building. As the building's closing time approached, the university's security forces moved in and detained Dean Shelley and many of the students. Watching all of this was a case study in what not to do. I never fully understood what caused the lack of preparation on the university's part, but it was a useful lesson for events in my not too distant future.

I really don't know why I took German. It was the dumbest academic decision I would ever make. I really believe that I have a kind of undiagnosed dyslexia. I can read, write, and speak just fine. Spelling is sometimes a problem. I have always enjoyed the benefit of a great memory, but I don't think I'm capable of learning another language. I first noticed it when I took Latin in high school. Since I was going to be a doctor, Latin was supposedly a good idea. It was useful in my college biology courses, but I didn't really learn Latin; I memorized it. That was good enough to get me through the minimum requirements. I also noticed it in my music. I took up playing the French horn in high school. I loved playing it and had a propensity for it. By the time I was a junior, I was first chair in the concert band.

The French horn is keyed in F. The problem arose when I was given music to play that was written for some of the French horns that were keyed in E flat. Other horn players could transpose the music in their heads as they read it and play the piece correctly. I couldn't do that. I would take the E flat horn music home, get a sheet of blank music paper, and physically write out the transposed music, so I could read and play it.

Many years later, I was asked to evaluate the Defense Language Institute at Monterey Bay California for the U.S. Department of Education when the institute sought degree-granting authority. The Defense Language Institute is an extraordinary institution. It is the federal government's vehicle for training those in service to our country to be fluent and proficient in foreign languages. They have been at this for years and understand the science behind foreign language learning and instruction. They understand that it starts with inherent ability. You can't teach aptitude; you're born with it, and I wasn't.

Why German? Spanish, French, Italian, maybe, but German? What was I thinking? I had a sympathetic instructor in the class. She took pity and gave me a passing D grade. I received a letter from the dean's office my junior year reminding me that if I intended to graduate, I would need to complete three more semesters of German or four semesters of another language of my choice. I had a dilemma, and fate stepped in.

I happened to meet a visiting science major from Illinois State University (ISU). He let me know that a bachelor of science degree at ISU did not require a foreign language. I became immediately interested in Illinois State University. While it didn't have the stature and prestige of the University of Illinois, it had a great reputation, particularly in the quality of undergraduate instruction. I didn't care about prestige. ISU was an excellent university, but most importantly, I wouldn't have to take German. I decided to transfer.

One day, I got on a bus for the fifty-mile ride to Bloomington/Normal, home of ISU. I made an appointment with an admissions counselor and discussed the university's transfer requirements. I was notified that because I was in good academic standing at the University of Illinois, I would be accepted automatically to ISU, and all my credits would transfer as well. I asked for an admissions application to fill out while I was there. The counselor suggested that I wait until the end of the spring semester, so I would only need to send one set of transcripts. I told him that I didn't want to wait because I was concerned about getting my application in before they closed transfer admissions. I will never forget what he said: "Young man, Illinois State University is the oldest public university in the state, and we have never closed transfer admissions. Wait until the summer, and you'll be fine." With that assurance, I got back on a bus and returned to Champaign.

When the spring semester ended, I filled out my application and requested my transcripts. I asked the registrar if I needed to do anything else because I was not planning to return. I was advised to fill out a form withdrawing from the university. I then packed up my belongings and headed home to Chicago to find a summer job.

One of the best jobs I ever had was in the summer of 1966 when I became a coin collector for Illinois Bell Telephone Company. There are probably millions of people walking around today who have never seen a pay telephone, but in 1966, they were everywhere. One of my friends, Lance Arnell, suggested that we go to the National Urban League to seek a job referral to one of the many companies offering summer jobs to minority students. We were both sent to work at Illinois Bell.

Every day, fleets of trucks left central offices, fanned out to collect coins from thousands of pay phones across the city, and returned at the end of the day with tens of thousands of dollars in nickels, dimes, and quarters to be sorted and counted. It amazed me how much money could fit in the small rectangular box at the bottom of a pay phone.

The district office I was assigned covered downtown, the Loop, the Near North Side, the Near South Side, and Lake Front. Every morning we were given a stack of IBM punch cards with the address, location, and phone number of each phone to be collected along with a set of individual keys unique to each one. At that time, the early computers predicted when a phone would be full and in need of collecting. Each driver would collect about eighty phones a day depending on their locations. We loved train stations, large hotels, and especially McCormick Place Convention Center because they had huge banks of phones lined up next to each other. I loved the job. I worked alone through all the best parts of the city, seeing things and places I'd never seen before.

I was conscientious and on my first day wanted to do a good job. I quietly went about my collecting and surprised everyone back at the office when I returned early. When the rest of the staff came in at the end of the day, they were not pleased. They explained to me that I should never come in early again. I was told to "pace myself" and spread my work over the entire day. It was a summer job for me, but it was their regular gig, and they didn't need some eager college kid messing up the workload for the rest of them. I understood and did what I was told.

I loved the freedom, the access I had, and now the extra time to explore. I collected Mister Kelly's nightclub, where I fell in love with Nancy Wilson and listened to Sarah Vaughan rehearse for her show. I collected the downtown beaches and ate my lunch with a breathtaking view of the water and other inspiring sights lounging on the sand. I watched movies when I collected movie theaters. I collected the Playboy Mansion when Hugh Hefner lived in Chicago. The things I saw there were, well, awe-inspiring.

Chicago was the railroad passenger center of the country. No train passed through Chicago. They all originated or terminated there. Luxury rail service was still alive, and the train stations for Union Pacific, Santa

Fe, New York Central, and the Pennsylvania Railroads were often filled with celebrities and entertainers from all over the world. I collected the pay phones in the dressing rooms of two burlesque theaters on State Street just south of Van Buren. This was pre-porn America, and the dancers' stage performances would be considered downright boring against today's standards. But in those dressing rooms, they took delight in trying to shock and embarrass this twenty-year-old college kid. They succeeded, and for that, I am eternally grateful.

As the summer of 1966 neared its end, things were good for me. That was about to change. By August, I was concerned that I hadn't heard anything from Illinois State University. I wasn't worried about getting in given the assurances I had from the admissions counselor, but I was worried about getting housing. I wanted to stay in the residence halls until I had a better sense of the other options in my new town.

I called the admissions office at ISU to find out why I hadn't heard from them. The person I spoke to told me that I had not been granted admission because they had closed transfer admissions before my application arrived. I was alarmed. I recounted the conversation I had with the admissions representative in the spring. She told me this was the first time they had ever closed transfer admissions. I responded that I expected them to honor the commitment of the representative I spoke to and allow me to enroll. I asked to speak with that person and was told he was unavailable and not speaking with denied applicants.

The next day, I got on a train and went to ISU to plead my case. I badgered my way into a meeting with the person who told me to wait. If I had filled out the application during my earlier visit when I wanted to, I wouldn't be in this mess. The representative admitted that his advice had been incorrect, but this was the first time they'd closed transfer admissions, and no exceptions could or would be made. I was troubled, but I decided to return to the University of Illinois and transfer at the end of the fall semester instead. I took the bus ride back to Champaign and went directly to the registrar's office to reenroll. I was told I would have to reapply but that the application deadline had passed. I was academically homeless and devastated. It also meant I would lose my student deferment, and I would almost assuredly be drafted into the service and the Vietnam War.

During the 1960s and '70s, there were suits filed against the gerrymandering of selective service, or draft districts. Because Chicago housing was racially segregated, selective service districts were drawn from White neighborhoods that had fingers reaching into Black neighborhoods. There was ample evidence presented in these court cases to demonstrate that African American young men were being drafted in numbers far greater than their representation in the districts.

At the end of each year of college, I lost my student deferment and was classified "draft eligible." Every year I appealed, and my student status was restored. I never knew why my draft board pursued me so aggressively. Now I wasn't in school at all. I was convinced that my whole world was at stake and in danger. I was opposed to the war, and I did not want to go to Vietnam.

Unlike many people at the time, I have never been antimilitary. I have always loved history, and I know and believe in the necessity of maintaining a strong national defense. I would later hear a general make a comment that "if the lion and the lamb are going to lay down together, it's always better to be the lion if you have a choice." I agree. There were many reasons why I opposed the war: moral, political, strategic, racial, and so on. And candidly, I felt some fear as well. I lost friends in that war, and others came back altered from their experience.

I did not want to go, and I sat in the Student Union Building at the University of Illinois contemplating the end of my life as I knew it. The expression on my face must have been telling because a distinguished-looking gentleman I didn't know approached me and asked if I was OK. I told him no. Actually, this guy was not a gentleman. He was an angel. His name was Warren K. Wessels, and he was associate dean of the College of Agriculture at the university. He inquired as to the nature of my distress, and I explained the situation to him. He said he thought what happened to me was unfair. I agreed. I had followed the rules and did everything I was told to do, and because of that, I got screwed. If I had filled out my application when I wanted to, I would have been admitted. If I hadn't formally withdrawn from the University of Illinois and just not gone back, I would have been free to return when ISU went sideways on me. But I did as I was told by responsible people in authority, and as a result, I was in trouble.

In matters of religion and faith, my beliefs are uncertain. I have always been afflicted with an inherent belief in logic and evidence. When I was a child, I never believed in Santa Claus. It never seemed plausible that in one night Santa could visit every child on the planet, and there was no way he was going to get past the double dead bolt locks on our apartment on 61st and Vernon. I never believed in the Tooth Fairy either. It just never made sense to me. On the other hand, I've always been awe-struck by the beauty, power, and wonderful complexity and order of the natural world. I've also been aware that people and opportunities have come into my life in ways that couldn't be explained by chance. In my psychology courses, I learned about Carl Jung's concept of synchronicity "to describe circumstances that appear meaningfully related yet lack a causal connection."

Be it faith, fate, luck, or synchronicity, I prefer to call it God. Sometimes God sends angels, and that day, he sent me Professor Wessels. He asked to see my documents and for my permission to call the admissions office at ISU. I said sure, and he left to go make the calls. I don't know what they said to him, but they really pissed him off. He took me to his office and immediately enrolled me as a student in the College of Agriculture at the university. I was back! He told me that I didn't have to take any agriculture classes, but I took the genetics course that I would have normally taken under the Biology Department from the agriculture school out of respect for my benefactor.

While I never saw Dr. Wessels again, I have never forgotten him or what he did for me. Thereafter, at each institution I served, I would tell my colleagues about his Samaritanship, which became known as the "Wessel

Principle." If an official gave a student bad advice, then the institution would do everything in its power to make the student whole.

One day, after I had been president of Thomas Edison for a while, it occurred to me that while I had told countless administrators and faculty members that story as a cautionary tale, I had never adequately expressed my appreciation to Dr. Wessels himself. I didn't know if he was still at Illinois, still working, or still alive, but I had to try to find him and thank him. I was successful. After a long career, he had just retired from the university. I sent him a long letter reminding him what happened and what he had done for me and the effect it had on my life and career. After I sent the letter, we were able to talk by phone. I was profuse with my expressions of gratitude. He had no recollection of any of it. For him it was not memorable; it was a common random act of kindness. Warren Wessels is an angel.

I finished my fifth and final semester as an undergraduate at the University of Illinois, and in January 1967, I began the second semester of my junior year as a biology major and chemistry minor at Illinois State University. While I didn't know it at the time, moving to ISU would change the arc of my life and put me on the path that has continued to this day.

Transferring from the University of Illinois to Illinois State was like moving from a city to a small town. While the University of Illinois had twice the enrollment of ISU, it had much more than that. It had world-class research centers and laboratories; faculty, researchers, and graduate students from all over the world; a magnificent performing arts center; and a 75,000-seat football stadium, huge basketball arena, and a cosmopolitan vibe that was incongruous with being located among the cornfields of central Illinois.

With over 17,000 students, Illinois State University was certainly not a small college, but Normal, Illinois, was the smallest town I would ever live in. It was another "twin city" with Bloomington, its bigger sister. Bloomington had the benefit of being the international headquarters of State Farm Insurance Company and Illinois Wesleyan University, a smaller liberal arts college. The only thing in Normal was the university. "Downtown" comprised a movie theater, a bank, and a few stores stretching over three blocks. There was almost no off-campus housing for students. This tiny, primarily White conservative town did everything in its power to ignore the university, which was laughable because the student population of ISU was much larger than the population of the town.

The sale, possession, and consumption of alcohol was illegal. Fortunately, Division Street, which divided Normal from Bloomington, was less than a mile from campus, and the National Liquor Store was on the Bloomington side of the boundary. We all referred to it as "the Bank." Every Friday after class, you could witness streams of students walking down Main Street on their pilgrimage to the Bank to make their withdrawal for the weekend. The tiny Normal police force preoccupied themselves playing cat and mouse in attempts to catch careless students with alcohol, mostly beer.

While Illinois State University didn't have the sophistication, size, or stature of the University of Illinois, it did have an excellent faculty committed to the education of its students. The contrast between the institutions was striking. There is no question that the quality of my undergraduate education at Illinois State University was superior to my experience at the University of Illinois.

When I was still in Champaign, I took the introductory psychology course. It was the largest single course at the school with over two thousand students the semester I was enrolled. I sat in the large lecture hall with about three hundred of my classmates and watched Professor Dulaney's taped lecture on video monitors positioned around the room. In one of his lectures on learning theory, he said, "Learning is most effective when instruction is personalized and takes into account the individual background and circumstances of the student." All of us in the room erupted in spontaneous laughter at the absurdity of our situation given the comments of our professor. All the students enrolled that semester took our midterm and final exams in the university's beautiful auditorium using computerized answer sheets. Our results were posted on a bulletin board using our student ID numbers. I never met Professor Dulaney.

At ISU, I met and spoke with all my professors. At the University of Illinois, the professors were well-respected scholars and authorities in their field, but I was always a spectator from the audience as they lectured from a distant stage. My professors may not have been famous at ISU, but they were scholarly, accomplished, and within reach in a classroom where I could engage, speak, question, and sometimes debate with them.

I left five semesters of accumulated friends back at the University of Illinois, so I spent the weekends of my first semester at ISU back in Champaign. Illinois State University was quiet, sleepy, and frankly boring compared to what was going on at the larger campus fifty miles away.

Of the 17,000 students at Illinois State, there were only 135 Black students, mostly from Chicago, with a smaller group from the Saint Louis region. As was the case at University of Illinois, out of necessity, we all had to find and know each other. If you were Black at Illinois State, you were automatically part of a fellowship, though there were no fraternities, sororities, or social clubs. We liked each other and got along. We had to.

As my first semester at Illinois State progressed, the expense and time commitment of my studies forced me to spend more of my weekends on my new campus with my new friends. I am grateful for the deep friendships I made at both universities, many of which continue to this day. I value those relationships more than any credits or credentials I earned at either place.

While ISU accepted all my credits in transfer, the distribution of those credits left some gaps that would require summer school. I would have to earn nine credits in six weeks. Most schools won't let you enroll for more than six credits; however, because I lived in Chicago, I registered for a three-credit course at three different schools.

While this provided a solution to my ISU graduation problem, it created additional challenges. It was expensive and limited the hours I could work. The heavy load had me in class from morning until night with a complicated commute between three campuses. Though I was interested in fulfilling the graduation requirement, life has a habit of teaching you some of its most important lessons from experiences that aren't part of any curriculum. That summer, I got a lesson in sexual harassment.

I was pleased to see that one of my friends from the University of Illinois was enrolled in one of my classes. A distinguished-looking professor with graying temples taught the class. I knew that taking nine credits in one summer session was ambitious, but I also knew that the grades would not transfer, only the credit. I wanted the best grade I could get but would be satisfied with a C in the course. I didn't even buy the textbook. There were about forty students in the class, and we met Monday through Thursday mornings, ending just before lunch.

On the last day of the first week, the professor stopped me as I was leaving to compliment me on the quality of a report I was selected by my classmates to present. I appreciated the acknowledgment. I thought nothing more about it and raced off to the next leg of my marathon day of classes and the intercampus gauntlet of buses and subways.

About a week later, I borrowed my friend's book the day before our first exam. Even though I was anxious about my preparation, I felt confident that I had at least gotten the C I needed. In class the following Monday, the professor handed back the graded exams to everyone except me. I raised my hand and told him that I hadn't received my test. He looked puzzled, said that he had given back all the exams he had, and didn't know where mine was; he then announced to the whole class that I had done very well and received an A. I was obviously pleased but surprised. My friend was ticked off. She'd bought the book, studied for the exam, and gotten a B, while I hadn't done any of that and gotten a higher grade than she did. I understood her frustration but figured that I'd just gotten lucky. I hadn't.

The professor would often stop me on the way out of class with some harmless banter, and it was clear that I had gotten his attention. At least, I thought it was harmless, and I was pleased to know he thought I was doing well. The grade for the course was determined by the grade on the midterm, which I had already "aced," along with the final exam and a paper.

Two weeks before the end of the term, he asked us to write down the topic we'd chosen for our papers and hand it to him as we left class. After I handed him my topic, he asked me to hang back a minute. He then showed me a handwritten note from one of my classmates, who had drawn a small circle over an *i* instead of a dot. He pointed to it, said it had "erotic" connotations, and asked me to join him for a drink after school. I was stunned. He was hitting on me. I had been clueless, but this time his intentions were very clear. I told him that I had to rush off because my next class was downtown. That was true. It gave me time to think, but I didn't know what to do. I didn't tell anyone. It dawned on me that he had given me an A and could just as well give me an F. What was always clear to me was that there was no way that I was going to do anything with him, whatever the consequence. I was anxious but also angry.

The next day after class, he stopped me again and asked when we were going to have that drink. I told him that my class schedule was a problem and that I didn't get back from my last class until ten at night. He said that he didn't think that was too late and that he could meet me. I told him I would get back to him. I confided in my girlfriend what was going on. Of course, she was enraged, too. Then, I remembered that her uncle, who I knew and liked, owned a bar around the corner from my class.

The next day, I told the professor that I would meet him after class at lunchtime for a quick drink at this particular bar. I told him that after school was just too late, and I was too tired. He accepted. I was miserable. That evening was my friend Eugene's twenty-first birthday, so the gang went out to celebrate. We all drank too much. The next day, I was in no condition to go to any of my classes, and it gave me a good excuse to skip my "rendezvous" with the professor. Instead, I had lunch with my girlfriend, who was working at Michael Reese Hospital. She asked me what I was going to do, and I told her that I really didn't know. I skipped the Wednesday and Thursday class as well. I knew that on Monday I was going to have to face him.

When he saw me, he was clearly agitated, like someone who had been stood up. I told him that I had gotten sick and had been at the hospital on the day of our "drink." I smiled inwardly; technically that was true. His countenance changed to one of concern. He asked again about rescheduling our drink, and I told him that the doctor told me, because of my stomach, I couldn't drink for a week. I offered to have lunch with him in the school cafeteria. He said we'd stay in touch and reschedule when I was feeling better.

At the end of the week, I took my final exam and turned in my paper. I asked if I could have my paper back when he finished reading it. He said yes, and he would arrange a time when I could pick it up. I felt I was almost home free. When I turned in my final exam, he gave me a slip of paper with the time and day I could come to pick it up. He also gave me his home phone number. I took a friend with me to his office to pick up my paper. First, though, I stopped at the registrar's office to see if he had turned in his final grades for my course. He had.

He wasn't there, but he had left a note for me to call him at home. I asked him if he had my paper there, and he said he didn't; it was at his office. He asked me for my phone number. I told him I was finishing school, didn't live with my parents anymore, and wouldn't have my own phone until after I got back to Illinois State. He asked me to send him my number when I had one. He said he would send me my paper when I let him know where to send it. I never got my paper. I got an A in the course, and I got away but not unscathed.

Just as I learned a life-altering lesson from an angel named Wessels, I also learned something unforgettable from a demon professor. I learned a hatred and intolerance for people in positions of power engaging in predation against people who have no way to protect or defend themselves. Later I served in executive leadership positions at six large organizations. I was always committed to use my influence to protect people against what I went through. I completed my three courses and returned to Illinois State University for my final year before graduation.

Chapter Three

Education is not the learning of facts, but the training of the mind to think.
—Albert Einstein

I have always objected when political leaders and public figures assert that the reason for going to college is to get a job. They cite data that shows that college graduates on average have higher incomes than non-graduates. That is true but not for the reasons they think. High-capacity people outearn low-capacity people, and higher education is a vehicle for developing high-capacity people. It teaches people how to learn, think critically, self-discipline, and self-motivate. It aligns behavior with consequences and accountability. It promotes team building, communication skills, and problem-solving. None of these constitutes a ticket to a particular job.

Less than 25 percent of college graduates in the workforce are in jobs related to their undergraduate major. I majored in biology and minored in chemistry, but I haven't been in a science lab since I finished my undergraduate degree. Of course, that is different if you are a teacher, nurse, architect, accountant, and so on, but for most of us, it's true. Vocationalizing college also marginalizes legitimate and important vocational training that prepares people for highly skilled jobs that often provide higher incomes than college-educated professionals. If you doubt that, you'll be reminded of it the next time you call a plumber, electrician, or mechanic. It also makes no sense to ask an eighteen-year-old what they are going to do for the rest of their life. By the time I reached Illinois State University, I was beginning to experience a change in my own plan.

For as long as I could remember, I was certain that I was going to be a doctor like Uncle Doc. When I was ten, I required an appendectomy. He reviewed the procedure with me in detail, including the anatomy and surgical technique and instruments he would use. When the procedure was over, he packed up my appendix in a bottle and gave it to me. I still have it. I have six medical doctors in my family. They weren't average doctors; they were extraordinary in their fields. Though I still love science, I realized that I didn't have the passion for medicine to be a doctor, especially not like the ones who came before me.

I was interested, even fascinated, by the science involved, but I wasn't in love with it. I knew that without that deeply felt passion, I could not sustain the discipline and commitment necessary to have a successful career in medicine. I realized that I didn't want to be a doctor; I wanted to be Uncle Doc, and that wasn't enough to get me through what I'd have to do. I think if Uncle Doc had been a plumber, I would have wanted to be a plumber, too. I no longer pursued a career in medicine.

For the first time in my life, I didn't know what I wanted to be, but I did know that I needed to finish college. I still love science. I'm fascinated by the mysteries of the natural world, medicine, Einstein's and Hawkins's mind-expanding reconceptualizations of the physical universe and time, and the pursuit of objective truth through evidence-based decision-making. I'm disturbed by an era of "alternative facts" and ideological pseudoscience. I'm horrified by the kind of thinking that cost Galileo his life when he committed "the heresy" of pointing out that the earth revolved around the sun and people who deny climate change and evolution, despite overwhelming evidence to the contrary.

I returned to Illinois State University in the fall of 1967 to finish my senior year. The country was caught up in social upheaval. The civil rights movement was in full bloom, and so was the antiwar movement and the women's movement. Questioning, examining, reexamining, and redefining was taking place everywhere. The one and only Black graduate student enrolled that semester was James Tate. Jim was a year older than me; we had both attended Hirsch High School and played in the band together. Jim was doing some graduate work in biology in preparation for medical school at Howard University. There were only two African American members of the faculty, a well-respected math professor, Dr. Charles Morris and Dr. Delano Kimberly Cox, a maize geneticist and former classmate of my brother's, whom I had met during my frequent visits to the Kappa House. There was only one Black member of the administration, Harry Shaw, who worked in the advancement division of the university. There was a small chapter of the NAACP, and Charles Morris was its advisor. While Charles Morris, Kim Cox, and Harry Shaw weren't students, we embraced them in our fellowship. We had great respect for them, and they would have great influence on us.

Early in the fall semester, we began having discussions about how we might impact, change, and reform the university to make it more accessible, responsive, and welcoming to people of color. We also wanted more diversity among the faculty, administration, student activities, and campus life. These discussions led to the formation of the Illinois State University Black Students Association, and I was elected its first president. We began to form strategies for approaching the administration, specifically, the newly appointed university president Samuel Braden.

We also had to think through precisely what it was we wanted. Campus protests were going on all around us, and some of them were violent. Some protests were well planned and thoughtful; others were groups of alienated people mindlessly acting out. We had no intention of destroying the university; we just wanted to change it. We methodically formulated what we thought were reasonable and achievable "demands," in hopes that the administration was willing to work with us.

African Americans made up approximately 12 percent of the population of Illinois. We felt that it was rational that a public university's student body should reflect the same proportionality as the population of the state. We recognized that there were "pipeline" issues for the faculty and administration, but we thought 12 percent was a sensible, aspirational goal. We discussed tactics and risks involved in demanding diversity in the speakers and entertainment invited to campus and the hiring of people of color among the executive ranks of the university.

We decided to occupy the administration building and issue our "nonnegotiable demands." We discussed the possibility of being arrested, expelled, or beaten. After weighing the risks, we decided to proceed. About fifty students volunteered for the occupation, although the support among Black students was almost total.

Given our size, we did not attempt to occupy the entire building but limited ourselves to the president's office suite on the top floor of Hovey Hall, the administration building. As the president, I was our spokesperson, and we gathered in an orderly, disciplined manner at the Student Union Building and marched next door to Dr. Braden's fifth-floor office suite. Having done reconnaissance, we knew that the hallway outside his suite was large enough to accommodate us. We also knew that he was on campus and would likely be in his office.

I approached the receptionist and indicated that we were there to see Dr. Braden, and we did not intend to leave until he met with us. After what seemed like a long time, although it probably wasn't, we were informed that he would meet with a small group of us. The officers of the BSA and I were ushered into his conference room and invited to sit down. Shortly thereafter, Dr. Braden came in. I read the list of demands and handed him a written copy. Braden was serious but not intimidating or intimidated. We had some brief dialogue. He had some questions, but they were more for the purpose of clarification than antagonism. He said that he needed some time to confer with his colleagues before he responded but assured us that he fully intended to do so. We both agreed that there would be a follow-up meeting. We reported to our colleagues in the hallway that we felt heard and agreed to leave the building. We exhaled, debriefed with our leadership, and felt we had achieved a promising beginning. No one was arrested, expelled, or beaten. President Braden seemed genuinely sympathetic and interested in working with us.

Our first negotiating session was scheduled for about a week later. Representing our side were Al Perkins, Ron Montgomery, Deborah Lindsey, Jim Tate, and myself. Prior to the meeting, our team met to discuss tactics and strategy and even role-played. Jim decided that since he was leaving soon for medical school that he would play the "bad cop"—hostile, militant, and demanding. I would be the mitigating "voice of reason," standing between the university and Armageddon.

On the day of the first meeting, we arrived a few minutes early to get a feel for the room. We were shown in and invited to sit on one side of the table. Soon after, two people entered and introduced themselves as representatives of President Braden. The first was Kenneth "Buzz" Shaw, executive assistant to the president, and the other was Paul Wisdom, associate dean of the faculty. If you wanted to know what Dennis the Menace would look like at thirty years old, it would be Buzz Shaw. Paul Wisdom was incredibly tall, about six feet seven or eight. I would later learn that both Shaw and Wisdom had been all-American basketball players: Paul at Dartmouth and Shaw at Illinois State.

We went through each of our demands, sometimes deploying the tactics we had practiced and sometimes not. By the end of the meeting, both sides agreed to a common set of objectives, and we decided that the next meeting would focus on implementation strategy. By the end of the next meeting, our negotiations had transformed into a collaboration. I didn't know at the time, but two more "angels" had come into my life. Buzz Shaw and Paul Wisdom would become two of my closest friends and mentors, and Buzz would become the reason that I would choose a career in higher education.

Because of our collaboration, the university agreed to pursue four major objectives: to increase the enrollment of African American students, increase the recruitment of Black faculty and staff, provide speakers and entertainment that enhanced the diversity of campus life, and reexamine the curriculum to reflect greater diversity in academic inquiry and course offerings. We wanted to increase Black student enrollment, but we didn't want to recruit students who wouldn't be successful and couldn't handle the rigor of the university.

From my freshman days at the University of Illinois, I always wondered why some students were successful and some were not. They were all smart. They wouldn't have been admitted if they weren't. This was before the days of remedial courses. You were expected to show up with the background and preparation necessary to be successful or suffer the consequences. I believe that nonintellectual variables differentiated those who would succeed from those who would not.

The university was not going to change for us, not right away at least. We had to find students who could succeed in it as it was. In the 1960s, both universities were harsh places for students of color. It was my view that the students who survived or thrived were the ones whose personalities and self-concept were strong enough to deal with the alienation, confront it, and overcome it.

Following our discussion with the ISU administration, the university agreed to support us in a Black student recruitment initiative to bring 150 new Black students to the university for the fall class of 1968. We had permission to offer admission to 175 students using criteria of our own design. We organized recruitment teams who enlisted current Black ISU students to go back to their home communities and use their contacts and credibility to persuade potential students to enroll. If they could deal with being stuck in Normal, Illinois, we could guarantee admission as well as room, board, and some additional assistance.

All the students we recruited qualified for some federal financial aid, although it was not a requirement. We also made it clear that just because we had "flexibility" in the admissions requirement, this was not a remedial program with compromised standards. To reinforce this point, we named the initiative the High Potential Students (HPS) program. We wanted to recruit students who had the fortitude, capacity, and perseverance to succeed in a place that was at best indifferent to their presence and at worst overtly hostile.

A panel of us interviewed every candidate. We were looking for three things: evidence that they possessed threshold academic capacity to handle the rigor of the university's programs; good communications skills; and that they demonstrated self-confidence and strength of ego to manage the consequences of being Black in the ISU/Normal environment. We did not necessarily select the students with the highest grades or test scores. Some of them were marginal in their academic records, but they all knew what they were getting into and felt ready for the challenge.

Those of us who planned and executed the project felt a strong sense of obligation to these students. We all felt a great responsibility for their welfare and success. Most of the teams were sent to Chicago, but teams were also sent to Peoria, Rockford, and the Illinois side of the Saint Louis area. Each team comprised a student delegation accompanied by a member of the administration driving a university vehicle. We launched this armada in the spring of 1968. In fact, we exceeded our numbers because as word spread, we began to attract other Black students who heard what we were doing and wanted to become a part of it. We even attracted two new graduate students, one from Alabama State and one from Grambling University. Whether we recruited them or not, we embraced them all.

When the fall semester of 1968 began, we increased the Black student enrollment of the university by over 150 percent. It was executed smoothly and without a hitch. The success of this initiative went a long way to reinforce the collaboration and trust between the Black student community and President Braden and his administration. The strength of that relationship would prove invaluable, as future events would test us all.

Chapter Four

Your profession is not what brings home your weekly paycheck, your profession is what you're put here on earth to do, with such passion and such intensity that it becomes spiritual in calling.

—Vincent van Gogh

Off-campus housing was difficult to come by for all students but nearly impossible if you were Black. People wouldn't rent to us, and buying property was difficult, too. Housing discrimination in Normal was severe. We were lucky; an African American woman owned a large house near campus and rented to us. She worked as a domestic for a wealthy White family in the suburbs of Chicago. She lived in their home and rarely visited her house in Normal. We called her "Granny." She was a feisty woman and enjoyed a glass of Hennessey when she was in town. We loved her and were very protective of her and her house. We voluntarily fixed up the place and kept it in good repair. We were all good friends, shared freely, and enjoyed each other's company. We were also all active in the BSA and the HPS recruitment program.

Ever since our takeover of the president's office, the Normal police began to patrol past our house and sometimes even park out front. I guess they wanted us to know they were watching. We were the closest things to "campus radicals" they'd ever seen. They were there so often that we even got to know one of them when we would stop by his patrol car to chat. It helped allay their fear of us and relax rather than view us as a threat. We were making progress and feeling hopeful about the future, and then our world changed.

On April 4, 1968, Martin Luther King Jr. was assassinated. We were horrified and grief-stricken. The grief turned to anger, and the anger turned to rage. Later that evening a classmate stopped by. He had tears in his eyes and handed me a large bag. Inside was a microscope from one of the science labs. He knew that I had a biology professor who was not one of my favorite people. He told me that he started a fire in this professor's office and had taken the microscope as a souvenir for me. I was angry. I told him that what he had done was mindless, stupid, served no purpose, and put me at risk by bringing evidence of a crime to my house, which was currently under police surveillance. He left quietly and took the microscope with him. I was relieved to hear that the fire was minor and caused no real damage. While I was against what he did, I understood and shared the rage he felt.

I left Normal and returned to Chicago for spring break. The day I got back, the tension in the city was palpable, and that night all hell broke loose, with some of the worst rioting the nation had ever seen. People felt that hope had been murdered along with Dr. King. People that have no hope feel that they have nothing to lose, and people with nothing to lose are dangerous people indeed. The entire country was engulfed in rebellion. The violence incited by the rioters and the response of law enforcement were out of control. The country shifted to the brink of a treacherous place.

When I returned to campus, life was hectic. I continued to work on the HPS program, while balancing my coursework. I was anxious about what I was going to do after graduation. One day Buzz Shaw asked me to work with him, Harry Shaw, and Charles Morris on a grant proposal to allow us to implement the three objectives that emerged from the collaboration between the BSA and the university. We completed the grant application and submitted it before the end of my last semester. We were successful, and the grant request was funded.

Buzz invited me to work at the university after graduation and go to graduate school tuition-free as an employee benefit. My title would be faculty assistant to the dean of the faculty and associate director of the High Potential Students program. Though Charles Morris would be titular acting director, I would have operational responsibility for running the program. Charles was widely respected by the academic community. Besides, no one was going to take seriously a twenty-two-year-old Black kid from the South Side of Chicago with a bachelor's degree. I saw their point. I didn't care about title or salary. I just wanted to see what we had started brought to fruition. I believed that we had begun something significant that would change people's lives and transform the university. However, it wasn't the only offer I had on the table.

I applied for an entry-level management position at the suggestion of my former manager at Illinois Bell. I did not think the interview went well. My interviewer, who was not much older than me, was patronizing, condescending, and dismissive. The encounter brought to my mind that definition of minority groups: "different, and the difference is held in low esteem." It was clear to me that he was skeptical as to whether I would be a good fit for the company. We finished the interview; I took the screening and placement exam and left. I was told that either way I would be contacted about the outcome.

I was invited back for a follow-up meeting. This time the vibe was different. I was warmly greeted, and after some pleasant small talk, he informed me that I was being offered a position with the company as district traffic supervisor, at a starting salary significantly higher than what I expected from ISU. I had received a high score on the exam and was selected for a management position. I was congratulated.

Given his earlier attitude, I thought it was OK to have a little fun at his expense. He deserved it. I asked what my percentile rank on the exam was. He said it was among the highest percentiles in the company. I smiled and nodded. I started to ask him what his score had been, but I didn't see the point. He looked at me at the first interview and immediately assumed, without knowing anything about me aside from my appearance (and I don't mean the suit I was wearing), that I wasn't qualified.

I had no idea what being a district traffic supervisor meant. I didn't know what the job entailed, and I had no idea what being a part of one of the world's largest corporations would be like. Illinois Bell Telephone Company was a part of "Ma Bell," AT&T. The AT&T Bell System has no analogous counterpart today, and it was one of the largest corporations in the world, before the government later broke it up. As the nation's largest utility, it was an efficient, benevolent, and well-managed monopoly, but it was a monopoly nonetheless.

I thought I would give it a shot, and if I didn't like it or if they didn't like me, I'd return to ISU. Besides, I had some time before I had to let ISU know if I was returning, so I accepted the position and marched off to join the ranks of corporate America.

The Traffic Department was statewide and enormous. The state was separated into divisions, and the divisions were separated into districts. Each district had three types of telephone operators separated into distinct operator groups with their own technology and training support depending on their function. There were three types of offices and operators. The first was Directory Assistance, reached by dialing 411. The second was Intercept, to handle numbers that had been disconnected or changed. The final office was by far the most important and would be one of the scariest places I would ever work. It was called Dial Service Assistance, or DSA. If you needed assistance in placing a call, you reached an operator by dialing the letter O. This was long before the days of 911, and when a DSA operator received a call, it could be anything: a medical emergency, a crime in progress, a fire, an urgent plea for help, a child playing with the dial, a psychotic rant from a mentally disturbed person, a suicidal person, or a lonesome soul in the middle of the night who just wanted to hear another voice.

The training these people received was outstanding, and the service they performed was heroic. I gave them the same respect usually reserved for firefighters, EMT, law enforcement, and first responders. I've heard of more than one operator talking people through the delivery of a baby. These were special people who never got the attention, recognition, or compensation they deserved.

The operators in each office were divided into sections headed by a supervisor. All of the operators were women, and all of the managers were men, and until I showed up, they were all White. I met an African American woman who had just graduated from the University of Wisconsin and was hired as a group chief operator. The two of us integrated the Traffic Department.

Bob McCann, division traffic manager, invited me to have lunch with him in the executive dining room at corporate headquarters. During the course of the conversation, I began to realize that the attention I was getting was because my appointment had broken the color barrier. Normally, a newbie peon in an entry-level management position wouldn't have access to the division head, but I think I became Bob's project. Aside from ethical considerations, Bob understood that in 1968, the absence of African Americans in the management ranks of a regulated utility was not a good idea. It made the company vulnerable to public criticism, potential regulatory problems, and even litigation. He pushed to change that, and I was the result.

The next time I would have lunch in the executive dining room would be with the company's chief human resources executive. Again, it was not lost on me how unusual it was that I was having lunch with such a senior executive. I asked him why they had hired me. I was educated as a biologist and chemist. I wondered why the phone company found value in that. He smiled and said that with the exception of the technical areas, such as accounting, engineering, and so on, Illinois Bell assumed that no undergraduate had any knowledge that was useful to the company at all. He went on to explain that the company hired people with college degrees for its management ranks because they knew how to learn, think, communicate, problem solve, work in teams, and were self-disciplined and self-motivated.

He said people with those skills could be taught everything they needed to know to contribute to the success of the company. He did not believe in vocationalizing higher education either.

If I was going to supervise telephone operators, I needed to be trained as an operator, and I was. The training in Directory Assistance and Intercept was easy. The training in DSA was nerve-racking. Fortunately, I was never confronted with any real crisis. The training was excellent, and we debriefed unusual situations to see what we could learn for next time or expand our training when confronted with something new. We were also obsessive about the quality of the service we offered. I saw the tangible value of organizational culture as a contributor to success in the marketplace.

I valued the use of relevant, useful data in evidence-based decision-making in determining what worked and what did not. I observed the consequence of analytical thinking and the clear and precise identification of company goals and performance objectives. I never forgot what I learned, and I continuously applied these lessons to the different circumstances I would find myself in going forward. Yet I remained conflicted. While I saw much to admire, I also saw other things I did not.

You didn't have to be particularly perceptive to know I was different. Everyone knew who I was. Though I was certainly not the only African American in the company's management, I never remember seeing another Black face in the executive dining room. As far as I could tell, I was "it" in the Traffic Department. I knew that I would be under scrutiny, and people would notice how I conducted myself. I was used to that. After all, I had gone to two all-White universities.

I knew that Bob McCann was trying to "evolve" the company, and I played a role in that, though I wasn't sure I was invested in it. At ISU, I felt I could contribute to changing the country, not just one institution or corporation. It was ridiculous that the management of the company was segregated, and that absolutely needed to change. At ISU, I could advocate for access to meaningful education, the ability to vote, the opportunity for people to choose the community they wanted to live in, or the right to purchase a home or to swim on a public beach. People were literally dying for these causes. Which change and challenge did I want to be a part of?

I made my decision after a meeting with Elmer Carlquest. Carlquest, a senior vice president and officer of the corporation, was head of the Traffic Department. One day, my boss informed me that Bob McCann was taking me to meet Carlquest. Again, I knew that this wasn't routine. Carlquest had the biggest office I had ever seen. I was impressed. The office itself made the statement that we were in the presence of someone important. Carlquest sat behind his desk, and McCann and I sat across from him. There was a lot of small talk. Carlquest asked me if I knew how much money my boss made. I told him I did not. He told me, and again, I was impressed. He then told me that there was no reason why if I applied myself, one day, I too could become a district traffic manager. While I think he was attempting to give me a "work hard and you can be successful" speech, that is not how I took it. The district manager was two promotions away from my current position, and while I was still brand new, it didn't take much to figure out that he saw a limited future for me. While I am not sure that was his intent, it was one more attempt to stunt my aspirations because of my race. In a respectful way, I wanted to let him know that I had heard him, but it wasn't OK. My response was, "What kind of effort is necessary to get in your chair?" McCann and Carlquest both turned red and took a minute to recover. He quietly responded, "Anything is possible." On the way out, McCann chuckled.

The next day, I called Buzz Shaw at ISU to accept his offer. Two weeks later, I called Bob McCann and told him I was leaving the company. He was not happy, and I appreciated his position. Part of his displeasure was that he thought I had used the company as a high-paying summer job. That wasn't true, but I understood why he may have thought that. The truth was that my values, passion, and interests aligned very well with my work at the university and not so much with the success of a huge company that had major issues with race, culture, and diversity. At the company, I could have had a career. At the university, I found my calling.

Upon returning to ISU in the fall of 1968, I moved into an apartment with my friend Al Perkins and quickly enrolled in graduate school. While the university's offer of free tuition was an amazing employee benefit, I understood that it was an unspoken requirement of my new job in academia. I wanted to pursue my graduate studies in biology, particularly molecular biology and genetics. The problem was that science courses came with heavy-duty laboratory requirements. I was now working full-time and wanted to earn my master's degree in two years. That was doable but not if I pursued biology. While I will always consider myself a scientist, at the time, the credential was more important to me than my interest in scientific studies.

Fortunately, when I had decided to evade the rest of my German requirement in Champaign, I had filled the space it left in my schedule with psychology courses. My brother likely influenced this. Just as I had, he'd enrolled at the University of Illinois as a premed student, and just like me, he figured out that he did not want to chase Uncle Doc either. He switched his major to psychology and, after graduating from Champaign, earned his PhD in clinical psychology at Western Reserve University (now Case Western Reserve). Because I had so many "electives" in psychology, I had satisfied all of the prerequisite undergraduate course requirements to apply and be admitted to the master's program in guidance and counseling.

To say that I had a full-time job was an understatement. The two hundred new students we recruited with the HPS program were now on campus and fully engaged. Transplanting two hundred self-confident, cocky activists from Chicago and the Saint Louis area to Normal, Illinois, brought change, but it also brought drama, and lots of it. There would be a continuous cacophony of issues and challenges, mini protests, and occasional conflict. Much of this happened in the evening or late at night. I was in the middle of all of it, and it frequently conflicted with my coursework. I finished in the two years I had set for myself, but it was often a struggle.

The reporting structure for my new position was a little convoluted. I reported to Buzz Shaw, who was executive assistant to the president. For the purpose of this particular program, Buzz also reported to Richard Bond, vice president and dean of the faculty. Because I was faculty assistant to the dean of the faculty, I reported to Bond, too. I was also associate director of the High Potential Students program. Charles Morris was interim director of the HPS program as well as a professor of mathematics. On paper, it made no sense, but it worked well.

Paul Wisdom, who was a member of the original "negotiating team" during the previous year's protest, was associate dean of the faculty and was a member of Bond's staff. The fact was that Buzz Shaw, Charles Morris, Paul Wisdom, and I were a team. We trusted and respected each other and were almost always on the same page; who worked for whom never came up. I believe that structure and alignment between responsibility, authority, and accountability are important, but in the end, structure is no replacement for a team of good people unified around a common purpose. The organizational chart was bizarre, but it worked for the university, our students, and the changes we were trying to make.

The university was organized into colleges and schools each headed by a dean. The deans reported to the vice president and the dean of the faculty. One day, Paul Wisdom called and told me that Dean Bond wanted me to join the weekly Council of Deans meeting. As a member of his staff, he thought I should attend. The deans, all gray-haired, distinguished-looking men, arrived, and I waited while they took their seats around the table. I assumed that they each likely sat in the same seat at every meeting, and I didn't want to infringe on anyone's turf. In addition to the school deans and Paul, another associate dean of the faculty, David Sweet, joined us. I was twenty-two years old and felt like the kid at the grown-ups' table at Thanksgiving dinner, though they never treated me that way. I was respectful, knew that I was out of my league, and tried to listen and learn as much as possible.

Sometimes at the end of the workday, I would stop by Bond's office, and often Bond, Wisdom, or Sweet would provide me with an in-depth tutorial on the spoken and, more importantly, unspoken dynamics of the meeting. It was an invaluable education from the highest level of the university's leadership. Buzz would also have frequent discussions with me as to how things were going from the perspective of the president's office.

One day at the deans' meeting, there was a discussion to change the way the university calculated student grade point averages when a student repeated a course. In the current practice, if you repeated a course, the higher grade would stand. The proposed change would use both grades in calculating the student's grade point average. I was concerned about the change for two reasons. First, I felt the grade should reflect the level of mastery of the content or "outcome," without regard as to what it took to achieve it, and second, I knew that many students used repeating courses to maintain good academic standing. At one of the after-hours conversations with Bond, I raised my concerns. He supported the new proposal because he thought it strengthened "academic rigor." I asked if I could do some research on the matter. I was particularly concerned about the effect on minority students.

Illinois State, like its fellow institution in Champaign, was a selective admissions university. I took a representative sample of the general student population and then looked at the transcripts of all the African American students. I recalculated their grade point average assuming that the proposed new policy was in place. The findings were dramatic. For both groups, the academic attrition rate went up, and the retention and graduation rates both went down. Bond asked that I present and defend my findings at the deans' meeting. At the end of a robust discussion, Bond acknowledged that the research and ensuing discussion had changed his mind. The deans agreed. I was validated and happy that I made a difference with my contribution.

Bond told me in our usual after-hours briefing that he was pleased with my work. He also told me that the reason he invited me to be a part of the deans' council had nothing to do with symbolism. He recognized that despite my youth, I had experiences and insights that neither he nor other members of his team had. He expected me to continue to participate and contribute to council discussions. His comments were both gratifying and humbling.

The progress at the university continued with recruitment efforts for Black faculty, staff, and students. George Taylor was recruited from Howard University to become associate dean of students. Ronald Jackson joined us from Washington University in Saint Louis as assistant director of admissions. Darryl Norton joined the Speech Pathology and Audiology Department. Lucille Smith worked with me in the HPS program. Sidney and Claire Hibbert joined the Theater Department as well as others. I cannot remember them all. All these new faculty and staff were welcomed, embraced, and engaged in our expanding community.

When I returned to the university to work, I stepped down as president of the Black Student Association. A fellow student and friend, Frank Bowen, succeeded me, but I never completely got out of the game. I felt relieved to give up the reins, so I could focus on the HPS program and the broader agenda that had come out of our initial demands. I missed James Tate but was happy that he went on to graduate from medical school.

I also found myself in charge of a campus speaker series. One of our original demands was for the university to begin programing that invited speakers and public figures to campus who would diversify the campus dialogue. I was responsible for managing, inviting, and hosting the speakers and guests. While it was demanding, it gave me a lot of one-on-one face time with some extraordinary people. Andrew Young, Jessie Jackson, Charles Hamilton, Val Grey Ward, and Fred Hampton, among others, were my personal guests when they arrived on campus to speak. It was an exciting and turbulent time.

There was a protest organized to address the housing issue for Black students, faculty, and staff in Normal. An open housing march began at the university and proceeded through "downtown." The march was orderly and, though integrated, mostly White. It was encouraging to see so many

White faculty and students marching in support of fair and open housing in Normal.

Ordinarily, Normal was a sleepy town, but on this night a number of citizens were awake, agitated, and angry. The marchers were attacked with rocks, sticks, and bottles. The police intervened, and order was eventually restored but not without injury. My friend and colleague George Taylor was hit and wounded by a bottle thrown by one of the townspeople. One of the consequences of the march and the ensuing violence was that it awakened many White students and faculty to the need to support civil rights and open housing. Eventually, the students and faculty started to register to vote in Normal and took over the town. It was a good thing.

Not all the drama we faced had to do with racial or social justice issues. Because of the lack of off-campus housing, Charles Morris bought a large house and converted it into a residence for students. A group of African American female students moved in. It was probably a good investment for Charles, but I don't think that's why he did it. Being a landlord for a bunch of college kids could be a challenge, particularly for someone who was as busy as he was. I think he did it because of the pressing need for students of color, and he saw a way to help. It also provided a safe place for us to hang out. I will never forget watching Neil Armstrong take the first steps on the moon on the television in the lounge area of that house. Hanging out in a house full of good-looking college women had other appeals as well.

As a community, we never felt entirely safe at ISU or in Normal. Many of us had been the objects of racial slurs and occasional threats. Because of my high profile, it was a regular occurrence for me. For the women living in this house, it was a real concern. We had no faith in the police to protect us. As a result, we established an emergency telephone chain so that if something happened over there, a series of calls would go out to summon the cavalry.

One night I got the call. It was one of the girls crying and asking for help. She said that Jerry Butler was in the house with a knife and to come over right away. She said that others on the phone chain had been called

as well. I was baffled. Jerry Butler was a freshman HPS program student
of small stature and friendly temperament. I could not imagine him acting like this, even if he had been drinking. I didn't take him seriously as a
threat.

When I drove up, several of the girls were out front on the lawn. They
told me that Butler had a knife and had one of the girls in the living room.
I walked in and immediately realized that the Jerry Butler I knew and
expected to see was not the one standing in front of me. Instead, there were
two guys, both my size or bigger, one with a knife in his hand at the throat
of the other guy who was sitting in a chair. One of the women was standing
in the middle of the room, trembling, tears rolling down her cheeks, with
her blouse unbuttoned. Another girl in the room explained to me that these
guys showed up, said they were on their way to Chicago from Tennessee
State University, heard about the house, and decided to stop by and visit.

The scenario that led to this was a little complicated, but it came down
to the question as to whether or not the girl would take her clothes off to
save someone's life. She said yes, and this other Jerry Butler pulled out a
knife, held it to his companion's neck, and told her he would slice his throat
if she didn't disrobe. He apparently convinced her that he was crazy enough
to do it. She unbuttoned her blouse and then froze.

I asked these two guys who I had never seen before, "What the f-ck?"
By now, other members of the cavalry were showing up, and I felt a little
more secure. I also knew that at least one of them was probably armed. I
asked the girl if these two guys were together, and she said yes. I took her
by the hand to lead her out of the room, explaining that if this guy cut his
friend's throat, it wasn't on her. She left. With the girl safely out of the
room, we now had to figure out how to deal with these two idiots. We had
enough challenges as it was, let alone having to deal with this. I cannot
share with you what we told them, but they clearly understood they were
not welcome to come back, and those of us with cars literally escorted them
out of town.

Chapter Five

We can choose courage or we can choose comfort, but we can't have both.
Not at the same time.

—Brené Brown

Robert Bone was President Braden's brilliant predecessor. He served as the university's president for over twenty-five years and transformed the institution from its teachers' college roots to a robust research university while maintaining a focus on quality undergraduate teaching and learning. He had a photographic memory and was multilingual. During World War II, he served in military intelligence and was active in support of the French Resistance movement prior to the Normandy invasion.

Dr. Bone assembled a group of the finest educators and leaders of any school in the country. Many of them went on to become extraordinary college presidents in their own right: Buzz Shaw, Jim Fisher, Jim Koch, David Sweet, Richard Bond, Michael Adams, and others. I could not have been exposed to a more capable group of mentors and influencers. While I worked most closely with Shaw, Wisdom, and Bond, I also frequently worked with the president's entire cabinet and leadership team. In addition to Bond, Richard Hulet was vice president for student affairs, Eric Johnson was vice president for administration and finance, and James L. Fisher was vice president and chief advancement and public affairs officer. They were all immensely talented, and to this day, I haven't worked with or observed a more gifted executive team.

James (Jim) Fisher was young, charismatic, and energetic, with an infectious personality. He knew how to own every room he entered. He was articulate and erudite and often quoted Greek philosophy. He was always impeccably dressed and gave off an air of sophistication that gave the impression he had grown up in a country club or on a yacht. He didn't. He grew up in Decatur, Illinois, with modest working-class parents, dropped out of Milliken University, and joined the Marine Corps. After completing his service, he graduated from ISU on the GI Bill, where he caught the attention of President Bone. He went on to earn a PhD in psychology from Northwestern University. He worked at Northwestern for a while but was recruited by President Bone to return to ISU to join his administration. When we took over President Braden's office, we took over Fisher's as well because his office was a part of the president's suite.

Every day at lunchtime, a group of administrators and faculty would get together to play basketball. I was invited to join them. Fisher was a regular fixture at these games and befriended me. Buzz and Paul played too, but they were in a completely different league than the rest of us. We would never let the two of them play on the same team. The games were always fun, and we enjoyed great camaraderie.

In 1969, the team began to unravel. It started in the spring when Jim Fisher was named president of Towson State College in Towson, Maryland, a suburb of Baltimore. Soon after, Paul joined him as his vice president and chief advancement officer, and finally, in the fall, Buzz joined them as vice president and chief academic officer. Buzz and Paul, the two people who started me on this journey—first as negotiators on the other side of the table, then as collaborators, and then as friends—left me. I was happy for them and grateful for what they had done for me, but I knew I would miss them. It turned out that I wouldn't miss them for very long.

The sixties was one of the most tumultuous and transformative decades in the country's history. It would see a major breach in the walls of America's version of apartheid and much progress toward achieving what America had promised to be. It was also the decade of assassinations: President John F. Kennedy, Martin Luther King Jr., Malcolm X, Medgar Evers, Bobby Kennedy, Emmett Till, Violet Liuzzo, Michael

Schwerner, James Chaney, and Andrew Goodman. Then, there was Fred
Hampton.

Fred Hampton was the extraordinary young vice chairman of the Chicago Black Panther Party. The Black Panther Party for Self Defense began
in Oakland, California, but affiliate chapters quickly formed in the urban
north. They were militant, high-profile, and provocative. When Fred spoke
at the university, he was popular, well liked, and well received. The Pan-
thers were controversial in that their strong advocacy of "self-defense"
included defense against the police and police brutality. They dressed in
semi-military garb and carried visible firearms. Their antipolice rhetoric
made them both hated and feared by law enforcement.

On December 4, 1969, a joint law enforcement team raided the apartment where Fred and eight of his colleagues were staying. Fred Hampton
was shot and killed in the bed where he slept. The only other casualty was
Mark Clark from Peoria, Illinois. Government authorities characterized
the event as a shoot-out between police and the occupants. Later, forensic
investigation would disprove that characterization. Over ninety shots were
fired by the police, and only two came from inside the apartment, one of
which went into the ceiling. It was a government-executed assassination.
The survivors of the raid sued the government agencies responsible and
settled the case with a $1.85 million award to the victims' and their fami-
lies. Fred Hampton was twenty-one years old.

The news of Fred's death hit the campus like a bombshell. These were
not distant public figures we lost. These were people that we knew and
considered friends. Mark Clark's sister was a classmate of ours at the
university. The loss was deep and personal. We were hurt, shocked, and
angry. Toni Seaberry, a HPS student and good friend, stopped by my
office and asked what would happen if someone lowered the flag in front
of the administration building to half-mast, because one of our students,
Alonzo Pruitt, had done just that.

My first reaction was one of frustration. Here we go again. The pace of
our activism was wearing me down. Fortunately, Toni snapped me out of it

by reminding me of the gravity of what just happened. For a moment, I felt embarrassed, but having been refocused by my friend, I left my office, went out on the quadrangle where Pruitt was standing alone by the flagpole, and joined him. Alonzo "Lonnie" Pruitt was a sharp, passionate, engaging, and articulate freshman who had entered the university that fall. We were not related, but because we had the same last name, people often thought we were. We greeted each other and said, "What now?" Neither of us knew.

Lonnie's actions were grief inspired and had no other purpose but to express his—our—collective sorrow for the loss we all felt. Soon, other African American students joined us; about twenty or thirty assembled. We were quiet. No one really knew what to say. After what seemed like an hour, someone from President Braden's office delivered the message that he wanted to see me. I asked Lonnie to come along.

When we got to the president's office, Dr. Braden informed us that our actions had attracted media attention and that he had received a call from the governor's office directing him to have the flag restored to the top of the mast. The governor's office chastised him, saying that only the governor had the authority to order the flag lowered at a state institution. While we were not happy, we accepted the president's position. After all, our actions were not directed at him, and we had not intended to put him in a difficult position. We had a respectful relationship with Dr. Braden and had not anticipated or wanted a confrontation with him over this. We went back to our colleagues at the flagpole, reported our conversation with the president, and silently disbanded. The flag was restored to its original height.

That spring on May 4, 1970, national guardsmen shot and killed four student protesters, injuring nine others, at Kent State University in Ohio. This act triggered immediate outrage on campuses across the country. More than four million students organized demonstrations and walkouts on campuses all over America. At Illinois State, a group of White students lowered the flag to half-mast. Black students were also sympathetic and supportive of the protest over Kent State, but we were curious if this event initiated by White students would receive the same response our actions had in December. We waited, and still no one raised the flag.

Troubled by what I recognized as a clear double standard, I went to Dr. Braden's office. The door was open, and I'll never forget I saw. The image of the man was haunting. He was hunched over his desk, with his jacket off and sleeves rolled up with his elbows propped up on his desk, cradling his head in his hands. He turned his head, saw me, and said, "I wondered when you were going to show up." He told me that when the students lowered the flag, he sent for their leaders and explained the governor's position, but this time was different. With campuses in uproar throughout the state and around the country, the governor's office cowed and told him to use "local discretion." He was on his own.

I suggested a solution; Malcolm X's birthday was about two weeks away on May 19. I proposed that the flag remain at half-mast for the length of time it had been permitted for us in December, then raised, and, on May 19, lowered again for the entire day to commemorate the loss of all victims of social justice causes. That should take care of everybody and offend no one, or so I thought. President Braden liked the idea and directed that it be done. Our small chapter of the Students for a Democratic Society (SDS), the group who lowered the flag, embraced the idea, and everyone was satisfied for the time being.

On the morning of May 19, I woke up early and walked to my office. As I approached the quadrangle, I noticed a crew of White construction workers gathered around the flagpole. The flag was at half-mast, and a security guard was stationed at the base of the pole. I watched as a construction worker shoved the security guard to the ground, shimmied up the flagpole, raised the flag to the top, and cut the cord so that it couldn't be lowered again. Then he yelled that they would be back if anyone tried to lower it again.

It appeared that the security guard was relatively unharmed, so I went straight to the president's office to find out what was happening. As expected, there was a flurry of activity. The campus administration took the construction workers' threat of violence seriously and called the local Normal police. I was told the police refused to respond because they agreed with the construction workers and opposed lowering the flag!

The state attorney general's office was then contacted to find out how we could protect ourselves and legally keep outsiders off our public campus. This situation quickly escalated from a social-justice, free-speech issue to a security and law enforcement matter. The attorney general's office advised the university to create a defined physical barrier around the flagpole so it could be designated a nonpublic space. It was the only legal way to restrict access to the general public. They said if anyone breached the barrier, it would be considered trespassing and serve as grounds for arrest.

Maintenance and campus security personnel restrung the flag and returned it to half-mast. University vehicles were then arranged in a circle around the flagpole. It reminded me of a scene out of a western movie when they "circled the wagons." Later that day, a substantial contingent of Illinois State Police sporting riot gear arrived.

I had been receiving a number of death threats at both my home and office as a result of press coverage during the December events and in the days leading up to the May 19 commemoration. Additionally, a number of African American students came to me to express fear for their safety. We decided to organize a peaceful "gathering" on the quad at the opposite end from the flagpole. We felt we would be better protected if we assembled in a group close to the state police. Some of the students brought baseball bats and softballs with them, with no intention of playing ball. The tension in the air was palpable, and no one knew what would happen next.

Late that afternoon, the state police began to pack up, and the "wagon train" dispersed. We were told that the state police had identified and spoken to the construction crew and "persuaded" them that it was not in their interest to pursue the matter. The police felt the threat had been neutralized. We breathed a collective sigh of relief, disbanded, and went home. When we left, the flag was still lowered to half-mast.

I headed home, looking forward to decompressing after such an exhausting day. Unfortunately, it wasn't over yet. At around nine o'clock that evening, the dean of students, Ed Smith, called to let me know that the local Normal police had received a call from the wife of one of the construction workers. She was concerned because he and his coworkers had come back to their house and, after a few drinks and heated conversation, left to hunt someone down for retribution. That someone, it turned out, was me.

The Normal police suggested that I come to the police station so I could be "looked after," until the situation was resolved. They didn't know where the construction workers were, but they knew where I was and offered me "protective custody." All I could think of was how the Normal police had refused to respond to the university's call for assistance that morning and couldn't imagine they had any real interest in protecting me. Ed agreed and called campus security to pick me up and take me to their headquarters. I wasn't sure how the ISU security officers felt about me either, but at the very least, I knew they weren't happy about the attack on their colleague that morning. I tried to make myself comfortable and settled in for the night.

Around three o'clock in the morning, a call came in that police had finally located the construction workers, who had sobered up and gone home. After receiving further "counseling," from the Normal police officers, they agreed to let the matter go. Assured that the threat was over, campus security drove me home. Unfortunately, I continued to receive occasional threats. This was the only time in my life I would ever spend a night in "jail."

In the aftermath of the flagpole incident, the Black members of the campus community petitioned the university to name the Student Union Building after Malcolm X. This idea originated with the students; however, Charles Morris and the rest of the faculty and staff supported it. Personally, as much as I had been influenced by Malcolm, I thought going after this would be a bridge too far. The media had identified Malcolm with the extreme dogma of Elijah Muhammad and the Nation of Islam, though he had evolved beyond them. At the end of their lives, Malcolm X and

Martin Luther King Jr. essentially had more in common than differences, but in 1970, that was not the perception. Nevertheless, our community had decided to pursue this course, and I was on board.

When President Braden received our petition, he responded by saying he would only take it to the Board of Regents if it had the endorsement of the University Faculty Council and the Student Government Association. I think President Braden passed the ball to the campus governing bodies because he didn't think they would support it. Frankly, I didn't either, but we had been given both a path and a challenge. Charles Morris took the lead in managing the campaign to get the council's endorsement, and I had the responsibility for winning over the Student Government Association. We organized our teams, designed our respective strategies, and went to work. To everyone's surprise, including ours, we were successful. In separate votes, the ISU faculty governing body and the Student Government Association voted to endorse naming the Student Union Building after Malcolm X.

In Springfield, the reaction was swift. Legislators called for punitive budget cuts and other sanctions if the university took this action. Members of the Board of Regents also raised objections. One of them, Percy Julian, the famous African American chemist, met privately with us to express his concern and opposition. We were grateful for his presence and respectful. We made our case to him, but he was unmoved. We parted amicably.

Soon after our meeting with Dr. Julian, President Braden invited a large group of us to his house. He explained that he felt constitutionally obligated to transmit the recommendation of the student and faculty governing bodies to the Board of Regents, but he would do so with his "disapproval." He made the kind of decision that presidents are sometime required to make to protect the institutions they lead. I think he expected that we would be angry. We weren't. We were sophisticated enough to know that he could not support our position without subjecting the university to immense harm, and we understood his decision. It was another testimony to the trust, respect, and relationship he had established with us. The "flagpole incident," the largest of many demonstrations ISU had during the '60s, peacefully concluded.

An unfortunate consequence of this unrest was the resignation of Dr. Braden. While his announcement was a surprise, it was understandable. Dr. Braden was an educator; he didn't take on a presidency anticipating protests, takeovers, violence, threats, and marches where people threw bottles at demonstrators. In his resignation statement on June 11, 1970, he said, "I simply find that I no longer enjoy grappling with the problems which confront a college president today."

Samuel Braden was a kind and elegant man who successfully led the university through three of its most turbulent years. We were the only public research university in the state that sustained no significant destruction or violence. That was testimony to Braden's leadership and an African American activist community who valued transformation over disruption. The Braden era was brief but impactful. The university put programs in place that substantially increased the numbers of minority students, faculty, and staff. Unlike its peer institutions, the academic performance of these students matched or exceeded that of the general student population.

The progress made under Braden's leadership paved the way for Al Bowman's appointment in 2004, as the first and only African American president of the oldest public research university in Illinois. Though it took nearly thirty years, I can't tell you how proud I was that the work we started came to fruition in this way. The principal convocation center at the university was named the Samuel Braden Auditorium. The acknowledgment was well deserved, and fortunately, it was done while he was alive to enjoy it.

Dr. Braden conferred my baccalaureate diploma at his first commencement and my master's at his last. Students went home for the summer, and the campus was quiet while everyone benefitted from a much-needed break. Now that I had earned my graduate degree, I was appointed the first director of the High Potential Students program, the job I had been doing for some time but now officially with a new title and salary to match. Things had come together quite nicely.

Despite the violence, riots, and assassinations of the decade, there were also intermittent examples of kindness, tolerance, and heroic statesmanship and cooperation across race, gender, class, and political groups to strive for a more equitable and just society. The entire world united when Neil Armstrong became the first person to land on the moon. There were excesses to be sure, but the country survived and ended the decade better and healthier than when it began.

Richard Bond went on to a successful presidency at the University of Northern Colorado and then served as a state senator. David Sweet became the founding president of Minnesota Metropolitan State College and then president of Rhode Island College. James Koch was appointed president of the University of Montana and, later, the Old Dominion University in Virginia. Michael Adams became a distinguished and much-loved president of Fairleigh Dickinson University in New Jersey. Buzz Shaw had successful presidencies at Southern Illinois University, the University of Wisconsin system, and Syracuse University. James L. Fisher led Towson State University through the greatest transformation in the school's long history before becoming president of the Council for Advancement and Support of Education (CASE).

This incomparable repository of talent at Illinois State University assembled by President Bone would greatly enhance leadership in higher education across the country for years to come. This group was a testament to his remarkable ability to identify and nurture exceptional talent. Every one of these extraordinary leaders credits Dr. Bone for recruiting, mentoring, and developing them professionally. I'm sure President Braden was grateful for it, and I was fortunate and humbled to be befriended by and learn from these wonderful people. I could not imagine having a more empowering incubator in which to begin my journey into higher education.

When you are a long-serving university president, you accumulate acknowledgments along the way. You shouldn't do this work to receive attention; nevertheless, it is gratifying when the things you've worked to achieve are recognized. One of those occasions for me occurred in 1994 when I was invited back to Illinois State to accept an honorary degree.

Conferring an honorary degree is the highest honor a university can bestow. Each time it's happened to me, I have been both honored and humbled by the recognition, but to receive this from ISU was touching, given all the trouble I caused and how much of my heart I put into the place. Things came full circle when the ceremony was held in Braden Auditorium, and I was able to dine with President Braden along with other invited guests. It had been twenty-four years since I had seen him, and he looked well. We greeted each other warmly, and I told him I was grateful for his approval given all the headaches I'd caused him. We both agreed that the end result was worth it.

While I was glad he was on the platform during the ceremony, I wish he could have placed the hood on me. He had conferred my bachelor's and master's degrees, after all. It was the last time I saw Dr. Braden. I was deeply moved by the occasion, and I will never forget it or him.

This would not be the last time I would be acknowledged by my alma mater. In 1996, I was awarded the Distinguished Alumni Award, and my portrait was hung in the student union building. Finally, I returned to ISU one last time to be inducted into the Illinois State University Hall of Fame, along with Jim Fisher, Buzz Shaw, Jim Koch, and K. Patricia Cross. Pat Cross and I had the opportunity to work together often over the years. She was an important scholar, researcher, and author on adult learning theory, and she made major contributions to the development of adult higher education through her pioneering and universally respected work. She wrote and spoke about many of the founding principles adult-serving colleges and universities, including Thomas Edison State University, were built upon.

We had a great time. It was a heartwarming reunion in a memorable place that had nurtured us all.

Chapter Six

I saw courage in both the Vietnam War and in the struggle to stop it. I learned that patriotism includes protest, not just military service.

—John Kerry

Every draft-age man in America remembers where he was on December 1, 1969. In response to protests and lawsuits about inequities with the draft, the selective service system abolished student deferments and instituted a lottery. The numbers were randomly drawn and your place in line was determined by your birthday. On practically every campus in America, draft-age students were drinking, half grieving because they were going to be drafted, and half celebrating because they weren't. I will never forget the number that freed me to live my life—277.

Soon after graduation, I received a call from Buzz Shaw inviting me to Towson to interview for the position of dean of students. Buzz was vice president for academic affairs, and Jim had persuaded Richard Gillespie, chair of the Theater Department, to accept the student affairs vice presidency. Though he wasn't particularly interested in administration, Dick cared about what was happening on campuses around the country and at Towson, and the activist community and the students respected him. He acknowledged this invitation as an opportunity to shape policy as opposed to reacting to it.

Buzz and Fisher suggested that I would be a good addition to the team and encouraged Dick to interview me. I took an immediate liking to him. He was kind, dedicated, and passionate. It was great seeing Buzz, Paul, and Jim again, too. I was offered the position of dean of students at the oldest and largest of the state colleges in Maryland. I was twenty-four years old. I would have broader institutional responsibilities, and I would be reunited with my team of mentors and friends. I happily accepted.

While I took a small cut in salary, I've never taken a job for the money. My new compensation was comparable to my peers, and most importantly, I loved the work. I reported directly to the vice president for student affairs, and because Dick insisted on maintaining his hand in theater, I became chief operating officer of the division to relieve him from many of the administrative duties of vice president. When Dick was unavailable, I represented the division at President Fisher's cabinet meetings. The first time I attended a cabinet meeting with Jim at the head of the table and Buzz and Paul as vice presidents, I was thrilled. It felt good to have the band back together.

I flew back to Normal to meet with Vice President Bond, Charles Morris, and the High Potential Students program staff, all of whom I had recruited, to tell them I would be leaving. Not only was I fully integrated within this community; I had helped create it, and leaving was tough. It was like leaving home all over again. And Baltimore? I had never thought about living in Baltimore. Even though as a practical matter, I had left home when I went away to college, I was never more than 125 miles away from the South Side and everything familiar to me.

Baltimore in 1970 was a gritty, blue-collar, working-class town that had seen better days. The city had not recovered from the riots and flight of the middle class that afflicted many cities, but it still enjoyed a solid industrial base. The steel mills at Sparrows Point, several large clothing manufacturers, one of the busiest seaports in the country, and a significant seafood industry offered a stable range of jobs. You could attend a ballgame for one of the three professional sports teams—the Colts, the Orioles, and the Bullets—and, of course, feast anytime on the famous Chesapeake Bay crabs.

Politically isolated, Baltimore was a hole in a donut. It was solidly Democratic and had a large urban minority population. It was surrounded by suburban, White, Republican Baltimore County, which actively worked to keep the city encapsulated. What is now a beautiful, developed inner harbor, which revitalized the downtown and created an economic development engine for the entire region, was at that time populated by abandoned, rat-infested wharfs. While it had robust cultural assets, including a symphony, opera company, and art museum, it did not share the urbane sophistication of its neighbor forty miles to the south in Washington. Towson, Maryland, was the county seat of Baltimore County, and Dale Anderson was its disagreeable county executive. His predecessor was a former governor and vice president of the United States under Nixon, Spiro Agnew. That should give you a clear picture of the county's political climate.

Maryland is one of the "border states," a southern state that was not allowed to secede from the Union in the Civil War. It was a slave state and practiced legal segregation until it was dismantled by the courts. That legacy left it with a "dual system" of higher education. Morgan State College, Coppin, Bowie, and Maryland State were Black colleges. The University of Maryland system (which included the flagship research university at College Park and four other campuses), Towson, Salisbury State College, and Frostburg State College were all White. Following integration, Morgan, Coppin, and Bowie were joined with Towson, Frostburg, and Salisbury to become the Maryland State College system under a single board of trustees. There was a caste and class differential between the University of Maryland system and the Maryland State College system. The University of Maryland was favored in status, funding, and governance autonomy.

Legal segregation was no longer in place, but Towson for all practical purposes was an all-White school. Students of color made up less than 3 percent of its enrollment, and I cannot recall there being any full-time African American members of the faculty. There were two other Black administrators at the College, Julius Chapman, who was recruited to work on diversity issues, and Harriett Dandridge, assistant director of financial aid, but I was senior in rank and the most visible. The budget analyst at the state's Department of Budget and Fiscal Planning attempted to block the appointment when he found out I was Black. It took special intervention by Wayne Schelle, Towson's vice president for administration and finance, to move the appointment forward.

While I understood I was recruited for the contributions I could make to his leadership team, I also knew my appointment provided a visible statement of Fisher's commitment to make Towson a more welcoming place for people of color. He regularly included me in high-profile events with donors and people of influence. As a result, I received a lot of media attention.

Mary Lee Farlow was the director of housing and residence life. She was a competent administrator with a warm, inviting personality and a pronounced southern accent. One day she came to my office to discuss a problem. She had been confronted by an irate mother infuriated that her freshman daughter's roommate was Black. She demanded her daughter be assigned another roommate. She went on to say that she sent her daughter to Towson because she thought this would never happen there. Mary Lee explained that she spoke to the daughter, who was embarrassed by her mother's behavior. She followed up with the mother to let her know that the young women were happy with their arrangement and she had no intention of separating them. At that point, the mother furiously demanded to speak with her boss. That would be me. Much to our delight, she scheduled a meeting for the following Monday. That Sunday, the *Baltimore Sun* published a story and profile on me in its magazine section. She never showed up. She called Mary Lee, told her she had seen the article, and expressed her disappointment in the college. I was disappointed as well. I was looking forward to the encounter. As far as I know, the roommates continued their living arrangements without further interference from the mother.

Another interesting experience occurred when Buzz invited me and Julius Chapman to his community swimming pool to test a racially exclusive covenant that excluded Black people. Of course, I was game, although I couldn't entirely put out of my mind the riots and violence that had taken place when we integrated Rainbow Beach. Fortunately, the afternoon was uneventful, and I don't recall so much as a dirty look. Buzz didn't get any grief from it either.

Towson was a great learning experience for me. I learned a lot about management, facilities, procurement, construction, residence halls, and leadership not only in observing Jim, Buzz, and Paul but under their tutelage. Jim was a visionary, and the rest of us were aligned with him and committed to fulfilling his vision. After accompanying Jim and Paul on trips to Annapolis, to meet with political figures and the state bureaucracy, I was debriefed on strategy, tactics, and the personalities and personal relationships that often determine whether things happen or not. Jim was sincere and authentic, qualities that endeared him to powerful political figures and captains of industry just as much as bartenders and barbers. This invoked feelings of jealousy from some politicians and colleagues as he rose in stature to become one of the most respected, visible, and influential figures in Maryland higher education.

As president from 1969 to 1978, Jim doubled Towson's enrollment, constructed eleven new buildings, increased academic programs and faculty, and achieved university status. When he departed to become president of CASE, Jim's high profile led to overtures from both parties as to his interest in running for governor. He declined. His brilliant leadership of CASE was cut short when he suffered a heart attack, from which he fully recovered but which led to a decision to change his lifestyle. He stepped down from the presidency of CASE and became a prolific writer, authoring over fourteen books on leadership, governance, and the presidency. In honor of his exceptional leadership and contributions to the field, CASE established the James L. Fisher Award for Distinguished Service to Education.

Jim's first book, *The Power of the Presidency*, was one of the best books I've ever read on presidential leadership. In it, he writes about the importance of maintaining what he calls "social distance" as a leader. Simply stated, the president can never be one of the gang. There are public expectations of the institution and the office that the president can never forget. A relevant cliché is "familiarity breeds contempt." Among the many things that President Carter did that compromised his effectiveness was to erode the "social distance" between himself and the public. He was overexposed in the media commenting about mundane things. He was often seen carrying his own bags and didn't let cabinet officers ride in limousines. The problem is that no one wants the president of the United States, leader of the free world, to be "Joe Six-Pack" or "the Guy Next Door." When President Carter needed the public to take him seriously, many people didn't. Richard Nixon, on the other hand, took the symbols and trappings of office to the other extreme and became "the Imperial President." Franklin Delano Roosevelt, John F. Kennedy, and Ronald Reagan all understood it and got it right.

Fisher got it right too, but there is a significant exception. There is a very wise saying to the effect that the quickest way to lose a friend is to give them a job or loan them money. However, you can violate the principle and be better off for it, if you hire the right kind of friends. When Jim was president, the best friends he had were Paul, Buzz, and, sometime later, me. For us, our friendship with Jim was a great burden in our professional lives. We always understood that his success and that of the institution relied on our effectiveness. There was no way in hell we were going to let him down. We had great respect for the enormous responsibility and accountability of his office. We were appropriately deferential in public and when engaged in our work but affectionately irreverent when we weren't.

It was Jim who first encouraged me to seek a college presidency. From my work at Illinois State and then at Towson, I became enamored with the transformational power of the academy and higher education. I thought colleges and universities were wonderful places that empowered people, created new knowledge, and developed the human capital that the future of society depended on. Until Jim planted the seed, the thought that I should lead one had never crossed my mind.

Jim recognized that, at my core, I was an activist. I was engaged, involved, and wanted to follow Uncle Doc's advice to leave things better than I found them. Jim pointed out to me that I had an aptitude and intuition that allowed me to perform beyond my age. He was clear that my appointment at Towson was not a charitable act, and he fully expected a return on his investment. I was intrigued by his assessment, and I began to contemplate my future in higher education.

Academic freedom is a core value of the academy, but it is often under attack, misunderstood, and misinterpreted. While people jealously guard their right to express and advocate their point of view, they are sometimes less generous in acknowledging the same prerogative on the part of those who have opposing perspectives. Civil rights, race relations, the emergence of the women's movement, and the Vietnam War were all polarizing issues in 1970. It was a time of great turmoil, upheaval, protest, and, unfortunately, violence.

All of these issues affected Towson, but not with the same intensity as some other campuses. The major source of activism on the campus centered on opposition to the Vietnam War. We had protest marches, rallies, lectures, speeches, and teach-ins. I learned an important leadership lesson. Where possible and appropriate, leaders need to be transparent, articulate, consistent, and predictable in enforcing the norms of the community. It lowers the probability of miscalculation on all sides and can sometimes help to avoid unnecessary confrontation.

To do this, Fisher wrote and distributed a brilliant treatise on academic freedom, free speech, protest, and civil disobedience. From Gandhi to Martin Luther King Jr., he pointed out that the moral power of civil disobedience lay in the willingness to accept the consequences and punishment associated with breaking an immoral, unjust law or practice. He pointed out that the right of free speech and protest would be respected and defended, but the laws and rules governing the college would also be enforced. While the document was thoughtful, brilliantly written, and widely distributed, its greatest value was in defining reference points and standards the university employed to respond to the activism of the time.

The presence of military recruiters in our placement office angered anti-war activists on campus. Our challenge was to defend both the right of student protesters as well as the right of students who wanted to participate in the military. We developed contingency plans for a variety of scenarios. As a disruptor, I brought a certain practitioner insight to the process. The student protesters frequently picketed the administration building when the recruiters were present. We protected their right to picket, but we would not permit them to prevent access to students who wanted to meet with the recruiters.

One day, a group of approximately ten demonstrators, some standing and some on the floor, physically obstructed the hallway and entrance to the placement office. Campus security responded and notified the protesters that their actions were in violation of campus rules. They were told that if they did not move, they would be subject to campus disciplinary action. My recollection is that some of the protesters voluntarily left, others were escorted out by security, and some of those who were lying on the floor were physically picked up and carried away. Scuffles broke out, and some students were arrested. All of them were subject to campus disciplinary action. The incident became a major press event. There was heated debate on campus, in the surrounding community, and even in halls of the legislature in Annapolis on how the events were handled by the university.

Conservatives applauded Fisher for standing up to "leftist campus radicals," liberals decried the use of force, and radicals accused him of being a tool of the military industrial complex. Despite the fact that there had been contingencies anticipating such an event, not everything went as planned. The rumor mill took over, and the actual events were obscured in a cloud of myth and distortion.

Fisher appointed a commission to investigate the incident and report its findings and recommendations. I was selected to chair the commission. The other two members of the panel were Henry Chen, a faculty member who had great credibility with the activist community, and a student representative selected by the student government association. The three of us became known as the Pruitt Commission.

At our first meeting, we committed ourselves to conducting an objective, accurate, and fair investigation. We agreed that our conclusions would be fair and evidence based. I pledged to do everything in my power to achieve consensus among the three of us in the final report. We were empowered by the college to interview anyone needed and were provided access to any documents we required. We worked well together and issued our findings. The report was accepted by the community, achieved the commission's purpose, and allowed the campus to move on.

> To be black in the Baltimore of my youth was to be naked
> before the elements of the world.
> —Ta-Nehisi Coates

Growing up in Chicago you take the brutal winters for granted and you learn to live and cope with the cold, snow, and wind. There were no fashion considerations when dressing for school in the winter. You tried to stay warm and avoid exposed skin. Boys and girls alike walked into the school looking like the Michelin Tire Man, with layers of clothes, earmuffs, gloves, and scarves. I walked to school every day from kindergarten through high school enduring some of the most brutal weather imaginable. I had never heard of schools closing for weather until I moved to Baltimore.

One morning I heard an announcement on my radio that Baltimore city and the surrounding area public schools were closed due to the overnight snowfall. Further, the "snow emergency plan" was now in effect.

I could not imagine what had happened. I jumped up to look out the window expecting to see something catastrophic. Instead, I saw blades of grass poking through a light dusting of snow. I couldn't help but laugh as I got in my car and drove to work without incident.

Baltimore's reaction to snow would provide my first real insight into the difference between traditional-age college students and adult learners. One semester, I taught a course at Aberdeen Proving Ground military base. Towson had a large traditional, full-time student body and a sizeable part-time working-adult student body. One day we had unexpected, heavy afternoon snowfall, and classes were canceled.

I taught an early evening class for working adults, and even though the cancelation was announced on the radio, I was worried that my students might not hear it and show up anyway. I decided to make the drive out to Aberdeen just in case. On the way to my car, I could hear the traditional-age students cheering that classes were canceled as they headed to the local bars.

When I arrived, I was surprised to see the entire class. Even the students who had heard about the cancelation were there, and they had questions. They were relieved when I arrived and wanted to know the consequences of canceling the class. If the class was canceled, how would it be made up? Would they receive a tuition refund? I was pleased by their attitude. What a contrast from the kids back on campus who were celebrating their canceled classes. For my students, this course represented an investment of their time and expense, and they wanted their money's worth. It was eye-opening for me. That day we made a pact. No matter what the college decided about class cancelations, I would be there if they would. I never missed a class, and neither did they.

One of the greatest gifts Baltimore gave me was the opportunity to meet and get to know my cousin Levi Watkins Jr. Levi was two years older than me, and we had both relocated to Baltimore around the same time. He grew up in Montgomery, Alabama, attended Tennessee State University, graduated in 1966 at the top of his class, and became the first African

American admitted to Vanderbilt University's School of Medicine. Levi's mother and my mother were first cousins. His father, Levi Watkins Sr., was a long-serving, distinguished, and highly respected president of Alabama State University.

Though I had never met Levi as a child, I knew his oldest sister, Marie. She was a frequent guest at our house, especially on holidays when she was in graduate school at Northwestern University. Levi Sr. and Lillian had six children, and they were all exceptional. Marie went on to earn a PhD in math from the University of California, Berkeley, followed by a career as a researcher and department head at Bell Labs. Pearl was a gifted musician; Donald, an attorney; Doristine, an accomplished educator and school principal; and James, a cardiologist.

My mother and Lillian told me and Levi to reach out to each other since we were both new to Baltimore and didn't know anyone. We met and became instant friends. Levi was there to begin his internship and residency in cardiac surgery at Johns Hopkins Medical Center. As is the case with interns and residents, Levi had little time for social engagements, but somehow, he always made time for good music and BBQ ribs, two things dear to my heart.

Being single, young men in a new city, we enjoyed active bachelorhood. He was tall, crazy smart, and a product of the civil rights movement. He had a deep, abiding, and uncompromising commitment to social justice issues. Growing up in Montgomery, he attended Martin Luther King's Dexter Avenue Baptist Church. He was close to the King family, especially Coretta Scott King, and served as Rosa Parks's personal physician. After completing his residency at Johns Hopkins and Harvard, he became the first Black chief resident in cardiac surgery at Johns Hopkins Hospital. In 1980, he made medical history when he performed the first implantation of the automatic implantable defibrillator. In 1991, he was promoted to full professor of cardiac surgery and dean for postdoctoral programs and faculty development at the Johns Hopkins School of Medicine.

Though his achievements were great, they did not come easy. He grew up in the heart of the segregated south. When he integrated Vanderbilt University School of Medicine, he was not warmly received. He was frequently harassed and on one occasion had dog feces thrown on him. Despite this, he persevered and became the first African American to graduate from the school. Interestingly, he would later serve as a trustee of the university, and an endowed chair would be named in his honor at the medical school, where his portrait is hung. Tennessee State University, his alma mater, created the Levi Watkins Jr. Institute to promote and encourage students, especially those of color, to pursue careers in medicine and the STEM fields. His portrait is also hung in the Johns Hopkins School of Medicine. Most recently, the Johns Hopkins Outpatient Center in East Baltimore was named for him.

In Baltimore, he was most known for his social justice work and civil rights activism. He pressed Johns Hopkins to increase minority enrollment in the medical school and was instrumental in achieving a 400 percent increase in the admission of African American students. He was proud this was achieved without lowering the admissions standards of one of the most selective medical schools in the country. He was prouder still that his recruits graduated at or near the top of their classes.

His company was often sought out by celebrities—Oprah Winfrey, Maya Angelou, and others—but he was never interested in attention or publicity. What he really cared about was people, particularly those he perceived as powerless or voiceless. At Hopkins, he spent a lot of time with service workers and supported a local gospel choir they organized. He was outspoken but never about himself. He was assertive but always approachable and kindhearted.

On Friday evening, April 10, 2015, he and some of his colleagues were meeting a new group of students when he suffered a massive heart attack and stroke. Surrounded by some of the best doctors in the world, he passed away in the early hours of April 11. He was seventy years old. He lived his life on his own terms and died doing something he loved. The medical profession lost a gifted and innovative surgeon that day. The civil rights community lost a shining star, the people of Baltimore lost an articulate voice for social justice, and I lost a very dear and respected friend.

The last time I spoke to Levi was in February 2015. I was already contemplating my retirement, but I wanted to bestow an honorary degree on my accomplished cousin before I left. I told him of my intentions and asked if he would accept. I was anticipating that the college would receive university status soon and inquired if he would rather wait and receive his degree from "the university." He laughed and said he didn't care about things like that, and then after a pause, he said, "Let's do it this year." I told him that I was going to invite the family, and maybe we could have a mini reunion. We laughed, recounted stories, and reminisced about our social adventures when we were both young, single guys in Baltimore. I smiled for a long time after I got off the phone and looked forward to hosting him and some of the family in September, when Thomas Edison held its commencement ceremony.

In June 2015, the university's board of trustees approved the awarding of an honorary degree, posthumously to Levi Watkins Jr. Levi's sister Marie Watkins Garraway and his cousin Beverly Guy-Shefthall, with whom he was very close, accepted the degree on his behalf. It was a heartbreaking ceremony to get through.

Chapter Seven

Leaders run toward the fire.

—*Don Hart*

In April 1972, Dick Gillespie stopped by my office to tell me to expect a call from the president's office at Morgan State College. I asked Dick if he knew why, and he answered that he had a suspicion it was about a job. The next day, the call came to schedule my appointment with King Cheek, the president of Morgan. Though I had never met him, I had seen him and his wife at a conference in Chicago and attended his inauguration when he became president. I was curious and eager to meet him.

At that point, King Cheek had been president of Morgan for a little over a year after a short presidency at Shaw University. He and his brother, James Cheek, garnered national attention at Shaw when James was president and King was provost. No one objected to the nepotism because they were such a dynamic duo. It was almost like JFK and Bobby Kennedy. King was an innovative and creative academic, and James was an accomplished executive, fund-raiser, and visionary leader. When James left Shaw to become president of Howard University, King succeeded him as president. Not too long after, King was appointed president of Morgan.

My meeting with King went well, and the conversation flowed effortlessly. We spent a lot of time talking about higher education, the things we loved and the things we thought should change. It was clear that he had an exciting vision for Morgan that would build on its historic strengths, and he described a future filled with innovation and reform. I was impressed.

I was caught off guard when he asked me to work with him as vice president for student affairs. Despite Dick's comment, I did not see that coming. I responded that I was deeply honored by the offer and was inclined to accept, but I wanted to discuss it with Fisher before providing my answer.

When I returned to campus, Jim confirmed what I had by then figured out: he had recommended me for the position. Jim encouraged me to view this position as a step on the pathway to a presidency. There were only six institutions in the state college system, and Jim and King recognized kindred spirits in each other. Like Fisher, King was young, clever, and had a warm disposition. They became good and trusted friends. One led the largest and most respected White state college, and the other lead the largest and most respected Black state college in Maryland. After speaking to Fisher, I called back to accept. I would begin on July 1, 1972.

Before I left the meeting, King told me that he and his wife, Annette, were expecting their first child the following month and that her sister from Nashville, a schoolteacher, would be staying with them for the summer to help with the baby. Since she didn't know anyone in Baltimore, he asked if I would be willing to take her out. I remembered King's wife, Annette, and she was gorgeous, so I thought this might prove interesting, but I was a very active bachelor. I also worried about dating the boss's sister-in-law. I shared my concern with King, and he assured me that there was nothing to worry about as there were no expectations. After all, it would only be for the summer. His sister-in-law, Delores Walker, and I were married on December 30 of that year, 1972.

Leaving Towson was bittersweet. This time *I* was leaving Buzz, Paul, and Jim. I felt like a baby bird, flying out of the nest for the first time. I would be assuming major executive responsibility for the second largest organization in the institution. I hoped I was ready for it. I felt that I was, but I also knew that I had never been tested at this level, especially not without the comfort of my friends and mentors working alongside me.

I felt an enormous sense of obligation not only to Buzz, Paul, and Jim for their counsel and encouragement but also to King Cheek, who had taken a risk on this twenty-six-year-old kid. I understood that he would be held accountable for how I performed, and Buzz, Paul, and Jim had high expectations of their protégé. I was determined to not let them down.

I was grateful and deeply moved by the well wishes and congratulations I received from my colleagues at Towson. The most memorable was from Gene Dawson, head of campus security. At any college, it is important that the student affairs staff and campus security work closely together. He reminded me of a concert we hosted in our largest, indoor facility, for both the campus and off-campus communities. Due to the large crowd, the event promoter hired additional contract security. Gene was there that evening to oversee public safety, and I was there as the administrator on duty.

It was a warm evening, and the crowd milled around both inside and outdoors. Suddenly, I heard the unmistakable sound of two gunshots outside the building. Given where I grew up, I knew without a doubt what that sound was. With a lump in my throat, I immediately headed in the direction of the shots. At the same time, Gene Dawson came around the corner. We made eye contact, and in a split second, we exchanged a nonverbal look of "oh shit." When we got outside, we found one of the hired security guards with a pistol in his hand. Gene identified himself and took his weapon. The guard said some unruly patrons were threatening him, and he fired two warning shots to disperse them. Gene and I were both furious. It could have caused a panic and a stampede. People could have been seriously hurt. Gene took charge of the situation and handled it perfectly.

When he came by to say good-bye that day, he said some very kind and touching things, but what I remember most was his appreciation during that concert event when he ran toward the gunfire and found me right there with him. Together, we confronted a dangerous situation, and he felt I had his back. He told me he didn't know of any other colleague who would have done that, and he was really going to miss me. I was deeply moved, and I have never forgotten his words.

Don Hart, a good friend of mine, once told me that when you are on land, everyone runs away from the fire, but when you are on a ship, everyone runs toward the fire. For obvious reasons, if a boat fire isn't contained, everyone is at risk. I have learned that if you are in a leadership position, be it on land or at sea, you must always run toward the fire.

GOOD GENES

An acquaintance of mine died from a heart attack. What was shocking about this was that the guy was in his early fifties, ate right, exercised, and was in great shape. I called Levi and asked what do to keep from dying. I'll never forget what he said: "First, arrange to be born into a family with good genes, and then don't abuse your body." Unfortunately, you don't get to pick your parents or your family, but in many ways, I lucked out with mine. In life span, some like Levi or my mother, who passed at seventy-four, died too young, but some others lived for quite a long time. What they lacked in longevity, they sure made up for in brainpower.

There's always the debate between "nature versus nurture." What's more important, a person's environment and opportunity or a person's inherited capacity and genetics? I have one foot firmly planted in each camp. Things like environment, poverty, education, experience, and opportunity are important to a person's development, but it is also powerfully true that genes are a significant determinant in a person's potential.

Unfortunately, I don't know much about my father's family. I never knew either of my paternal grandparents; they both died when my father was young. My father was the eighth of nine children. He had three brothers and five sisters. They were born and raised in and around Texarkana, Texas, on the east Texas border with Arkansas.

Robert Pruitt, my father's brother, was head of the municipal employee union in Detroit and had come up in the labor movement with Walter Reuther. We visited him once when he was ill, and I remember the huge floral arrangement in his living room from Governor George Romney. Uncle Robert was polished, well-dressed, drove a beautiful gold Cadillac, and didn't go anywhere without his pistol. He was cool, and I liked him.

Though Robert was the only one of my father's brothers I ever knew, I was fully acquainted with all five of his sisters. They had all migrated to Los Angeles. My father's oldest sister, Bertha, had two daughters and a son. Of the nine siblings, only Aunt Bertha and my dad had children. I knew of my father's uncle, Wesley Pruitt, who had a school named after him in Atlanta, Texas. Unfortunately, when integration occurred in Texas and the rest of the South, most of the Black schools, including Pruitt High School, closed.

I know a great deal about my mother's side of the family. My maternal great grandfather was William F. Carmichael. He was White, his parents were from Scotland, and there is evidence that he fought in the Civil War for the Confederacy. He married Olivia Williamson in Crawford, Mississippi, on March 25, 1865. In the census of 1870, the first that recorded Black people, she is listed as "Mulatto." They bought a home in Canton, Mississippi, in February 1887. They had twelve children, ten of whom survived to adulthood. Among them was George Morton Carmichael, my grandfather; Etta Carmichael Varnado, Levi's grandmother; James Carmichael; and Lillie Carmichael Evans.

Even though their mother was "Mulatto," physically and for all practical purposes, William and Olivia's children were White. James, my grandfather's oldest brother, had light hair and blue eyes, yet for reasons no one in the family could figure out, they chose to be Black—and in Mississippi! All the men married Black women, and all the women married Black men. My maternal grandmother had beautiful chocolate skin.

The modern reality and perception of the South depicts a place that has vigorously and often violently enforced separation and demarcation between Whites and Blacks, but historically that was not always the case. Following the Civil War and prior to the end of Reconstruction, the relationships between the races were fluid and ambiguous. In fact, the first

African American elected to the U.S. Congress was Hiram Rhodes Rev-
els, U.S. Senator from Mississippi. It was also true that special "accommodations" were often made for the offspring of White men and Black
women.

James Carmichael was superintendent of the "colored" schools in Canton, but he frequently stayed at the Trolio Hotel, a Whites-only facility.
When he and his brothers traveled on the segregated trains, they rode in
the White section with impunity. Of course, that was not true for their
wives and brown children. Olivia Carmichael was illiterate and signed her
name with an X, yet all of her children were educated, and some even went
to college.

The intellectual capacity of that family from small-town Mississippi
would produce an astounding array of achievement. At this writing, there
are seven entities named after William and Olivia's descendants:

The Percy Abrams Sr. Senior Housing Center, Emeryville, CA
The GA Carmichael Family Health Center, Canton, MS
The Lillie Carmichael Evans School, Miami, FL
The Constance Lane School, Rockford, IL
George A. Pruitt Hall, Thomas Edison State University, Trenton, NJ
The Levi Watkins Memorial Institute, Tennessee State University,
    Nashville, TN
Jewel Williams Street, Canton, MS

While not directly from the Carmichael lineage, I want to mention the
Levi Watkins Sr. Learning Center, Alabama State University, Montgomery, AL, named after Levi's distinguished father. Levi's sister, Marie, married a wonderful man named Michael Garraway, who was on the faculty
at Ohio State University. Unfortunately, we lost Michael much too soon
to prostate cancer. Marie and Michael had three gifted children. The two
oldest were moved by their father's death to pursue careers in cancer
research. Levi A. Garraway became a professor of oncology at the Harvard University School of Medicine before leaving to continue his research

in the pharmaceutical industry. He was inducted as a fellow of the American Association for Cancer Research. His sister Isla Garraway is a professor and researcher in oncology at UCLA, and their younger sister, Doris, is a professor of French at Northwestern University in Chicago.

James Carmichael Rennick, great grandson of James Carmichael, was chancellor of the University of Michigan at Dearborn, chancellor of the North Carolina A&T University, and a vice president at the American Council on Education.

My brother, Joseph Pruitt Jr., was a member of the psychology faculty at the University of Southern California; he then went on to become director of the Crisis Services Unit of the Los Angeles County Department of Mental Health and clinical director of the Exceptional Children's Foundation, Los Angeles, followed by a long and distinguished career as a psychotherapist.

George Evans, after finishing first in his class at Meharry Medical School, became an iconic figure in Greensboro, North Carolina. Percy Abram III serves as head of school of the Bush School in Seattle. Beverly Guy-Shefthall is a professor of English and women's studies and founding director of the Women's Research and Resource Center at Spelman College. She is also an exemplar in the field of feminist literature, having authored more than ten books, thirty articles, and numerous published essays. She has received numerous honors and awards and, in 2016, was inducted into the American Academy of Arts and Sciences.

The list of high-achieving members of William and Olivia's offspring goes on and on. I hope those not mentioned will forgive me. What makes these accomplishments so extraordinary is that they were achieved in the face of significant racial, social, and economic barriers. Most of these individuals were the product of segregated, underresourced schools created by a society that had no expectation such achievement was possible.

Chapter Eight

Fair Morgan, as onward the years quickly fly, and thou livest in memory sweet.

—The Morgan State University Alma Mater

Morgan State University was a private college until 1939 when it was acquired by the state of Maryland. While its original mission was to prepare men of color for the ministry, it soon transformed into a teacher training school to prepare African American teachers for segregated schools.

The body of great scholars from the fifties and early sixties had begun to atrophy as distinguished faculty retired, and it became increasingly difficult to replace them with people of comparable stature. It was also challenging to compete with White schools who offered prominent Black faculty higher salaries and more robust research facilities. Additionally, the Maryland State College system regulations no longer allowed Morgan to build competitive salary and benefit packages to vie for the top talent it could formerly attract.

By 1972, Morgan was firmly rooted in the 1950s. This was not uncommon at historically Black colleges and universities (HBCUs) at the time. Tuskegee Institute and many of the public Black colleges were created to produce a workforce for a segregated America. Other institutions like Fisk, Howard, Morehouse, and Morgan saw their role as nurturing a Black intelligentsia for what Anna Julia Cooper and W.E.B. Du Bois described as the "talented 10th" of Black society. In the late 1960s, Bennett College, a Black women's institution, viewed itself as a "finishing school" for "educated ladies." Though "Bennett Belles" were required to wear stockings, heels, pearls, and white gloves to attend chapel on Sundays, the same students, with the support of their president, would discard the pearls, change clothes, and join students from North Carolina A&T University in demonstrations to integrate lunch counters in Greensboro. Many of these students were assaulted and arrested. At Spelman College, the same period saw the emergence of young activist Black feminist scholars. The contradiction between "old school" tradition and contemporary social relevance created widespread campus protests. Students felt oppressed by their own university administrations and faculty, who were operating from traditions that were no longer relevant. Most of the student demonstrations at HBCUs in the '60s were not about racism or segregation; rather, they were quests for better treatment, autonomy, and student engagement.

The disconnect between what was happening on the campus and what was happening in the country prompted the new president to charge me with creating a more contemporary and relevant campus experience. I began with the student code of conduct, which was rigid, paternalistic, and autocratic. While the code I inherited contained harsh and sometimes arbitrary provisions that violated due process, other aspects of student accountability were surprisingly lax. For example, if you were pregnant and unmarried or even suspected of getting someone pregnant, you would be expelled, but if you were dealing drugs on campus, you would not be turned over to the police.

College policy prohibited the Baltimore City Police Department from coming to campus uninvited. Campus security personnel were not allowed to press charges against students committing nonviolent crimes on college property. I supported the practice of keeping the police off campus, as many other colleges did, but I expected campus security to enforce the law, and that included turning offenders over to the police for prosecution when crimes were committed.

My first month on campus, I walked through the student union building and noticed a drug deal going down. When I asked the head of campus security about it, he replied that his hands were tied by the administration. The drug dealers recognized a sanctuary when they saw one and moved in. We worked out the necessary protocols with the city police and shut down the drug dealing in one week. I'm sure it didn't stop, but at least we moved it off campus.

King asked that I work with him and Stu Brooks, assistant to the president, in managing the institution's government relations portfolio. He added "Executive Assistant to the President" to my title. Some of what I consider our greatest achievements at Morgan included doubling the enrollment of the freshman class, reconceptualizing the placement office, creating WEAA Radio, and instituting full-time physician coverage in the campus health center.

We established the first Office of Veterans Affairs to serve returning Vietnam veterans who enrolled in the college. We recruited Earl Banks as athletic director, established a firm financial foundation for the athletic department, and won the NCAA Division II national championship in men's basketball.

I also recruited two of my childhood friends, Clarke Williams and John Townsend. Clarke was a math whiz and had a great head for finance. He became the business manager for the athletic program. It was because of Clarke that the athletic department's deficits disappeared. John Townsend played football at Morehouse and earned his masters at Illinois State. Upon his graduation, I was able to convince him to join Earl Banks's staff with the football team. Having two of my best friends at the university made living in Baltimore a lot more fun.

We faced many challenges. We were underfunded and suffered from declining enrollment and significant administrative overhead costs associated with the large percentage of students who received federal financial aid.

The enrollment affected not only our student revenues but the size of our state appropriation. Historically, well-prepared Black students in Maryland didn't have many other options; therefore, Morgan was not accustomed to competing with other institutions for students. As a consequence of the civil rights movement, many colleges and universities now pursued students who would have automatically come to Morgan. I never had any formal training in marketing, but I intuitively understood that our task was to differentiate ourselves in the marketplace, so bright, talented Black students would identify with us and enroll.

Colleges and universities didn't advertise back then. When I was at Towson, I met Dave Barton of Barton and Gillette, a well-known marketing and advertising firm. On several occasions, we discussed Morgan's enrollment challenges. Dave liked King Cheek and wanted to help me. We decided to produce a short promotional film for high schools, community events, church gatherings, and movie theaters.

Dave agreed to take on the project at cost. We could find no example where this had been done before, and he came to the project with great enthusiasm. We shot the film and evaluated it with focus groups. It tested well with both potential students and their families.

Before we launched, we solicited feedback from the Morgan faculty. Even though it tested well with the target audience, the faculty hated it, likely because it wasn't about them. While the film gave homage to the great faculty we had, most of the footage highlighted the quality of student life and postgraduate outcomes. Since we were not trying to recruit faculty with it, we decided to ignore their objections and launch it anyway.

We recruited Francine Ailer as director of admissions, aligned our marketing with the new film, and increased our contact with Maryland high schools. By the time I left Morgan three years later, we had doubled the enrollment of new students. The film was used to great effect for many years.

Haywood Harrison, the college's advancement vice president secured a sizable grant to start a public radio station at Morgan. Under Haywood's leadership, consultants and lawyers were retained to secure the necessary permits and licenses. Once this transpired, the responsibility to create and operate the station shifted to me. It was a source of great pride when WEAA went on the air. We attracted some great talent, and the station was a tremendous asset to the college and metropolitan Baltimore. The station is alive and well today, and when I'm in the area, I try to remember to tune in, always with a smile.

With the exception of the University of Maryland, College Park, Morgan was the only other school with a long-standing and robust tradition as an illustrious intercollegiate athletic program. We had especially strong football, basketball, and track programs. In addition to our successful basketball team, Morgan boasted a long roster of eventual NFL football players, track stars, and track records at the Penn relays.

When I arrived, the athletic program was struggling. Morgan was governed by its own board of trustees when the athletic program was built. When the system took over and the school lost its board, it fell into a "one size fits all" regulatory structure that didn't accommodate Morgan's unique mission, role, strengths, and capacity. The state college system bureaucracy straightjacketed all of the state colleges. Fisher fought it at Towson, but Morgan bore the brunt of it. We could not use state appropriations or tuition to support athletics, and it was grossly under resourced. The program was supported exclusively by student athletic fees, ticket sales, and fundraising. This did not have much effect on the other schools because they never had Morgan's storied athletic tradition.

A great source of institutional pride, Morgan's successful athletic program was central to the unique community and political support the college enjoyed. Our football games drew large crowds, but our basketball attendance was limited by the capacity of our gymnasium. Football was the only significant source of revenue for athletics, but it also had the greatest operating costs. With the president's concurrence, I recruited Earl Banks, our legendary football coach, to serve in the additional capacity as director of intercollegiate athletics.

The major fundraiser for athletics was the annual Grambling/Morgan Classic in Yankee Stadium. Both schools benefitted economically from the substantial crowds, but it was more important to Morgan than to

Grambling. It was a cultural experience with ancillary events and entertainment surrounding the game. While it was always a financial success,
the disappointment for me was that we could never win the game!

Grambling had a notable, well-funded football program led by a
remarkable coach. We had an impressive program and coach but meager
funding. During the three years I was there, we eliminated the deficit and
restructured the finances of the program to make it self-supporting. Sadly,
we never did beat Grambling.

Many years later, I was invited by President Earl Richardson to place
the hood on my friend Jim Fisher when Morgan awarded him an honorary degree. I took great satisfaction in seeing that the football field had
been named after Earl Banks.

I had been at Morgan a little over a year when King Cheek informed
me that he was leaving. I was devastated. The reason I had left my friends
at Towson was to build something important with this charismatic and
visionary young leader. Since I married his sister-in-law, we had become
close personal friends as well as colleagues.

King Cheek left Morgan State College in 1974 after three years in office.
He was appointed president of a new, innovative consortium of institutions called the Union for Experimenting Colleges and Universities. It was
a confederation of about fifteen diverse institutions; some were large and
prestigious, others were small and obscure, but they were all high quality.
Each institution was led by a creative president who wanted a degree-
granting innovation laboratory in which to experiment with different
models of higher education. The Union, as it was called, was licensed by
the board of regents of the state of Ohio and was accredited by what is now
the Higher Learning Commission.

By this time, Jim, Buzz, Paul, and now King were all encouraging me
to pursue a college presidency. I knew that to follow their advice, I would
need to earn a terminal degree. While I was sincerely interested in further study, my major objective was to secure the appropriate credentials.
I was practical about it and explored several options.

It was King Cheek who suggested the Union. The Union was ground-breaking at the time in that it encouraged an integration of different fields to create new, specialized, and individualized disciplines. They were looking for accomplished adults who could benefit from the freedom allowed by this model to produce high-quality outcomes and research. I was confronted with a dilemma of conscience. The safest option would be to go with Johns Hopkins—prominent, well known, and respected. The riskiest was the Union Graduate School, new and innovative but unknown with an uncertain future. The Union stood for everything I believed in pertaining to the future of doctoral education. The challenge was deciding whether it was a reasonable risk. I took the leap and have never regretted it.

My doctoral studies were a combination of organizational development, management, leadership, and higher education. The chair of my doctoral committee was Leo McLaughlin, former president of Fordham University. I received my PhD from the Union in 1974.

Later, I would serve on the Union's board of trustees for twenty-three years and chair during its most challenging period. We navigated the tragic and unexpected death of President Bob Connelly, a failed succession, and the appointment of President Roger Sublett, who led the university through a transformational renaissance. At the conclusion of my service in 2011, I was awarded an honorary degree.

When it came time for my doctoral research project, I wanted to do something that was both relevant and useful to my chosen path. Uncle Doc always used to tell me: "If you want to learn how to do something, learn from someone who does it well." One of the personality theorists I most admired was Abraham Maslow. Whereas many psychologists were preoccupied with understanding pathology, emotionally healthy people fascinated Maslow. His most famous contribution was his "hierarchy of needs." He was particularly interested in the characteristics of "self-actualized" people, the healthiest state in his taxonomy.

In the '60s and '70s, campuses were in turmoil, and college presidents were dropping like flies. Two professors who wrote a book on presidential leadership concluded that presidents were fundamentally well-intentioned people who were casualties of the times, that contemporary colleges were unmanageable, and that leadership didn't make much of a difference. I asserted that the most important element in a university's success was the efficacy of its president's leadership.

I observed great presidents like Theodore Hesburg at Notre Dame, Kingman Brewster at Yale, James Fisher at Towson, Benjamin Mays at Morehouse, and many others who safely led their institutions through troubled waters. I decided to take my uncle's advice and learn from exemplary people who had "done it well." Not all presidents are successful, and I wanted to understand the attributes that differentiated the effective ones. In 1988, my research was validated when it was used as the prototype in a large national study contained in *The Effective College President* by James Fisher, Martha Tack, and Karen Wheeler.

In 1974, when Tom Frazier was named interim president, I was concerned but shouldn't have been. In the short time that Frazier led Morgan, he accomplished one of the greatest transformational achievements in the school's history. There were two Morgans: one was conservative, out of touch, and preoccupied with the illusion of a glorious history that had long since passed; the other Morgan was youthful, active, and relevant to contemporary conditions. King Cheek stimulated the latter, and Tom Frazier was firmly rooted in the former. However, he understood Morgan's achievements were made possible because the school had its own autonomous board of trustees who were able to recruit and support effective presidential leadership like Martin Jenkins and his predecessors. Frazier wanted to free Morgan from the state system bureaucracy and return it to its own board of trustees. He was absolutely right, and his vision united the two Morgans.

Morgan held considerable political influence in Maryland. HBCUs were important engines of the civil rights movement through the activism of their faculty and students and their influential alumni. Most of the Black members of the state legislature were Morgan graduates. Parren Mitchell, the first African American member of Congress from Maryland, was a member of the faculty, and much of his campaign support derived from the campus community.

Politicians of all races wanted to appear supportive of the college. Tom Frazier's push for independence was not well received by the state college system or the state bureaucracy, but he was steadfast and fearless in his pursuit. After all, he was interim and had nothing to lose.

We worked as a team in support of Frazier's vision of an autonomous Morgan with its own board of trustees. Homer Favor (dean of the School of Urban Studies), Horace Judson (vice president for academic affairs), Haywood Harrison, Stu Brooks, and I went to work in the community and the state legislature to advocate for the passage of the legislation and create the conditions to secure the governor's signature. In addition to its own board of trustees, the bill also granted Morgan university status and expanded its mission. It was a great triumph for Interim President Frazier, and I hope his historic contribution is well noted and celebrated at what is now Morgan State University.

All of us who were involved in the achievement were very much aware that we had done something truly important. After a momentary stumble with the president who followed Frazier, the new board recruited Earl Richardson as Morgan's president. Richardson, with the support of his own board, built Morgan into one of the finest universities of any ethnicity in the country. None of Richardson's transformational leadership achievements would have been possible without the structural changes brought on through Frazier's determined and fearless leadership.

A period of severe financial distress also occurred during Frazier's tenure. To avoid running a deficit, we had to cut costs, lay off staff, and eliminate obsolete programs. It was the first but, unfortunately, not the last time I would have to lay off members of my team. This was one of the most distressing times in my life because these cuts included my friend John Townsend. Eliminating his position was not my decision, and I was upset that I couldn't save him. Fortunately, his leaving Morgan led to a long and successful coaching career in the Big Ten and the Ivy League.

Terminating people for poor performance is an uncomfortable but necessary part of management. Some executives fail because they lack the strength to do it, even when it is critical to the health of the organization. You should not go into management if you do not have the will or ability to enforce accountability. However, layoffs are entirely different. It is horrible to inflict the pain of unemployment on a competent member of your staff simply because the organization cannot afford to keep them.

Following the passage of the bill, the trustees' first task was to recruit a new president after Tom Frazier went back into retirement. Any time an organization changes CEOs, it triggers a period of great uncertainty for the institution. It is especially true for cabinet officers and those directly responsible to the new chief executive. I hoped that the board would get it right. We were encouraged by the fact that the new trustees seemed to be experienced and competent people.

When Andrew Billingsley was announced as the next president of Morgan, both Judson and I were optimistic. We thought the progress we wrestled out of the place would continue and a great new chapter for Morgan lay ahead. We looked forward to serving on Andy's leadership team. We were wrong.

Andrew Billingsley took office early in 1975. To be fair, Andy and I got along fine, but I was horrified by how he treated others. He bragged to me once that while at Howard, he had fired three deans in five minutes. He was often unpredictable. The environment and morale deteriorated rapidly, and after several months, I concluded that I couldn't work for him.

For the first time in my professional life, I was going to have to look for a job. Buzz had recruited me to Illinois State, and Towson and King had invited me to Morgan. Now it was up to me to figure out what to do next. I started by reaching out to friends and colleagues, one of whom was Jerry Durley, who was doing similar work at Northern Illinois University. He told me a friend and former colleague of his, Fred Humphries, was serving his first year as president of Tennessee State University and was looking for a new vice president for student affairs. He knew Fred well, had great respect for him, and thought we would make a great fit. Shortly after Jerry nominated me for the position, I was contacted by the search committee and invited to interview. This went well, and Fred offered me the job. I was delighted and accepted. We moved to Nashville, and I assumed my new position in October 1975.

Leaving Morgan was bittersweet. While I was only there for three years, we had accomplished a lot. The resolution passed and presented to me by the board of trustees upon my departure included a listing of specific achievements we had accomplished that would benefit the university for years to come. I also made some great friends at Morgan. I was sad to leave Buzz, Jim, and Paul at Towson and of course my cousin and good friend Levi Watkins. I was off to Tennessee State to begin my second vice presidency. I was twenty-nine years old.

1. George A. Pruitt. Courtesy of the Thomas Edison State University Archives.

2a. *Left to right:* Arnold Fletcher, Larraine Matusak, Ellie Spiegel. Courtesy of the Thomas Edison State University Archives.

2b. *Left to right:* George A. Pruitt, General Charles "Chuck" Yeager, Major General Francis R. Gerard, Trenton mayor Arthur Holland, Princeton mayor Barbara Boggs Sigmund. Courtesy of the Thomas Edison State University Archives.

3a. Morris T. Keeton and George A. Pruitt. Courtesy of the Thomas Edison State University Archives

3b. *Left to right:* W. Cary Edwards, Pearl Bailey, George A. Pruitt, John S. Watson. Courtesy of the Thomas Edison State University Archives.

4. *Top row, left to right:* Joseph H. Pruitt Sr., George A. Carmichael (Uncle Doc), Bertille Carmichael, Joseph H. Pruitt Jr. *Middle row, left to right:* Lillie Carmichael Pruitt, Willie S. Carmichael, George M. Carmichael, Evie C. Wilson. *Bottom row, left to right:* George A. Pruitt, Evie H. Wilson, Janice A. Wilson. Author's collection.

5a. The original members of the Thomas Edison State College Foundation Board. *Top row, left to right:* John Connelly, Edward Booher, Richard Hansen, Michael Scheiring, Richard Gillespie. *Seated:* George A. Pruitt and Chris Yegen. Courtesy of the Thomas Edison State University Archives.

5b. *Left to right:* Governor Thomas H. Kean, John Moore, George A. Pruitt, Harold Eickhoff, Donald E. Walters. Courtesy of the Thomas Edison State University Archives.

6a. *Left to right:* Trenton mayor Douglas Palmer, Governor Christine Todd Whitman, George A. Pruitt. Courtesy of the Thomas Edison State University Archives.

6b. *Left to right:* Leonard Coleman, Nomalizo Leah Tutu, Desmond Tutu, George A. Pruitt. Courtesy of the Thomas Edison State University Archives.

6c. *Standing, left to right:* Kenneth Hawkins, Bernard Crowell, Harvey Alexander. *Seated, left to right:* George A. Pruitt, Frederick S. Humphries, Calvin Atchison. Courtesy of the Tennessee State University Archives.

7. *Left to right*: George A. Pruitt, Congresswoman Bonnie Watson
Coleman, Pamela Pruitt. Author's collection.

8a. *Left to right:* Virginia Foxx, George A. Pruitt, Pamela Pruitt. Author's collection.

8b. *Left to right:* George A. Pruitt, Pamela Pruitt, Robin Walton, Congressman Robert "Bobby" Scott. Author's collection.

9a. George A. Pruitt appearing before the House Committee on Education, April 2017. Courtesy of the House Education and Labor Committee.

9b. *Left to right:* George A. Pruitt, Shayla N. Pruitt, Governor James Florio, Lucinda Florio. Courtesy of the Thomas Edison State University Archives.

10a. *Left to right:* Trustee Brian Maloney, George A. Pruitt, Trenton mayor Eric Jackson. Courtesy of the Thomas Edison State University Archives.

10b. *Left to right:* C. Richard Gillespie, Kenneth "Buzz" Shaw, George A. Pruitt, James L. Fisher.

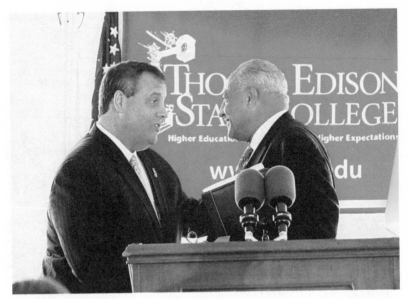

11a. Governor Chris Christie and George A. Pruitt. Courtesy of the Thomas Edison State University Archives.

11b. *Left to right:* George A. Pruitt, Congressman John Lewis, Pamela Pruitt. Author's collection.

Chapter Nine

In the land of golden sunshine, by the Cumberland's fertile shore.
—Laura Averitte, Tennessee State University Alma Mater

When I arrived in Nashville, I had no idea that I would be involved in one of the greatest adventures of my life and one of the most consequential leadership challenges of my career. Tennessee State University (TSU) was founded in 1912 as part of the "dual system" of segregated higher education in the South. Through its long and distinguished history, it was fortunate to boast the leadership of three exceptional presidents.

The first was the founding president, William J. Hale, who led the university from 1912 to 1943. He established an extraordinary foundation for a school that was uncommonly robust for a segregated university of its time. It was rumored that President Hale was the Black half brother of a White governor of the state and that the university benefitted from that relationship. I have no idea if it was true, but it was a credible myth if it wasn't. The second great president was Walter S. Davis, who led the institution from 1943 to 1968.

If Hale laid the foundation, it was Davis who built the university. The university was designated as a land grant university in 1958, and under Davis's leadership, new academic programs were introduced, the enrollment exploded, and twenty-four buildings were constructed. He also used the school athletic programs to break down racial barriers. If Hale founded it, and Davis built it, it was Fredrick S. Humphries who saved it. President Humphries led the university through ten of its most challenging years, during which its very existence would hang in the balance.

Although I had never visited the university prior to my on-campus interview, I felt a comfort and familiarity from the moment I arrived. President Davis was also from Canton. He was a close friend of Uncle Doc's and the rest of my mother's family. My uncle and aunt spent part of their honeymoon at the president's residence on the university's campus, and I have vague memories of the great man playing with me on the floor of my grandparent's living room when I was a child.

Davis recruited several of his lifelong friends and colleagues to join him at the university, and he made a special effort to make Tennessee State a friendly place for students from Mississippi. My cousin Levi and my mother's youngest sister, Evie, graduated from TSU, and my cousin Percy began there before transferring to California State Los Angeles.

Former President and Mrs. Davis were especially welcoming when I joined the university. They greeted me with open arms and treated me like family. The director of financial aid was Homer Wheaton, and his family and my family had been lifelong friends.

Barbara Murrell, who would become my "second in command," was from Greenwood, Mississippi. She was a graduate of the university and former "Miss TSU." When the Tennessee State football team played against Jackson State in Mississippi, there were no hotels where an African American homecoming queen and her court could stay. Dr. Davis arranged for Barbara to stay with Uncle Doc in Canton, so she could attend to her ceremonial duties at the game. The intertwining histories of the university, Dr. Davis, and my mother's family and friends made me feel right at home in Nashville.

I had certain expectations of what a great historically Black college would be. At Morgan, I was disappointed. At Tennessee State, I found everything I hoped for. The professionals, teachers, and scholars were efficient and experienced. They loved students, took pride in the institution, and had a real sense of camaraderie, community, and respect for each other. They honored the institution's great history of achievement without limiting themselves to its past. They were innovative and ambitious, and in Fred Humphries they found the perfect leader to forge ahead and secure its future. Little did we know what was in store. Our ability, character, and spirit would be tested in ways we never imagined, and in the end, our true colors burned bright.

Fred was from Apalachicola, Florida, attended Florida A&M University, and went on to earn a PhD in chemistry from the University of Pittsburgh. He assumed the presidency of Tennessee State in January 1975 and was met with great challenges the minute he set foot on campus. Before Fred arrived, the Tennessee Board of Regents, the university's governing body, signed a contract with a technology company to install a new student information system and to manage the computer center. The new systems were installed, and an external vendor was secured to manage the data processing. The first test of the vendor's new systems and management would occur in the fall of 1974, and it failed miserably. The old system had not been retained as backup, and all previous data was lost. An adequate solution for the spring semester had not been found by the time Fred arrived.

His first challenge was to improvise a manual registration system for over six thousand students with no data processing support whatsoever. It was a major crisis. Class schedules, course registrations, housing rosters, financial aid, fee assessment, and payments had to be processed manually. This early test of the campus community and the heroic collective effort they displayed to pull it off was a testament to Humphries's leadership. The board of regents tried to blame the campus for the debacle, but the paper trail was clean and unambiguous. The vendor had been imposed on the university by the regents' staff, and they screwed up.

Finger pointing and threats of litigation commenced at the system level, while the campus struggled to make sure students were in classes by the beginning of the semester. They pulled it off. The vendor contract was terminated for nonperformance, and what was left of the university's IT staff began the difficult process of jury-rigging systems to regain data processing capacity.

By the time I arrived, some primitive systems support had been restored. Admissions, registration, financial aid, and housing all reported to me. It was impossible to manage these critical university functions without adequate data processing support. We worked shoulder to shoulder with the IT team to construct patchwork systems to get us through the day-to-day, while at the same time working on the design and construction of an integrated system to restore normal operations for the long term. It was a daunting and tedious challenge.

When Fred became president, he also became a defendant in a federal desegregation lawsuit. The litigation began in 1968 when a group of community activists, alumni, faculty, and friends of Tennessee State University sought an injunction to prevent the proposed expansion of a center of the University of Tennessee located in Nashville. The plaintiffs contended that this action would create competition and perpetuate a segregated dual system of higher education. The state, in its defense, argued that the center did not have campus status, could not grant degrees, and existed solely to offer a few evening classes to part-time students; therefore, it was not a competitor or a threat to Tennessee State. The court agreed and did not grant the injunction.

Soon after the court ruling, the University of Tennessee proceeded to expand the Nashville center into everything it said it was not. It elevated the center into a branch campus, which it called the University of Tennessee at Nashville (UT-Nashville), gave it degree-granting authority, built a sprawling new campus facility in the heart of downtown Nashville, and expanded its academic offerings and budget. At the same time, the state began reducing its support for Tennessee State University.

A new lawsuit was filed in response to this change in circumstances. In 1973, another group of plaintiffs, "Richardson et al.," intervened in the case and proposed that the University of Tennessee at Nashville merge into Tennessee State University. Among the plaintiffs was a group called Tennesseans for Justice in Higher Education. Their counsel was Avon Williams, a brilliant civil rights attorney and state senator from Nashville. He was fiercely independent with unimpeachable integrity. The demographics of Nashville produced enough support to keep a distinguished civil rights attorney and activist in a safe senate seat and empower him with the independence to take on the state, the University of Tennessee, and the rest of higher education in federal court.

Many professionals were drawn to Nashville from all over the world, resulting in a diverse and cosmopolitan population uncharacteristic of the Deep South. It was home to over fifteen colleges and universities, which invited the nickname, "Athens of the South," complete with a full-size replica of the Parthenon. The largest and most prominent of these institutions was Vanderbilt University.

The presence of Tennessee State, Fisk University, and Meharry Medical College and Hospital, combined with independent Black-owned businesses, banks, architectural firms, law firms, and a large publishing company that produced hymnals for Black churches all over the country, resulted in a thriving economy driven by African Americans.

As president of Tennessee State, Fred found himself in the unusual position of appearing as a defendant in a lawsuit in which he publicly supported the plaintiff's position. The other defendants in the case were Governor Ray Blanton, the University of Tennessee, and the chancellor and board of regents system, which TSU was a part of. Governor Ray Blanton was by statute chair of the board of regents, but functionally the vice chair of the board exercised the power and influence in the governor's absence. In the entire time I was there, I never saw the governor at a board of regents meeting.

The conflict joined in 1975 when venerable and respected Cecil Humphries retired as chancellor of the board of regents system and was replaced by Governor Blanton's friend Roy Nicks. There was no search or selection process for the chancellor of the board of regents. Ray Blanton's sponsorship was more than sufficient. For Tennessee State University, this was the worst choice imaginable. Nicks, as head of UT-Nashville, was TSU's greatest antagonist. He was outspoken in his contempt for

TSU's leadership, faculty, and capacity. He often publicly ridiculed the notion that Tennessee State could assume the role of UT-Nashville in the state's capital.

There was an opportunity during the proceedings for questions prior to the board's vote on the appointment. Fred asked to speak and was denied. When the board relented, Fred questioned whether Nicks could be an advocate for the university given his derisive comments in the recent past. His question was considered impudent. Systems expect conformance and obedience from its member presidents, especially in public. The fact that Fred was Black and asked this question in the presence of the governor rendered his audacity particularly disturbing to Nicks, the governor, and some members of the regents. This meeting in Nashville was only seven years and two hundred miles from the assassination of Martin Luther King Jr. in Memphis. This was not the progressive "new south." This was still very much "old south" Tennessee. They did not care or respect that Fred was defending his university and protecting the legacy and future of African Americans in Tennessee.

Nicks's public response to the question was appropriate. He indicated his support of all six of the public universities and the community colleges within the board of regents system. He had a habit of turning red when he was angry, and that day he was red as a beet.

The lawsuit, which called for a merger of the two institutions with Tennessee State as the surviving entity, was pending in federal court. In fear of that, the state soon adopted, with great fanfare, a new two-school statewide desegregation plan to present to the court in defense of the status quo.

The two-school plan explicitly marginalized Tennessee State University, reducing its enrollment to 4,000 students while simultaneously expanding the University of Tennessee at Nashville to 16,000 students, including new graduate and doctoral programs. Fred understood that this two-school plan would result in the demise of his institution, and that was something he could not and would not endorse. Fred again offended the higher education hierarchy, when in a response to a reporter, he indicated that the plan was the second-best solution to the problem. However, the state's considerable African American community took notice of Fred's courageous defense of the university, and his popularity and reputation rapidly grew. This was disturbing to Nicks, the regents staff, and elements of the state's political culture. Fred earned the support of the Legislative Black Caucus, Black ministers and community organizations, and alumni groups in Memphis, Chattanooga, and Knoxville as well.

Sterlin Adams, a plaintiff in the lawsuit, was executive assistant to the president. Sterlin was from Memphis and had deep community ties there. Previously a member of the mathematics faculty at TSU, he was incredibly bright and a fearless activist. As a supporter of the plaintiff's position, Fred didn't think it was an issue that his executive assistant was a plaintiff in the case. Roy Nicks, however, considered it a significant problem, so much so that he insisted Fred fire Sterlin. Fred refused.

By the time I arrived in October, Fred Humphries was a threat to the governor, the leadership of the board of regents system, and the University of Tennessee. I came to Tennessee to join a university leadership team, but I soon realized that I had landed smack in the middle of a major civil rights battle. People who involved themselves in this type of struggle had a lot more to fear than job loss, but when I came to understand the nature of the cause we were pursuing and the character and integrity of my colleagues, I was all in.

Fred, Sterlin, and I were joined by other members of this admirable team. Harvey Alexander was one of the finest chief financial officers I had ever met. Bernard Crowell, vice president for academic affairs, and Fred were former colleagues and friends. Calvin Atchinson, the chief advancement vice president, was a longtime member of the TSU community.

The chancellor and the head of the board of regents system confronted Fred after he refused to support the two-school desegregation plan. They threatened there would be "consequences" if he didn't get on board. The situation in Tennessee was not about a coherent system strategy around an educational policy. It was about civil rights and social justice involving the survival of an iconic institution vital to the African American community.

The state was slowly starving Tennessee State while pouring resources and new programs into the University of Tennessee at Nashville. There was an abundance of testimony and evidence produced in the trial to support the notion that the state was building UT-Nashville, while stifling TSU for an eventual closure of TSU or acquisition by UT-Nashville. We could see the writing on the wall. We agreed that Nashville didn't have room for two public universities, but we were committed to Fred's vision that Tennessee State University would be the surviving institution. For a Deep South state like Tennessee in the midseventies, that outcome was inconceivable.

Fred understood the responsibility placed upon his shoulders. He responded to the chancellor and system board chair that he was aware of the gravity of the situation, but given the magnitude of the stakes for the university and people of color all over the nation who depended on this institution and the survival of its legacy, he was steadfast in his position. He was willing to accept the "consequences" of his advocacy. The proponents of the plan argued that the two-school solution guaranteed the survival of Tennessee State, but no one really believed that.

The leadership of the board of regents system was furious. They didn't expect Fred to put his principles ahead of protecting his job. They also understood that if they fired Fred over his defense of the university, the political aftershock would be severe, particularly for a Democratic Party and governor who relied heavily on African American support in the face of an increasingly growing Republican presence.

They also knew that Fred would likely be called to testify in the federal desegregation trial, and they had no idea what he would say. They had already threatened to fire him, and that didn't work, so they needed a new plan. The chancellor wanted to regain some leverage over Fred to influence his testimony and invent a plausible rationale for terminating him. That's when the siege began.

We were inundated with requests for information, investigations, and "review teams" looking into the finances and management of the university. There was much to examine, particularly focused on the business operations, especially the controller's office, financial aid, admissions and records, and athletics. The debacle caused by the collapse of the data systems wreaked havoc on administrative operations. Years of underfunding of capital improvements and maintenance left important elements of the campus infrastructure near collapse.

Athletics was quickly dropped from the inquisition. Football coach John Merritt and track coach Ed Temple were larger-than-life celebrities, and the regents' staff decided to leave them alone. Admissions and records and the financial aid office reported to me, so I was directly in the line of fire. We did have legitimate weaknesses in these areas, but they were not of the university's making; nor were they the fault of the competent and hardworking staff and leadership.

Tennessee had a sophisticated funding formula for allocating resources to public higher education. The Tennessee Higher Education Commission collected an exhaustive amount of data to ascertain the cost of delivering instruction by discipline and level. Based on this extensive "cost study," they could decide the level of appropriation allocated to each institution. In theory, it was an efficient and transparent way to allot resources.

Unfortunately, the application of the formula for Tennessee State didn't take into account the demographics of our student body, capital funding, or infrastructure support. The enrollment at TSU was approximately six thousand students, yet we had more students on financial aid than institutions with enrollment at least three times our size. The institutional matching funds requirements of financial aid along with the disproportionate administrative costs associated with such a large proportion of needy students were burdensome. Our hefty facility and deferred maintenance deficit combined with a dilapidated capital infrastructure and desperate need for new data processing support left us at a huge disadvantage in the formula.

Of all the administrative challenges we faced, the most difficult was in student accounts receivables. Uncollectable receivables went back thirty years in some cases. At any other institution, these receivables would be written off to clean up the balance sheet. To write them off, we were required to obtain permission from state government, and that permission was not granted. Fred and Harvey Alexander invested new resources and recruited a talented new controller, Sandra Davis; however, the state's refusal to approve the write-off was not an accounting decision but a political one. Without adequate data processing support and the ability to clear the receivables, we couldn't get an "unqualified audit," and with a defective audit, the case was made that the president was incompetent.

There was a heroic effort led by Ed Wisdom to disentangle ourselves from the company the regents hired to manage our IT and begin the herculean task of rebuilding our data processing support from the ground up. Ed had to concoct short-term stopgap measures while simultaneously designing the architecture of permanent new management systems, technology platforms, and staff recruitment and training.

The siege surrounded us on multiple fronts. We had to keep current operations running effectively, address and fix the consequences of years of underfunding, defend the school from the chancellor and his staff, and manage the community building that served as the basis of our political support all while preparing for the upcoming desegregation case.

For years, the state denied the university's request for funds to repair and upgrade the boilers that supplied the campus with heat and the network of underground cables that provided electricity. It was just another ploy to starve TSU while generous investments were made in UT-Nashville. Right on time, and on Fred's watch, these systems began to fail. We experienced power blackouts to large sections of the campus. The staff and the resources of the physical plant were stretched to the breaking point. Their valiant efforts were insufficient in the face of worn-out and obsolete equipment that had long outlived their life span.

As was the case with Towson and Morgan, I was once again feeling like the mayor of a small town. I was responsible for the housing and care of several thousand students. It was an on-call, 24/7 responsibility. Fred and I spent many a night in a utility tunnel at 3:00 A.M. watching our physical plant staff attempt to restore power to our residence halls. We weren't qualified to assist, but we wanted to understand what our people were up against, so we would have firsthand knowledge in framing a response and pursuing a solution. We were new and needed to figure out whether these problems were with our systems or with our people. We quickly discovered that our staff was competent and experienced and demonstrated a tireless commitment to the university. The challenges and conditions that the physical plant staff endured were indefensible. It was infuriating that the state neglected the campus to this extent. This would never have been inflicted on or tolerated by any of the White colleges or universities.

Of course, we were blamed and criticized for the blackouts, but we were able to produce documentation of our requests for funds and external consulting reports that made it difficult for the chancellor and his staff to hang the responsibility on the university administration. Our students and student government were supportive of us. We trusted them and they trusted us. Even though they had to bear the consequences of the conditions, their support for our president and his team, including me, never wavered.

Just when we thought things couldn't get any worse, they did. In the middle of a record-setting cold spell with all of Nashville covered in snow and ice, the boilers failed. We had no heat. We had lived through some uncomfortable and inconvenient conditions, but this was dangerous.

We were forced to close the university and evacuate the students. We reorganized the academic calendar and started "spring break" early. Most students were able to go home, but many were stranded in the residence halls. We quickly made arrangements for housing and transportation.

There is no manual for these types of contingencies. Our team were masters at improvisation. Titles, rank, and position all went out the window, and it was "all hands on deck." I wasn't crawling around in utility tunnels, but I carried bags and quickly learned how to drive a bus without time for the appropriate training and licensure.

This time there was outrage. The story made the national news, and local press and politicians demanded an investigation. When the students returned, they organized and conducted a well-disciplined and peaceful march to the state capital, demanding attention. Again, the chancellor's staff tried to blame the administration, and again the documentation, evidence, and consultant reports refuted the allegations. The state provided emergency assistance, and the heating plant received upgraded boilers and associated improvements.

Nevertheless, the siege didn't let up, and we continued to play defense. Most of the attacks, while infuriating, were ineffective; however, one of the grenades got through and landed directly in my wheelhouse. When the data processing system collapsed without backup, the university lost the capacity to calculate a student's cumulative average. Every semester we manually calculated and individually audited candidates for graduation to make sure they satisfied the degree requirements. Given our substantial enrollment, this was a phenomenal challenge for our registrar's office. We had no ability to calculate the cumulative averages for the rest of the students and therefore could not determine whether they maintained the grade point averages necessary to continue. In other words, we couldn't identify the students who should have flunked out.

The board of regents staff was aware of this. In fact, they knew their mismanagement of the data processing vendor's contract had created the problem in the first place. We were able to monitor standards of progress for federal financial aid recipients, but this problem would not be resolved until data processing support could be restored. The burden on the bursar, registrar, and financial aid departments was crushing.

The siege put all of us under a great deal of stress. None felt it more than Cass Teague, director of admissions and records. Like many seasoned TSU professionals, Cass had spent his career at Tennessee State. The loyalty, dedication, and tireless effort Teague showed in leading his team through the crisis will never be known or fully appreciated beyond those of us who supported and worked with them through that difficult period.

Over 90 percent of our students received some sort of financial assistance. Homer Wheaton and his team in financial aid made exceptional efforts to keep the office functioning in spite of the impediments they had to overcome. As with admissions and records, the staff at financial aid was experienced, competent, professional, and dedicated; however, they were understaffed, and the physical condition of their office was deplorable. I could tell we had a problem, but Homer was reluctant to ask for assistance.

He was a proud man and thought he and his team could work out any problems they had. He finally opened up to me. He candidly shared what he and his team were up against, and I was able to make the case to the president that we needed additional investments to the financial aid infrastructure to provide the service our students and university depended upon. I had to identify resources within the student affairs division that could be repurposed for this additional support.

Because the state had an enrollment-driven funding formula and we lacked the capacity to dismiss students for academic reasons, the chancellor accused the president of padding enrollment to get state-appropriated funds to which we were not entitled.

The chancellor announced that he was sending an investigative team to report back to the legislature. The "investigation" was a fraud. They already had monitoring teams overseeing most areas of our administrative operation. Practically everything we did was under their scrutiny and with their full knowledge. The only upside of the siege was that they had no plausible deniability because they were constantly in our business. The idea that they had suddenly uncovered a "plot" was ludicrous, when we had records of discussions with their staff going back months, if not years. The investigative team interviewed members of our staff and poured over student records. Meanwhile, the person who led the group acknowledged that the whole thing was theater and that he had already written the report and findings before they arrived.

The report determined that a small team of staff could have calculated the cumulative averages with hand calculators in a couple of weeks. Again, a committee of the legislature held a hearing. Though no one from the university was invited, Sterlin and I invited ourselves.

We sat in the hearing room along with a sizeable student contingent who came to offer their support. Fortunately, Avon Williams was a member of the legislative committee. In the public hearing, Avon objected to the fact that no one from the university had been invited to respond. Avon and Sterlin Adams were very close. While I had met and knew the senator, our relationship was casual and businesslike. He and Sterlin, on the other hand, had known each other and worked together for years.

During a break, I was able to speak with Senator Williams. I explained that we had been working on this problem around the clock for months, and we were about a year away from getting it under control. I also told him that the chancellor's report was a work of fiction, although I used more direct language. I suggested they could settle the matter by letting the chancellor's team have at the records with calculators, and if they were successful in the time frame they indicated, then I would resign. On the other hand, if they were not, then my counterpart of the chancellor's staff should resign. The senator thought that was an interesting proposition.

I don't know what Avon said to the chancellor and some of the other legislators over coffee before the hearing resumed, but the chancellor looked over at me and turned crimson. Fred tasked me with writing the rebuttal to the chancellor's report, and the issue was not pursued. As I predicted, we had sufficient IT support restored within the year and were able to manually load previous grades of currently enrolled students to calculate cumulative averages once again.

One of the things I hated most was the damn "Fourteenth Day Report." It was the official university enrollment census of all the students with "zero balance" on their accounts as of the fourteenth day of classes. Every year, we would have hundreds of students arrive on campus without the money to pay for their tuition and fees. This was true at many historically Black colleges and universities. Most of our students had some combination of federal, state, or private financial aid. Some family contribution was usually necessary to close the gap between what they had and what they needed. Many of them thought if they got close enough, we would find a way to work it out for them. We tried very hard, and for many we were successful. Unfortunately, we couldn't help them all and had to send some home.

From the day the students showed up on campus, it was another all-hands-on-deck situation to save as many as we could. Although we never talked about it and didn't want it known for obvious reasons, all of us at some point reached into our own pockets to save a student whose story was so compelling we couldn't let them fail because of their poverty or family circumstances.

At the end of the fourteenth day, the bursar's office had to certify the list of students who made it and those who would be sent home. As I was leaving for the day, I saw staff in the bursar's office briefing Fred about their last-minute attempts to save as many students as possible.

Fred took off his coat and joined in, and I followed. We finished at 4:00 A.M., but we saved over two hundred students. We were all worn out, but we learned how to streamline the process and felt satisfied that we had done some good. We still had to send many students home. I also learned how important it is for senior executives and especially the president to understand how things work operationally. You always need to keep your sights on the big picture, but so much success or failure occurs where the rubber meets the road.

The quality of our human capital was tremendous. It stretched all the way back to President Davis, who assembled one of the most talented team of professionals any university could ask for, and that legacy was still in evidence by the time Fred and the rest of us joined. This was one of the finest communities I would ever have the privilege of belonging to, and the external threat we faced together formed a unifying and lasting bond.

On November 11, 1977, weighing seven pounds, eleven ounces, at slightly before 11:00 in the morning at Meharry Medical School Hospital, our daughter Shayla Nicole Pruitt was born. In my psychology courses, I had read about "peak experiences," but I don't think I'd ever really had one until the first time I laid eyes on my daughter. It felt like every emotion I was capable of experiencing was laid out on the keys of a piano, and they were all pressed at the same time. I have never felt like that before or since.

If we had a boy, we had already agreed that his name was going to be George Carmichael Pruitt. Despite the fact that my mother and father had both come from large families, my mother's maiden name would not survive beyond Uncle Doc. He had the last Carmichael name, and the Pruitt family name would not survive my brother and me, unless I had a son. We had a more difficult time coming up with a girl's name. One day we saw an article about the Ebony Fashion Fair and its commentator, Shayla Simpson. We both liked the name Shayla, Delores came up with Nicole, and the matter was settled.

While it often felt like being at Tennessee State was like working at the Alamo, in so many ways it was a wonderful place to be. I had great respect for the faculty, the colleagues I worked with, and the campus culture, and I loved our students. We also knew how to have a good time. It was an enjoyable time in my life.

As we approached the trial date of the desegregation case in federal court, the anxiety level on campus increased. Everyone was aware of the consequences of the outcome of the case. Though the intensity of the siege increased, we managed to achieve some major victories. Ever since the power outage and breakdown of the heating equipment, Fred was able to secure increased capital funding. As a result, we built a new physical education, athletic, and convocation complex. It was the most significant capital investment in the university in years. It included a ten-thousand-seat arena for basketball, convocation, performances, indoor track and field events, and an Olympic-size aquatic center. It also included an Olympic-size outdoor track for the world famous Tiger-belles women's track program.

The center was named after Howard Gentry, a legendary football coach at Florida A&M and then at Tennessee State University. He served with distinction as director of athletics for many years and was a part of the "golden age" under Walter Davis. Howard was a member of my cabinet until his retirement. He was active and well respected within the National Collegiate Athletic Association (NCAA). I was pleased that the new athletic and convocation center was named in his honor. It was a well-deserved acknowledgment of an extraordinary career. The Howard Gentry Center opened with a sold-out inaugural performance by Stevie Wonder.

Replacing Howard Gentry was a challenge. We knew that there weren't other obvious choices out there with his experience and stature. Given the history and visibility of athletics at Tennessee State, we wanted to get it right. Fred was an undergraduate at Florida A&M, which had a storied athletic tradition of its own. He was proud, competitive, and liked to win. He also understood how important TSU athletics was to the support the university benefitted from across racial and political party lines.

I sought the advice of several sports icons to aid the selection and hiring process, including the renowned Davis-era TSU basketball coach John McLendon and John Merritt, TSU's celebrated head football coach. Merritt was a legend in his own right. He was an iconic character who had been recruited personally by President Davis, and his record and impact were spectacular. Under Davis and McLendon, TSU became the first histori-cally Black college to integrate a national college basketball tournament. Led by one of McLendon's former players, New York Knicks Hall of Famer Dick Barnett, the team not only integrated the National Association of

Intercollegiate Athletics tournament but won the championship three times.

When I arrived at Tennessee State at twenty-nine years old, some wondered how I would handle leading a management portfolio with such giants as Merritt, Ed Temple, and Howard Gentry. Ed Temple coached Olympic gold medalist Ralph Boston, Wilma Rudolph, and the famous Tigerbelles, who would go on to achieve many world records and Olympic medals. We also had a successful basketball program under coach Ed Martin.

John Merritt came to TSU from Mississippi and was considered one of Walter Davis's "people." We liked, respected, and trusted each other. Merritt was an excellent coach, and he was supported by two of the most proficient assistant coaches the country ever produced. Alvin "Cat" Coleman was the offensive coordinator. He was from Canton, Mississippi, and a friend of my mother and the Carmichael family. The other was Joe Gilliam Sr., the defensive coordinator. Merritt, Coleman, and Gilliam were a troika: Merritt was in charge, but Coleman and Gilliam were his wingmen. They were a powerful team, inseparable and brilliant, and the results showed.

NFL Hall of Famer and Super Bowl champion with the Chicago Bears Richard Dent was one of "my" students at TSU, but Merritt had also produced Claude Humphries, the Atlanta Falcons great; Ed "Too Tall" Jones, the Dallas Cowboys legend; and "Jefferson Street" Joe Gilliam, the Pittsburgh Steelers quarterback. There were many other TSU football players who went on to have successful NFL careers.

"Jefferson Street" Joe had a particularly tragic story. Joe was Coach Gilliam's son and one of the most remarkable quarterbacks who ever lived. I heard Terry Bradshaw, Hall of Fame quarterback with the Pittsburgh Steelers, say on national television that, "if Joe Gilliam hadn't been ravaged by drug addiction, then no one would have ever heard of Terry Bradshaw." The world lost a gifted athlete, and Coach Gilliam lost his son.

We had all heard rumors about Merritt playing loose with the rules to win. Gentry and Merritt both assured us that wasn't true. We believed them, and I never saw any evidence to the contrary. Many competing coaches were jealous, and some of the stories we heard were just plain ridiculous. My favorite was that Ed "Too Tall" Jones came back from the Cowboys and played a game at TSU to help them win.

Both the President and I were very clear that we admired and respected them and were invested in their success under one condition: neither of us would tolerate any purposeful violations of NCAA rules. We also wanted the students to thrive academically and leave the university well educated. It was never a source of conflict. It's what we all believed in. As an undergraduate at the University of Illinois, I saw firsthand where that was not the case. At Towson, Morgan, and Tennessee State, we were committed to the ethical treatment of our student athletes.

After a national search, we offered the position to Sam Whitman, who was at Fisk University at the time. Having grown up in TSU athletics, including serving as a coach, Sam was known and well respected. Fred approved the recommendation, and I offered him the job.

We had a number of other challenges occurring simultaneously. During the Iranian Revolution of 1979, our Iranian students were divided into two factions: one side loyal to the deposed Shah and one side loyal to the Ayatollah, who overthrew him. Sometimes this division resulted in clashes between the factions. To complicate things, the Iranian hostage crisis inflamed anti-Iranian sentiments against students of both factions. We stayed in constant contact with various law enforcement agencies to protect our students from off-campus threats, both foreign and domestic.

The crises continued when one of our football players collapsed and died at practice one day. He received immediate and competent medical treatment but could not be saved. We were a close-knit community, and the loss was devastating. Then, the medical director of our health services committed suicide. Carr Treherne was a pillar of the Nashville community. He was a long-serving senior member of the Meharry Medical College faculty. He was charming, outgoing, and much loved. His loss and especially the circumstances surrounding his death were shocking.

Dr. Treherne had attended Meharry with Uncle Doc, and they were friends. He had befriended me as well, and I felt very close to him. He was also one of the attending physicians at the birth of my daughter.

Meanwhile, as the court date approached, the intensity of malicious public attacks on the administration increased. The confrontations between Fred, the chancellor, and his staff were often quite heated. Fred was steadfast and courageous in the face of the assault. The chancellor's quick temper caused him, on occasion, to lose control and blurt out statements that exposed his conspiratorial nature. On one occasion, when Fred got the better of an exchange with him in a public meeting, the chancellor acknowledged that he had been secretly recording their phone conversations.

When the trial began, the plaintiffs, through documents obtained during discovery, were able to construct a compelling argument that the state had in fact taken steps that, if allowed to continue, would eventually result in the subordination of Tennessee State University to the University of Tennessee at Nashville.

We knew the courtroom would be packed, so none of us attempted to attend the trial. I expected Sterlin to be there, and of course, Fred would be there as a defendant in the case. For us, the most important aspect of the trial was Fred's testimony. When Fred was called to testify as a defendant in the case, he did so for two and a half days in support of the plaintiff's position!

We were enormously proud of him and proud to be a part of his team in this important moment. Everyone else was infuriated and wanted to run him (and us) out of Tennessee. Before Fred left the stand, he was then asked if anyone had threatened him or intimidated him into giving testimony that was different than his true beliefs. He responded affirmatively. Avon then asked him for the source of the threats, and he named the chancellor and the chair of the board of regents.

Once his testimony concluded, Fred lost most of his leverage. We expected that the system would now come after him. Fred was positioned well from a political stance with a gubernatorial election approaching and enormous support from the Black community across the state. Also, Avon laid the groundwork for a wrongful termination suit if they attempted to remove Fred in retaliation. Nonetheless, we all felt at risk and waited for the other shoe to drop.

It did, in the form of a special board of regents meeting that was called to address the "Tennessee State situation." They decided to hold the meeting at East Tennessee State University in Johnson City. The location choice in the secluded hills of East Tennessee was strategic. They wanted a site that was isolated and as far away from the state's African American communities as they could get. We heard that Governor Blanton planned to fly in by helicopter to chair the meeting and suspected that Fred's removal from office was imminent. I expected that Sterlin Adams, Ed Isibor (the outspoken dean of the Engineering School), and I would be purged soon after.

It was a long and somber drive to Johnson City. I was resigned to our fate but confident we had done the right thing. We had no regrets, and my admiration for Fred Humphries couldn't have been stronger. The word of what was happening spread swiftly, and people started organizing in the minority communities around the state. Groups chartered buses in Memphis, Nashville, and Chattanooga to come in support of us. This alarmed state officials, and special details of state police were sent to Johnson City for crowd control.

The night before the board meeting, we heard rumors about last-minute drama developing. It seemed that Nicks and the board leadership had miscalculated the timing of their retribution. Democrat Jake Butcher was in a dead heat with Republican Lamar Alexander in the governor's race. The Butcher team worried that pushback from the African American community could cost their candidate the election. Alexander's campaign sent quiet sentiments of support for Tennessee State. The chancellor was in a bind.

We got word that the regents staff had stayed up half the night redrafting the script and resolution for the meeting the next day. Governor

Blanton canceled his attendance. When the meeting was called to order, we didn't know what to expect. The chancellor presented a litany of charges describing administrative and management troubles at the university, specious allegations generated by the siege. It was the "Bill of Particulars" the chancellor had compiled to justify Fred's termination. Instead, a resolution was introduced to place Fred on a six-month probationary period to demonstrate whether he had the capacity to lead the university. They punted. They postponed an action until after the election. They never mentioned Fred's support for the merger. Fred didn't care for the unfair, public reprimand, but we had survived to fight another day. I was relieved.

Fred and I checked out of the hotel and set out on the 321-mile drive to Cincinnati for a Tennessee State National Alumni Association meeting. We didn't talk much on the drive. We drove through a severe storm and passed a burning tree that had just been struck by lightning. Apropos given all we had been through.

We arrived in Cincinnati late that evening and went to our rooms exhausted. Fred was reinvigorated by the time he addressed the alumni. The buses carrying our supporters departed Johnson City without incident. Their show of support was inspirational. A statewide caravan of buses and people to fill them doesn't just happen spontaneously. It requires a lot of work, relationships, and organizational talent. I've always credited Sterlin Adams for this, although I don't recall us ever speaking about it. That has always been a characteristic of his, quietly getting things done without attention or credit.

The federal judge in the desegregation case ruled in our favor. He found that the state of Tennessee had in fact acted in a manner so as to perpetuate a dual system of higher education in violation of the Constitution. As a remedy, he ordered that the University of Tennessee at Nashville be merged into Tennessee State University.

Back on campus, there was jubilation. It was a historic victory, and we were elated. UT-Nashville was awash in tears and disbelief. The state immediately appealed the decision but lost at the appellate level as well. The court's decision was groundbreaking and unprecedented. To be sure, there had been plenty of court-ordered desegregation mergers since the *Brown* case, but none at the higher education level and none in which the historically Black institution survived and took over the predominantly White school. Our communities always suffered the consequences of losing these important social institutions and anchors. This victory was momentous.

The next significant event occurred when Lamar Alexander was elected governor. Soon after, Governor Blanton was indicted and arrested on charges of selling pardons. At the urging of the FBI, Alexander was sworn in as governor at midnight before his inauguration. Sometime after that, Jake Butcher was convicted and sent to prison for corruption stemming from his involvement with the Knoxville World's Fair.

With Blanton and Butcher both headed for federal prison, and a Republican governor and a federal judge looking over his shoulder in the merger, Nicks's influence dwindled. Life became considerably better for us, and Fred Humphries's "probation" was never mentioned again.

Creating one institution from two very different schools and cultures presented a new challenge for us. Fred's vision reaffirmed the university's historic commitment to the Black community while also welcoming students and faculty of all races. He continually pointed out that Tennessee State was the only institution in the state that had never turned away a student based on their race. It was a beautiful vision, but for people in Tennessee, it was disorienting. They understood what a White university was. They understood what a Black university was. After years of inflammatory diatribes and invectives led by the chancellor, the UT-Nashville and White communities of Tennessee couldn't envision a historically Black college with competent African American leadership and faculty that could be good enough or hospitable for them.

Fortunately, when Nicks left UT-Nashville to head to the board of regents, he was replaced by Dr. Charles Smith. Smith was the exact opposite of Nicks. Although he was loyal to the University of Tennessee, he was statesmanlike, collegial, and civil. He helped to change the relationship between the two institutions and after the court ruling did his best to facilitate the merger.

The UT-Nashville faculty was more resistant. They wrote proposals conceptualizing the merger as a consolidation of equals, resulting in a new identity. Some even suggested that the postmerger institution should have a new name. Fortunately, the language in the court order was specific and unambiguous. UT-Nashville was to be merged into Tennessee State University. The surviving institution, with all its history and traditions, was to be Tennessee State University, and the process for the execution of the absorption of UT-Nashville into Tennessee State would be court supervised.

As a magnificent cherry on the top of this achievement, the University of Tennessee at Nashville campus was later named the Avon Williams Campus of Tennessee State University. I can't think of a better or more well-deserved tribute to an extraordinary man.

My responsibility was to oversee the onboarding of the student affairs staff and programs. Usually in a merger or acquisition the resultant redundancy is eliminated. However, our merger plan maintained everyone's employment for a time. There wasn't any redundancy in student affairs due to the different missions and locations of the two campuses. UT-Nashville was an evening school for adults, so their students didn't require staff for student activities. Their existing student affairs structure stayed intact.

Bruce Hancock, their chief student affairs officer, reported to me and became a member of my senior staff. To his credit, Bruce did everything he could to make the transition work, and my team was gracious to him and his staff. While there were some hiccups and bumps, including some continuing skirmishes with the former UT-Nashville faculty, by and large, the merger was competently executed. This was no small feat, given the size, complexity, and cultural differences involved.

Personally, this was an exhausting but formative learning experience for me. I don't want to overstate my role. Community groups, activist faculty, and alumni began this struggle in the courts years before Fred Humphries arrived as president. This was a movement involving many people over a number of years including multiple plaintiffs in several court actions. By the time Fred arrived, the issues were already defined, and the battle joined. My principal role was in defending the president's flank when he was under attack in areas under my supervision and scope of responsibility. A small group of us felt we shared a foxhole together. The great respect and admiration we had for each other forged lifelong friendships. By the time the "merger wars" ended, we were all drained, but the pace didn't let up. Just when we thought we were through with mergers, another one popped up.

Peabody College was one of the few independent schools of education in the country. It was physically across the street from and closely associated with Vanderbilt University, but it was not a part of Vanderbilt. Vanderbilt students and Peabody students took courses on each other's campuses. They enjoyed a unique privilege with the NCAA in that students at Peabody were eligible to participate as student athletes on Vanderbilt sports teams. It was an exceptionally close and symbiotic relationship. However, the president and trustees of Peabody concluded that while they currently possessed substantial assets, the school was not sustainable as a freestanding institution. Accordingly, they approached Vanderbilt with the proposal of merging with them. It seemed obvious and reasonable, but to everyone's surprise, Vanderbilt said no. Faced with the prospect of going it alone, they began to approach other potential partners.

They had serious discussions with Duke University, but the logistical and geographical issues proved insurmountable. To everyone's surprise, especially ours, they approached us! Even though we were both in Nashville, the historical and cultural differences between our two institutions were substantial, but Peabody was a distinguished and prestigious institution, so we took the matter under advisement.

We didn't think they were serious, but as our conversations became more substantive and included the board of regents staff, it became clear that they were. We all thought that the circumstances were amazing. Documents were prepared, and the matter was placed on the board of regents' agenda for approval. We were expectant. The day of the meeting, we were greeted with the news that at a special overnight meeting, the Vanderbilt Board of Trustees voted to acquire Peabody College. We were all blindsided, including the board of regents staff. We had wasted a lot of time and money, but it did make sense. It's the deal they should have made in the first place. I learned a lot about the mechanics of mergers and acquisitions. It was a fascinating experience.

My time at Tennessee State was difficult, demanding, and the most gratifying experience of my life. During my time there, I fought in a small battle of a much bigger war. It was a movement. You don't often get a chance to battle in a just crusade against forces of evil in a high-consequence, high-stakes contest and prevail against all odds.

Chapter Ten

The first step towards getting somewhere is to decide you're not going to stay where you are.

—J. P. Morgan

From early on in my career in higher education, I regularly attended the annual meetings of the American Association of Higher Education (AAHE). The AAHE was a large and diverse association, and its meetings were regularly attended by thousands of presidents, administrators, faculty, state higher education officials, other association officials, some corporate leaders, and even the occasional graduate student. At its zenith, there was no other organization like it. Its programs were rich, and its speakers were eminent national leadership figures.

Some of the most informative and useful discussions took place in impromptu meetings in the bars and restaurants of the Chicago Hilton. It was a fertile plot that planted the seeds for many of my future professional relationships.

I began to find myself on panels and discussions at the conference. The first time I met Bill Clinton was at an annual AAHE meeting held at the Washington Hilton. Then Governor Clinton of Arkansas had been invited to address the association. He was one of a handful of "education governors."

I was asked to serve on a panel to comment and respond to Governor Clinton's remarks following his address. The panelists met with him in the small anteroom leading just off the platform where he would speak. It was the first time I would be exposed to his charisma and infectious personality. I was impressed by how quick and knowledgeable he was on a host of subjects. He made quite an impression. I remember thinking he would make a great president someday and hoped he would run in the future.

While attending an AAHE meeting, my good friend George Ayers, president of Massasoit Community College, asked me to meet with two of his colleagues. One was Larraine Matusak, president of Thomas Edison State College, and the other was Morris Keeton, president of the Council for Adult and Experiential Learning (CAEL). We first met when George was a vice president at Minnesota Metropolitan State College, working for my good friend from Illinois State, David Sweet. CAEL was created by a small group of colleges in cooperation with the Educational Testing Service and the College Board. George and Larraine were both members of the CAEL board.

They approached me about serving on an advisory committee to assist them in involving HBCUs in CAEL's work with adult higher education and the newly forming practice of prior learning assessment (PLA). PLA is the practice of awarding credit through the valid and reliable assessment of college-level learning acquired in nonclassroom settings. To this day, some good but uninformed people misrepresent this practice by referring to it as "credit for life experience." No legitimate institution grants credit for experiences. College credit can be granted if the learning one acquired through experience could be certified through a creditable assessment. Because traditional college-age students rarely acquire college-level learning outside the classroom, this practice is appropriate and beneficial for experienced, accomplished adults.

Most of CAEL's member institutions were involved with adult education. HBCUs mostly comprised eighteen- to twenty-two-year-old students and did not see CAEL's work as relevant to them. However, some of these institutions were in or near cities with large African American adult populations. PLA could offer these institutions a new source of enrollment as well as new relationships with large businesses and employers interested in workforce development. I was asked to serve on a committee to enlist the participation of these institutions in CAEL's work. I had no idea at the time how much I would become involved in this area.

By 1981 we had accomplished a great deal. It was an outstanding record achieved against all odds and under difficult circumstances. Although I was proud to be a part of this leadership team, I was exhausted. All of us were, and though he never showed it, I knew that Fred must have been depleted as well. I loved working at Tennessee State and living in Nashville, but I began to contemplate my future. I had not given up on my aspiration to become a college president; indeed, my experiences at Tennessee State reinforced the notion that it was something I should pursue. I also wanted to leave before Fred did. I knew that the board of regents would make sure that the next president wasn't going to be anything like him.

While Fred's leadership achievements were celebrated by those who cared about TSU, HBCUs, and social justice, they were not appreciated beyond the campus. Fred had taken on the board of regents, the University of Tennessee, and the governor. The fact that we prevailed was something that, while tolerated and begrudgingly accepted, was not looked upon favorably. Fred's future there would not be without its challenges.

My work with CAEL continued, and in the spring of 1981, George Ayers asked if I would meet with him and Morris Keeton. CAEL was going through a period of rapid expansion and just received a new round of grant funding. In addition, it had invested in some new technology they believed would transform and greatly expand the organization. While Morris was the visionary behind the organization, they felt the need to recruit someone with management experience to serve as chief operating officer. They offered me the position of executive vice president, and I accepted. Delores and I had a wonderful community of friends and colleagues. I loved Tennessee State—its history, traditions, culture, and students—but it was time to move on.

I began preparations to leave Tennessee State and Nashville. Leaving was difficult. Choosing my successor was going to be more complicated than it should have been because of the politics of the merger. In my mind, there was only one obvious choice for my replacement: Barbara Murrell. Barbara was part of the wave of Mississippians drawn to Tennessee State by native son Walter Davis. She was an active student leader as an undergraduate, completed graduate school, and joined the student affairs staff shortly thereafter. She was a gifted, self-disciplined, experienced, and extraordinarily talented student affairs executive who was highly regarded by her colleagues, students, faculty, and community.

There was some speculation that Bruce Hancock, the former dean of students at UT-Nashville would be considered, but for a host of reasons, that wouldn't have made sense. I think Bruce recognized that as well and didn't really want the job. Fred appointed a search committee to screen potential candidates and make recommendations to him for his consideration. I am not sure if Barbara ever applied for the position, but I know that she had a list of people who nominated and recommended her, including me. The search committee recommended Barbara's appointment, and she was named the university's third vice president for student affairs and first woman. Knowing that Barbara was succeeding me made leaving a lot easier.

My friends and colleagues at Tennessee State gave us a warm, wonderful, and tearful send-off. As a parting gesture, Fred informed me that the university intended to present me with the Outstanding Service Award at its summer commencement ceremony. It was one of the highest honors the university could bestow. Tennessee State's authority to award honorary degrees was withdrawn in the '60s. There was concern that it might use its prerogative to honor such "provocateurs, instigators and troublemakers" as Martin Luther King Jr. or Thurgood Marshall. It was both humbling and deeply appreciated to receive this recognition from the people and university I loved.

CAEL's original name was the Cooperative Assessment of Experiential Learning. This group, initially supported by significant grants from two major foundations, brought together prominent scholars, psychometricians, and researchers to explore two fundamental questions: Is it possible to measure college-level learning acquired by noncollegiate means through some valid and reliable assessment process, and if so, could/should college credit be awarded in recognition of this learning? Both were answered in the affirmative. You could in fact measure college-level learning acquired experientially or through noncollegiate instruction or simple self-discovery activities. Since you could objectively demonstrate that learning occurred, then it followed that college credit could be awarded.

Two assessment methodologies came out of this work. One was standardized testing to measure college-level learning, such as the College Level Examination Program (CLEP), developed by the College Board, and the American College Testing Proficiency Examination Program (PEP). The other methodology was portfolio assessment.

In portfolio assessment, an individual assembles evidence demonstrating and documenting acquired college-level learning. The "portfolio of evidence" is then evaluated by content experts, usually a college faculty member, to determine if the standard of proof is met to justify awarding college credit. A lot of research and validation work was done by scholars and experts on both methodologies to ensure that these tools produced valid and reliable results. Together, these two approaches along with a few others came to be known as prior learning assessment (PLA).

This seminal work by the Cooperative Assessment of Experiential Learning would have a great impact on American higher education. The steering committee of the group was chaired by Morris Keeton, who was at the time provost at Antioch College in Yellow Springs, Ohio. The organization incorporated and changed its name to the Council for the Advancement of Experiential Learning and maintained the acronym CAEL. Morris Keeton left Antioch and became CAEL's founding president.

CAEL's headquarters was in Columbia, Maryland, a beautiful planned community midway between Baltimore and Washington. The transition to CAEL and the relocation to Columbia went smoothly. We bought a home within walking distance of my office, Delores accepted a teaching position, and we enrolled Shayla in Nature's Way preschool.

Delores was an excellent, experienced special education teacher, a rare commodity that made her instantly employable in every community we'd ever lived in. Since her job required her to leave the house early in the morning, it was up to me to get Shayla dressed, make her breakfast, and drop her off at nursery school. I executed breakfast, sometimes with McDonald's pancakes, and got her dressed, but doing her hair was quite a challenge. When I dropped her off at school, her teachers would good-naturedly laugh at my attempts and mercifully take apart what I had done to fix it so that by the time her mother picked her up, all evidence of my ineptitude had vanished. Those couple of hours I had with her in the mornings were precious, and bad hair days or not, I cherished every minute.

Because of my committee work with CAEL while at TSU, I already knew many of the staff and board members. My first task was to learn everything I could about the organization, its programs, personnel, practices, and finances.

CAEL was an institutional membership organization comprising approximately five hundred colleges and universities from around the country. CAEL's major sources of revenue were membership dues, conference revenues (principally from its annual national conference), and publication sales from the many books and monographs it published on assessment, experiential learning, and adult learning. Significant resources were provided by grants from multiple foundations, but CAEL's development and growth could not have taken place without the Kellogg Foundation.

Russ Mawby, legendary CEO of the Kellogg Foundation, saw the great potential of this work and invested heavily in it. While the CAEL national network consisted of hundreds of people, Morris Keeton was its visionary heart and soul. Morris was also one of the most extraordinary people I ever had the opportunity to work with. He had the rare combination of a powerful intellect and no discernible ego. He earned his PhD from Harvard when he was twenty-one years old and was recognized as a national scholar by the age of thirty. He was raised in Texas and, though he went to Harvard, spent most of his career in the Midwest. He did not smoke, drink, or use profanity and always wore a white shirt with a tie. Despite his conservative appearance, he was one of the most tolerant and nonjudgmental people I have ever met. He was revered at Antioch College in the '60s, which was a hotbed and center of the counterculture revolution. The reputation of his great intellect when coupled with an impeachable sense of personal integrity made him a sought-after collaborator by major foundations.

I have never been in a situation before or since where foundation officers called to offer money for projects that hadn't yet been applied for, but because of Morris, it happened regularly at CAEL. It was not uncommon at the end of one of these calls for Morris to sit at his typewriter, bang out a letter, send it off, and a couple of weeks later, receive a $400,000 check. In 1981, this was a lot of money. Many of these foundation officers knew that once Morris took something on, he would often overdeliver, invariably producing more than they paid for.

I am not sure if George Washington ever told a lie, but I doubt Morris Keeton ever did. He possessed a generous spirit and abiding kindness toward others. Sometimes I would go and sit in his office to explore a new idea or share some new insight I thought would advance our work. He would sit patiently with me, listen, probe, ask questions in a Socratic way, give me suggestions, and send me off to explore. In following up, I would often find that he had written a book or article on the subject years earlier. It wasn't easy to have a "new" idea around Morris.

As I began to explore the operations side of the organization, I became concerned about the accuracy of the revenue projections used to build the budget. One of CAEL's former vice presidents was Dr. John Strange, a scholarly and compelling educational entrepreneur from the University of Massachusetts. John was a visionary and earlier than most saw the potential for personal computers and emerging technology to change the face of higher education, particularly the arena of adult learning and prior learning assessment. John developed a piece of technology that we affectionately called the "CAEL Box." It was a small computer and software package that could be used to facilitate the portfolio assessment process. John perceived that there was a great market for this tool and that it would produce a significant new revenue stream. That old saying that timing is everything was certainly true with this innovation. We had a product that was way ahead of its market.

I had a sense of this, and when I checked actual sales against the projected demand, it was quickly clear to me that the revenue expectations were unrealistic. Also, the renewal cycle of our grant funding created cause for concern because while we expected several large grants to be renewed, others were less certain.

As chief operating officer, I worked with our finance person to recalibrate our revenue projections with more realistic assumptions. It was clear that if we did not make some significant changes quickly, the financial stability of the organization would be in jeopardy. I remember the day that our chief accountant and I sat down with Morris to go over the projections. I had made recommendations for several cost-cutting measures that would include reducing some of the staff. Morris listened quietly, reviewed the figures, and authorized me to execute the recommended austerity measures and staff reductions to stabilize our finances.

At Morgan, Tennessee State, and now CAEL, I found it necessary to lay off good people through no fault of their own. I always hated to be the instrument of pain for competent and high-performing people who lost their jobs due to external circumstances.

I was surprised to discover that CAEL's finances were as fragile as they were. I had been led to understand that this organization was growing, expanding, and had bright financial prospects ahead. Though I reviewed the finances and audit report prior to accepting the position, I realized afterward that Morris and the board failed to grasp the risk embedded in their ambitious revenue assumptions. After we executed the changes, I made a presentation to the board and informed them that our current position was tenuous, though stable for the time being.

Around this time, Morris became physically ill. It not only affected his health but his mental status as he became depressed. It was a challenging time for me because I had to assume greater responsibility for the organization than would have otherwise been the case. I had to look out for the professional welfare of CAEL but also provide additional support to our president. Zelda Gamson, in her wonderful book about CAEL, *Higher Education and the Real World*, referred to this moment when she cited a board member's comment: "What do you do when the magician has lost his magic?" (p. 103).

Our problems were compounded when we were notified that one of the Kellogg grants we were expecting was delayed. I was faced with planning for contingencies of further downsizing the organization if the Kellogg grant didn't come through. It was my judgment that CAEL had three indispensable people: the first of course was Morris, the second was Diana Bamford Rees, and the third was Pamela Tate.

Diana had been with Morris from the beginning when she left her position at Educational Testing Service (ETS) to work for CAEL. Diana's principal responsibility was the CAEL annual conference and all the regional and local conferences under sponsorship. She was energetic, competent, devoted to Morris, and just a great person to be around. Diana is the wonderful kind of friend, having once acquired, you never lose. She continued her work at CAEL for many years, until she retired.

Pam Tate was responsible for the CAEL publication series. She served as editor and sometimes contributor to the publications. New scholarship on PLA was generated by some of the world's great authorities on assessment and experiential and adult learning. The foundations that funded this cutting-edge work wanted the scholarly product of their investment widely disseminated. They funded the production of a series of books that defined the field and created the knowledge basis for the rest of higher education to expand into adult learning and PLA.

Pam, like other members of the CAEL inner circle at the time, was incredibly bright, driven, and an all-around wonderful person. When we began working together, we found out that we were classmates at the University of Illinois at Champagne, which gave us plenty of things to reminisce about.

Just as Diana had a lifelong impact on CAEL and its future, so did Pam. Upon Morris's retirement, Pam succeeded him as CAEL's president. The environment changed, and Pam repositioned the organization, while building upon the strength and body of work Morris created. She successfully led CAEL during the remainder of her working career and, when she retired, left a formidable legacy of her own. Fortunately, retrenchment wasn't necessary. Morris recovered, the grant in question was renewed, and we got CAEL through its rough spot.

About a year after I joined the CAEL team, Larraine Matusak accepted a position as a senior program officer at the W. K. Kellogg Foundation. Larraine was charged with standing up another one of Russ Mawby's visions, the Kellogg National Fellowship Program (KNFP). It was quite an opportunity and a perfect fit for Larraine, who had on occasion expressed her frustration with the smothering bureaucracy and difficult political culture of New Jersey.

Morris informed me that he received a letter from Eleanor Spiegel, chair of the Thomas Edison State College Board of Trustees, seeking his assistance in identifying a suitable candidate for Larraine's successor. He told me that it was something I ought to pursue, and with my permission, he intended to nominate me for the position. I was flattered and consented.

Thomas Edison State College was a new, innovative adult-serving institution that was a product of the same intellectual movement that created CAEL. Adults first entered the academy as a result of the GI Bill following World War II. These returning adult servicemen and women were expected to be a temporary population moving through the academy and then going away so the colleges could return to the eighteen-year-old high school graduates they were created and organized to serve. These adult students turned out to be the disruptors of their time.

The academy was ill prepared to accommodate the character and attributes of mature adult students. During my undergraduate years, the university had a physical education class called PE100, required of all students. It was essentially a physical conditioning course under the theory that young students should be of sound body as well as intellect. Each student on the first day of class and the last day of class was required to run a mile for time with an expectation that by the end of the course they would be in better shape than at the beginning. This was a requirement for all students unless there was a physical disability that prevented it. This is perfectly reasonable unless your freshman student is forty or fifty years old.

As adults began to flood the colleges in increasingly larger numbers, these contrasts and contradictions between adult students and traditional-age students became more pronounced. What do you do with an insurance executive who received their education from Prudential or Aetna, was promoted through the company, became a member of the Million-Dollar Roundtable, and taught the state insurance licensure course but was now told they had to take Introduction to Insurance to earn their college degree?

In the '60s, the Carnegie Commission, through a series of committees and publications, declared that what the country needed was a set of specialty institutions focused exclusively on adult learners. There was a substantial body of research and scholarly work that documented and differentiated the learning style and pattern of engagement of adults from traditional-age college students. It was unreasonable to shoehorn a mature adult into an institution that was designed and operated soup to nuts for eighteen- to twenty-two-year-olds going to school full-time, supported by their parents.

Growing out of this body of work, several states answered this call by creating institutions whose missions were dedicated to serving adults exclusively. There was even new language created to describe them. They were called "learners," not students, a subtle but important distinction, denoting the active engagement of adult learners and self-ownership of their education as opposed to the traditional students, where that responsibility is entrusted to the faculty.

In 1971, the State University of New York founded Empire State College. The New York Board of Regents created the Regents External Degree Program. The State of Minnesota created Minnesota Metropolitan State College. Connecticut created Charter Oak College, and in 1972, the Board of Higher Education in New Jersey created Thomas A. Edison College. The University of Maryland University College (UMUC) was founded in 1946 for the purpose of providing a college education to U.S. military forces overseas following World War II. UMUC developed over time into a comprehensive adult-serving institution joining its younger siblings. With the exception of UMUC, each of these institutions was founded within a couple of years of each other, and all of them were public institutions supported by their states.

In September 1982, I was invited by the search committee, chaired by trustee Alan Ferguson, to interview for the position of president of Thomas A. Edison State College. I was invited back several weeks later to interview with the full board of trustees chaired by Ellie Spiegel. I drove up for the interview from Maryland and returned home the same evening. My mother was visiting us from Los Angeles, and we were watching television when the phone rang at around seven in the evening. It was Ellie calling to offer me the position.

I announced to my wife, mother, and daughter that, having been in the house for one year, we would be relocating and moving to Trenton, New Jersey. Of course, my wife was aware of all the things that preceded this, but my mother was in total shock. Shayla, at four years old, didn't care; nor did she have any sense about how all our lives were going to change.

Chapter Eleven

Do not go where the path may lead, go where there is no path and leave a trail.

—*Muriel Strode*

Thomas Edison State College was one of the founding members of CAEL, and our pioneering work in PLA was a direct outgrowth of our association. After I became president at Thomas Edison, I was invited to join CAEL's board of trustees, and subsequent to that, I was elected and served several terms as chair and remained on the board for many years.

Thomas Edison State University remained a member and supporter during the entirety of my thirty-five-year presidency. In 2011 the board of trustees of CAEL awarded me the highest recognition available to an educator in the adult learning space when they bestowed upon me the Morris Keeton Lifetime Achievement medal, another acknowledgment that to this day is dear to my heart.

CAEL is often and accurately described as a movement. And like most movements it did not have a single point of origin, was not the vision of any single person, nor was it controlled by any organizing structure. The movement was conceptualized by such visionaries as Alden Dunham, Earnest Boyer, Morris Keeton, and many others. It was developed and disseminated by an extraordinary group of researchers and scholars, such as K. Patricia Cross, Harold "Bud" Hodgekinson, Malcolm Knowles, David Colb, Arthur Chickering, Urban Whittaker, and many others. They were followed by the great practitioners who took their research and learning theory and built institutions around them. They included David

Sweet, founding president of Minnesota Metropolitan State College; James Hall, founding president of Empire State College, of the State University of New York (SUNY); C. Wayne Williams, CEO of New York Regents External Degree program; and James Douglas Brown, founding president of Thomas A. Edison College. Each of these trailblazing institutions was created exclusively to educate mature adult learners.

James Douglas Brown faced the enormous challenge of creating an institution with no precedent or road map to guide him. The research identified two defining characteristics of the adult learner: the barriers of time and place and the substantial college-level learning many of them had already acquired experientially or through training in noncollegiate settings. Adults have jobs, families, and myriad other responsibilities that do not afford them the luxury of sitting in a classroom at 10:00 A.M. on Monday, Wednesday, and Friday. They also need to apply the college-level learning they already have to their degree.

These institutions were challenged to create delivery models to serve these learners who wanted to pursue their studies while simultaneously fulfilling other obligations where they lived and worked. Additionally, each of these institutions embraced prior learning assessment. Understanding that a new nontraditional model for delivering higher education would instigate criticism and questions about credibility, they were all staunchly committed to educational quality and excellence. With these pillars to guide them and with a common mission and sense of purpose, each of these new colleges developed its own unique approach to serving adult learners.

Thomas A. Edison College was founded by the New Jersey Board of Higher Education under the leadership of Chancellor Ralph Dungan. Chancellor Dungan, who was heavily influenced by the work of SUNY president Ernie Boyer, came from New York to lead a newly formed board of higher education.

Early in the college's formation, President Brown made the wise decision to use Princeton University as an incubator for the fledgling college.

Because his father, James Douglas Brown Sr., was a nationally respected educator and long-serving dean of the faculty there, President Brown was well known to the Princeton community, and they welcomed his new-found institution to the campus. The stature and status of Princeton University provided the credence and legitimacy needed for this novel and unproven form of higher education.

President Brown was also greatly influenced by the proximity of the Educational Testing Service (ETS), as well as its scholars and research culture. Many of Thomas Edison's early staff members came from ETS and brought with them a measurement culture that insisted on testing, validating, and documenting all the innovative and new approaches they would employ.

Minnesota Metropolitan and Empire State College both offered inter-disciplinary liberal arts degrees with curricula individualized for each student working with faculty. While neither were campus-based institutions, their models limited their geographical reach.

Thomas Edison took a different approach. It offered traditional degrees by academic discipline: biology, history, English, economics, and so on. It worked with subject matter experts from around the country, what we call "mentors," in defining each specialty by its constituent competencies. Biologists described the learning outcomes that a person with a biology degree would be expected to have. The curricula for each specialty area were so constructed, and the method for earning individual degrees was calibrated against these standards.

Today, all of higher education is focused on measuring the learning outcomes of its students, but Thomas Edison State College was one of the first institutions in the country to employ this concept from its very beginning in the early 1970s. The college embraced the principle that it did not matter where or in what forum the learning took place as long as proof of the learning could be demonstrated. This allowed the college to engage students wherever they lived and worked and to take advantage of any educationally appropriate assets available to them.

Students at the college had three primary methods for satisfying their degree requirements: transfer credit from accredited colleges or universities; courses from corporations, labor unions, and the military evaluated by the American Council on Education and determined to be equivalent in quality, depth, and outcomes of traditional college courses; and finally, through prior learning assessment. The college offered no classroom instruction of its own; nor did it have a teaching faculty; however, courses were facilitated by mentors, who were subject matter experts in their fields. The absence of classrooms and faculty raised a lot of eyebrows, but President Brown was able to demonstrate that the educational results achieved by Thomas Edison learners was equivalent or superior to those achieved by students in traditional classes taught by faculty.

With the support of the chancellor, President Brown created the Statewide Testing and Assessment Center at Thomas Edison, an entity that provided prior learning assessment not only for our students but for those attending the state's other colleges and universities. He established rolling admissions, allowing students to enroll at any time during the year and to graduate whenever they satisfied the requirements.

Brown was a brilliant but troubled man, and his six-year tenure was tumultuous. However, everything that followed was built on the sound foundation he created. Brown was succeeded by Larraine Matusak, who was forceful and brought a clear intellect and driven personality to the institution. She quickly became frustrated by the bureaucracy and challenging political landscape in New Jersey, and her tenure as president only lasted three years, but during that time, she made important contributions in building on Brown's work. Perhaps her two greatest contributions to Thomas Edison were in the talented professionals she recruited and the relocation of the college from Princeton to an elegant, historic, and architecturally important building in the state capitol complex in Trenton.

Trenton mayor Arthur Holland was an amateur historian. He knew that what is now The College of New Jersey, Rider University, and Mercer County Community College were all founded in Trenton and relocated to their current campuses in the surrounding areas. Mercer County Community College occupied the historic Kelsey Building before leaving town. As a consequence, Trenton was left without an institution of higher learning. That also left the Kelsey Building abandoned in the heart of the city's capital district.

The Kelsey Building was built in 1911 through the generosity of Henry Cooper Kelsey, a wealthy industrialist. Kelsey retained the services of Cass Gilbert, one of the nation's most accomplished architects, to design the structure that he intended as a monument to his deceased wife, Prudence Townsend Kelsey. Gilbert was the architect who designed the U.S. Supreme Court building in Washington, the Woolworth Building in Manhattan, the state capitol of Texas in Austin, and several other notable structures around the country.

Kelsey shared with Gilbert that his wife was particularly fond of the Palazzo Strozzi, a Renaissance-era palace in Florence, Italy. Using this palace as his inspiration, Gilbert designed an elegant five-story building with two distinguishing features. One was the prominent, ornate clock adorning the front of the building, and the other was the memorial room designed to honor his beloved wife.

Mrs. Kelsey was an avid collector of fine and historic china and porcelain and traveled extensively through Europe acquiring pieces. Ten percent of the entire cost of the building was spent on the room to house her collection. The centerpiece of the room is a beautiful gilded table, and the ceiling and walls are inlaid with hand-painted oil canvases. The devotion Kelsey demonstrated to his wife in the manner he memorialized her has never failed to touch all those who have had the fortune to see it.

The building was constructed to house the Trenton School of the Industrial Arts, and in Kelsey's bequest, there were two conditions. He wanted the building used for educational purposes, and he wanted to ensure his wife's collection and the room built to house it were maintained in perpetuity.

Mayor Holland was distressed that this elegant facility had been abandoned. He was also disappointed that the three institutions of higher
education born in the city of Trenton, had all fled. To make matters worse,
plans were in progress to demolish this stunning, historic landmark.
Opposition to this outrage intensified and State Senator Joe Merlino and
others joined the movement to save the Kelsey Building. It was successful,
and the state of New Jersey took ownership, but it had no tenant.

The mayor set out to convince President Brown that the Kelsey Building would be a perfect location for the new college to adopt as its home.
This arrangement would uphold Kelsey's legacy, and it would ensure the
presence of a college in the capital city. Brown agreed, but with some reservation. No one knew what kind of facilities and campus a college with
no classrooms or resident students would require.

Ramapo College and Richard Stockton College, which were created at
the same time as Thomas Edison, received significant grants of land from
the state and were in the process of building their campuses. The Kelsey
Building, while stately and suitable for an academic institution, was land-
locked, with no room to expand. Holland brokered an agreement with
Governor Byrne and President Brown to give Thomas Edison control over
the building's adjoining historic townhouses. As an additional incentive,
the state would provide for and fund its capital requirements within the
state capitol complex as it experienced future growth. All parties agreed,
but President Brown departed before the school could relocate.

President Matusak engaged with the state, oversaw the renovation of
the facility to accommodate the college, and relocated Thomas Edison
from Princeton's Forrestal campus to Trenton. Unfortunately, the agreement brokered by Mayor Holland between the college and the state was
never codified contractually or in statute.

On many occasions, during my work with CAEL, Larraine expressed her
frustration with Dungan's successor, Ted Hollander, and the impediments
she was continually faced with in conducting business with the state. She

was also disturbed about what she perceived as the inequitable treatment of Thomas Edison when compared to the eight other state colleges.

Larraine Matusak was the first woman president of a New Jersey public college or university. A presidential residence or housing allowance was provided in the compensation packages of all the state college presidents, well, all except the female president of Thomas Edison. The presidents of all the institutions were also provided college vehicles to support their work. That was true of Thomas Edison as well, except that her vehicle was a spectacularly ugly, stripped-down Plymouth that was acquired and intended to be refitted as a state police car, only it never got the refit.

As I began to prepare myself for the presidency of Thomas Edison, I was concerned about the way Larraine and the institution had been treated, but I had a long history, both in Maryland and Tennessee, of dealing with troublesome chancellors, systems, and state bureaucracies, so I was undeterred.

We found a home in Ewing, New Jersey, that would serve nicely as a "President's Residence" even though I had no assurance at the time that I would be successful in securing the support of a housing allowance. Bill Harris, a former classmate of mine and educator, who then was an executive at ETS and longtime resident of the area, recommended we look in Ewing. He knew it was important to us that Shayla receive a quality education at a racially and economically diverse public school, and I trusted his advice.

Bill also introduced us to the superintendent of the Ewing school system, and when she found out that Delores was an experienced special education teacher, she immediately offered her a job. I moved into our house shortly before December 1, and Delores and Shayla joined me in January. The relocation went smoothly, Delores transitioned into her new job, and Shayla began kindergarten.

My mother returned to Los Angeles following her visit in October, but soon after we settled into our new home, I received a call that she had been diagnosed with advanced ovarian cancer. I was devastated by the news. We were told that her expected survival rate was five years following surgery. My mother's illness weighed heavily in the back of my mind as I threw myself into my work.

Soon after I arrived in Trenton, I was invited to attend a meeting of the nine state college presidents and the chancellor of the board of higher education to discuss the impact of the state's budget crisis. We were told to prepare for layoffs and potential salary reductions. There was even a rumor floating around that one of the colleges might close. That never happened, but I wasn't worried about us because our appropriation was so small that closing Thomas Edison would have had negligible impact. I guess we were "too small" to fail. At the end of the discussion, all my colleagues turned to me and said, "Welcome to New Jersey."

There is a progression institutions go through in selecting and onboarding a new president. The first phase is an interrogation. It's when the campus and the board challenge the candidates to demonstrate why they should be chosen to lead the institution. At the end of the interrogation phase, the board selects the person they want to recruit, and the second phase, or "seduction," begins. After the choice is made, they must now persuade the candidate to accept the position. This is the phase where they entice the candidate with all of the wonderful opportunities that lay ahead and all of the board support pledged to their success. The final stage is the "revelation," when all the bad news, problems, and warts are unveiled. If you are going to have a "what have I gotten myself into?" moment, this is the point when that happens.

In my orientation, I had a series of meetings with trustees and officers of the college who set forth the grueling problems that lay ahead. These were thoughtful conversations, and I received them with the appropriate reverence in which they were intended; however, given what I had gone through at Morgan, Tennessee State, and CAEL, I was not intimidated— in fact, I couldn't wait to get started.

I was continually impressed by the talent, commitment, and experience of the staff assembled by Brown and Matusak. They were collegial and passionate about the mission and new ground we were breaking. The elder statesman of the group was Arnold Fletcher, vice president for academic affairs. Dr. Fletcher was a fascinating renaissance man. He joined the adult learning movement in its infancy and was highly regarded and nationally respected for his contributions to the field. He was also an accomplished concert pianist and had a distinguished military career. He had been at Thomas Edison from the beginning and served as interim president twice. I greatly appreciated his wise counsel in understanding my new institutional home. By the time I arrived, Arnold was at the end of his career. He informed me that he intended to retire at the end of the fiscal year on June 30, 1983.

Rich Hansen, who was recruited by Larraine, was vice president for community affairs. Rich was affable and had previous experience in continuing education. John Bernard was vice president for business and finance. On several occasions, board members raised questions about the institution's fiscal management. While I had great personal affection for John, I concluded that the institution's finances would be better served under new leadership. John agreed that this might not be a good fit for him and decided to pursue other professional opportunities better aligned with his talents and interests.

The fourth member of the president's cabinet was Gerri Collins, executive assistant to the president and secretary to the board of trustees. Gerri was enormously efficient and perfectly suited to the special role she held. For the first ten years of my presidency, the two people closest to me were Gerri Collins and Anne Rue, my assistant. Gerri fulfilled the role of chief of staff, confidante, and adviser.

Presidents need people around them who are comfortable pushing back to prevent them from committing unforced errors. Sometimes when I was particularly exercised about something, I would write unfiltered letters to respond to the issue. Gerri would review important correspondence sent out over my signature. On more than one occasion, she'd come into my office, sit down, ask me if I felt better having written a letter, and then, with a smile on her face, tear it up and politely say, "You can't send this." After I calmed down, I always recognized that she was right, and I was grateful that she was there to protect me from myself and to keep me from doing something I'd later regret.

I was heartbroken when I lost her to cancer. When she got too sick to come to the office, I asked her to write the history of the college's first twenty-five years to help keep her on the payroll with health benefits. What she produced was excellent. It was the last project she completed prior to retiring, and we lost her not long after. Losing this talented, kind, and empathetic colleague was devastating.

It is not unusual for new presidents to arrive at an organization feeling that they need to clean house and bring in their own executive leadership team. This is almost always a bad idea. Long-term senior executives possess the institutional knowledge and context for the decisions and policies created to support the organization's mission. When institutions transition presidents, there is an inherent and sometimes destabilizing disruption. Decapitating the leadership compounds this. Nevertheless, a president is entitled to a team that is aligned with their vision and leadership style. No president can be truly effective without the support of a great team.

I informed the existing staff that I would begin recruiting my new team with them. If it turned out that the compatibility wasn't there, we would make adjustments. I promised to do everything I could to make changes in a way that respected their past contributions and minimized harm to their future prospects.

In the spring of my first year, I had to recruit two important cabinet-level positions, replacing Arnold Fletcher and John Bernard. We were fortunate to recruit Dr. Jerry Ice as our new vice president for academic affairs and Michael Scheiring for the position of vice president for administration and finance. Jerry had an extensive background in continuing education and adult learning. Mike had experience in state government, working in the administration of Governor Brendan Byrne and later as a fiscal officer with New Jersey Transit. Ice, Scheiring, Hansen, and Collins would form the nucleus of a leadership team that would stay intact for many years and help bring an infant institution out of childhood and through adolescence.

After eighteen years, Jerry Ice was recruited to a presidency at the Graduate School USA, and Bill Seaton became provost and vice president for academic affairs. Christopher Stringer, our exceptional controller, assumed the role of vice president for administration and finance when Mike Scheiring retired after over twenty years, and Mary Ellen Caro, our founding business school dean and retired executive at AT&T, accepted the new position of vice president for enrollment management and learner services. Natale Caliendo replaced Rich Hansen as the vice president for public affairs, and when Nat died in a tragic accident, John Thurber accepted the position. I later recruited Barbara M. Kleva to serve as the college's general counsel, and Robin A. Walton served as our vice president for community and government affairs.

In 2005, I began to hear some buzz around town about Robin Walton, a bright, impressive African American young woman who was doing good policy work in the community. My wife, Pam, also worked with her on the Trenton Public Education Foundation board and recommended that she meet with me. Robin agreed to come to my office for a meet and greet, but she was unaware that, from my point of view, it was a job interview. Just as King Cheek offered me a job after our first meeting, I invited Robin to join my office to assist me with some of the government affairs portfolio I had been managing on my own to that point. She was surprised but happily accepted. When I began to understand her ability and capacity, I turned over the government relations portfolio in its entirety and elevated her position to vice president. Given the nature of the public college presidency, we worked as a team hand in glove from the state house to Capitol Hill. I'm not Batman, but I had my own Robin. Just as Buzz, Paul, and Fisher mentored me, I took great joy in doing the same for Robin. I have taken a paternal pride in watching her grow into one of the most effective government relations professionals I have ever seen.

This executive team remained intact for the duration of my presidency. As an institution, we had very little turnover despite the attention our talented professionals attracted from other colleges and universities. I believe the reason we were able to maintain such continuity lies in the institutional climate we fostered and the community culture that emerged from it. We assembled a cadre of professionals who valued the freedom and autonomy to innovate without the burdens of countless committees and bureaucracy.

Organizational culture is a tangible and competitive asset in the marketplace just as much if not more than prices, goods, and services. Our culture energized our colleagues and enabled us to become an engine of quality and innovation. This environment nourished a team of professionals who felt valued, respected, and a part of something bigger than themselves. For many committed educators, this sense of community and professional empowerment is more valuable than titles and compensation. While we were efficient, serious about accountability, and proud of our ability to execute, members of our tight-knit community often remarked they felt like they were part of a family.

Though a high-quality executive team is essential, there are no roles more important in the life of a president than their office staff. When you enter the president's suite and close the outer door, these are the people inside the room with you. They know where you are 24/7. They know your calendar, who you speak with, who you meet with, the contents of your incoming and outgoing correspondence, and most of your personal information. They enjoy a level of familiarity with you not shared by anyone else at the institution. You are also more dependent and reliant upon this group than anyone else. You must have total confidence and trust in both their ability and loyalty.

As president, you are a symbol as much as an officer. You are under scrutiny no matter where you go and what you do in both your personal and professional life. There are public expectations regarding your behavior, appearance, words, and temperament. It goes with the territory, and you should not accept the position if you are not comfortable in fulfilling the expectations of your many publics. This also extends to the office staff and sometimes to the president's spouse or partner as well. The only two sanctuaries afforded a president are their home and office. When those doors close, you can be yourself because the people behind them are trusted, loyal, protective, and accepting. They see you at your best, and they see you at your worst.

When I first came to work at the college and closed my door, I had three wonderful people behind it with me: Gerri Collins; Gerri's secretary, Debbie Ellis; and my secretary, Barbara Shetsley. They were all extraordinary, and I was very grateful to Larraine Matusak for recruiting them; however, I would soon lose Barbara to parenthood and Debbie to an irresistible new career opportunity.

Fortunately, Gerri recruited a bright-eyed teenager a year out of high school, Linda Meehan, and I was able to recruit Anne Rue as my secretary. Anne was experienced and had impeccable skills and a wonderful and endearing personality. She is perhaps one of the most emotionally healthy people I have ever met, and she is a joy to be around. We were a wonderful team, and they would become my work family for a very long time.

Over the years, Gerri was succeeded by other wonderful people: Penny Brouwer, Esther Paist, Terri Tallon, and Linda Meehan, who supported my work in the president's office in various capacities. Melissa Maszczak succeeded Anne and Linda in the important role of managing me. Beverly Dash and Judy Lucas supported the executive assistant and chief of staff roles. While Terri and Beverly moved to other offices in the college, Linda, Melissa, and Judy were with me until the culmination of my presidency.

When I transitioned to the Center for Leadership and Governance, Linda accompanied me, while Melissa became executive assistant to the president and secretary to the board of trustees for the new president. In 2019, after working with me for thirty-five years, Linda retired. The departure of a long-serving and trusted colleague was certainly an adjustment, but like so many changes in life, they are often the source of new opportunity. I was delighted when I was able to recruit Melissa from the president's office to become my principal collaborator as senior fellow and director of the center.

Each of these professionals is meticulous in her work, intelligent, passionate about our mission, polished, and representative of an experienced and sophisticated executive office. I knew that whatever fires I ran into, this group was holding the hose and buckets behind me. The interesting thing about these positions is that if they are done well, no one knows what they do (this sometimes includes the president). But in any high-stakes office, if they make a mistake, everyone knows about it, and the president is accountable for it. It takes professional, self-aware people with low ego to toil quietly in the rafters while the president takes the credit for their good work. A good president knows this and takes care of these individuals, because they take care of the president. They are in the background while the president is the face of the institution, but the president is only as good as the people on his or her team.

For over thirty-five years, the core and heart of the university stayed mostly intact. This was representative of much of the overall staff as well, with very little turnover. I looked forward to coming to work every day, not just because I was excited by the opportunity to build this institution but because I delighted in the wonderful company I kept.

Larraine warned me that New Jersey was a special place, and she was right. It enjoyed one of the highest per capita incomes in the country yet had pockets of some of the worst poverty in the nation. You would think that a wealthy state whose residents pay among the highest per capita income taxes and property taxes in the country would have plenty of revenue to spend, which it does, but it also has a bizarre excess of government infrastructure that sucks up all of the money, leaving it in a constant state of fiscal crisis.

For a geographically small state, it has 565 municipalities, 555 school districts, 21 counties, and 738 fire districts. While Nashville and Davidson County, Tennessee, and Howard County, Maryland, each had to pay one police chief, one school superintendent, and one county executive, Mercer County, where I live, has 12 municipalities, school districts, and police departments. Each of these not only has its own mayor but its own school board and city council as well. Lay over that the county commissioners, and you have more government per square mile than anywhere else in the country.

While we need the teachers and police officers, we don't need the redundant bureaucracy, separate IT and HR departments, separate motor pools, dispatchers, tax officers, city clerks, and so on. The cost of paying for all of these superfluous layers of local government makes the economics of the state unsustainable. As a result, New Jersey has never adequately funded public higher education.

For the last forty years, we have had the highest college outmigration rate of any state in the nation. Public higher education in New Jersey was not valued and was so poorly supported that even though the Morrill Act of 1862 created public land grant research universities for the rest of the nation, New Jersey didn't have one until 1956, when Rutgers, a private institution founded in 1766, was acquired by the state. The New Jersey Institute of Technology (NJIT) was also founded as a private university and operated under contract until 1996 when it became an official public institution. The now defunct University of Medicine and Dentistry (UMDNJ) was organized in the late '60s and was composed of several medical schools. Because Rutgers, UMDNJ, and NJIT all had fairly recent and different beginnings, they had a governance autonomy much different than what was afforded to the nine state colleges.

Six of the nine state colleges were founded as teacher training institutions under the supervision of the State Department of Education. They later developed into comprehensive, multipurpose colleges. Thomas Edison, Richard Stockton, and Ramapo College all opened in the early '70s but amalgamated into the governance structure of the six former teachers colleges. In the late '60s, under the leadership of Governor Richard Hughes, governance, coordination, and oversight of higher education was vested in the New Jersey Board of Higher Education and the chancellor of higher education, who served as its executive officer. This history set up a class system among the schools. The research universities all had autonomous boards, but the state colleges were treated like bureaucratic state agencies.

The other unusual but well-known aspect of New Jersey's political culture is its reputation for corruption. I was no stranger to politicians who colored outside the lines, but in New Jersey, it was elevated to an art form. Fearful that higher education would be compromised by this unfortunate tradition of corruption, Governor Hughes and the legislature worked hard to create a structure to insulate it from inappropriate political intrusions. While the New Jersey Board of Higher Education was not created as a governing board, it was vested with broad powers and had great influence. The members of the board of higher education were appointed by the governor with the confirmation of the state senate; however, these board members were appointed for terms that went beyond the terms of the governors. The chancellor of higher education served as a member of the governor's cabinet but was hired and accountable to the board of higher education, not the governor, which, as far as I know, was a unique structure.

The trustees of the nine state colleges were appointed by the board of higher education. The chancellor and the board of higher education approved all new academic programs, had control over the levels of degrees offered, and made recommendations to the governor on the level of state support the institutions received. While the presidents didn't work for the chancellor, the fact that he appointed their trustees, approved any new programs, and had influence over their budgets made him someone they paid attention to.

In my early meetings with my trustees, they suggested I prioritize three challenges in no particular order. They were apologetic and embarrassed that they weren't able to offer me a residence or housing allowance entitled to other college presidents. Neither they nor I saw it as a compensation question, as much as a statement about the importance and value of the institution. While I certainly wanted the benefit, its symbolic importance as an acknowledgment of parity meant more to me than the dollars involved. (The car was pretty bad, too.)

The second issue involved a new bachelor of science in nursing (BSN) program intended for experienced registered nurses that lacked the baccalaureate degree. The program had been approved by the board of higher education (BHE) but never funded by the state. The trustees were concerned about the inequity of state funding compared to other public institutions and hoped we could generate more adequate support.

The third issue concerned the troubling atmospherics between the leadership of the college and the chancellor of the BHE and his staff. Larraine was incensed by what she perceived to be inequitable treatment by the chancellor, and the chancellor perceived that we were uncooperative and unresponsive to concerns he had about some of the college's practices. While the board was protective of the college's interest and felt there was a legitimate basis for Larraine's point of view, they were hopeful the tensions between the two organizations could be resolved to both parties' satisfaction.

In December 1982, the college enrolled approximately three thousand students, and the entire full-time staff complement was housed in four and half floors of the Kelsey Building. We shared the fifth floor with the New Jersey Capital Planning and Budget Commission, which was also a point of aggravation to the institution. Were we a college or another state agency?

I've always understood that so much of what happens within government is relationship based. At a luncheon, I found myself seated next to Ed Goldberg, associate chancellor. I mentioned that I received reports of tension between our organizations and asked if it was true. He was surprised by my candor but saw it as an opportunity and proceeded to set forth some policy differences that he perceived existed between us.

The principal issue was the department's objection to the college's credit and transfer policy from some unaccredited institutions. He felt this was troubling, and he wondered how we determined that the courses were comparable in quality, substance, and depth to maintain academic integrity in the absence of accreditation. While I didn't know the answer, I thought it was a valid question. I agreed to look into the matter and get back to him.

When I returned to the college, I found out he was correct, and we had on occasion engaged in this practice. The American Council on Education (ACE), through its "program on non-collegiate sponsored instruction," evaluated corporate training programs for their equivalency with traditional college courses. When this evaluation concluded that the outcomes of the courses were comparable, ACE then promulgated a credit recommendation in its directory, and hundreds of colleges and universities in the country accepted those credits in transfer. In fact, ACE contracted with Thomas Edison to do the evaluation of the work taking place in New Jersey. They also engaged in a similar practice with courses in training offered by the U.S. military.

After reviewing our practice, we decided to discontinue the acceptance of transfer credit from unaccredited sources unless they had undergone the ACE evaluation process and received its credit recommendation. We reinforced our standards and removed an irritant between us and the Department of Higher Education.

Following that, the chancellor, T. Edward Hollander (Ted) and I met for lunch, and I was eager to continue the dialogue. I enjoyed my first meeting with Ted. He was easygoing and sincere. He told me that I had not been his first choice for the presidency. One of his vice chancellors was a candidate for the job, and he was disappointed that he didn't get it. He also said that his counterpart, the executive director of the Tennessee Board of Higher Education, had told him that I was a troublemaker, to which I laughed and nodded in agreement.

Ted was Jewish, and we shared an intolerance for racism and anti-Semitism. We discussed the introductory meetings I had had with people of influence around the state. He was pleased by my outreach to the corporations and the nonprofits, but he was not happy that I met with legislators, cabinet members, and members of Governor Kean's staff. He felt that, as chancellor, he had an exclusive franchise as the voice of higher education with state government.

I responded that I appreciated his point of view, but a fundamental responsibility of a public college president is to advocate for their institution, especially with state government. He was concerned that the administration and legislature would receive competing messages if the presidents began advancing their own self-interests. He felt responsible for imposing some discipline on the individual institutions to manage a collective message in support of the broader public interest. He thought the higher education community should speak with one voice, and that voice belonged to him.

I appreciated the need for coordination and alignment, but I also expressed my belief in mission differentiation. The state did not have the resources to support twelve senior public institutions competing with each other in attempt to be all things to all people. Having said that, I explained that a choir has a better sound than a soloist, and as chancellor, he was in the unique position to organize the choir.

I expressed that our professional interests were interlaced, and it would be difficult for either of our organizations to be successful without the support and cooperation of the other. It was my hope that we would have open and candid communications, and I promised to align our positions when possible. I assured him that my advocacy for higher education would take place within the framework of the policy apparatus established by the board of higher education. He indicated that he appreciated my position, and it was the beginning of a mutually respectful relationship.

The first test of this agreement occurred when I began to pursue funding for our new nursing program and scheduled a meeting with W. Cary Edwards, Governor Kean's chief counsel. Cary was an outgoing, charismatic public policy wonk. Kean understood that the state budget was the most important policy-making tool a governor had. He entrusted Edwards with shaping fiscal policy and developing strategies and tactics in getting his budget through the legislature.

I introduced myself and explained that I was seeking assistance in securing funding for our innovative new nursing program. Thomas Edison had a unique capacity to provide educational opportunity for experienced, practicing nurses that no other college or university in the state could provide. Cary immediately grasped the unique nature of this program as well as the broader impact it would have on increasing the capacity of the nursing profession in the state. It was fortuitous that his wife, Lynn, was a nurse, and as such, the promise of this program and its importance resonated with him personally.

Cary and I stayed in touch through the legislative budget negotiations. When the budget was adopted on June 30, it was the *only* funding included for any college or university that had not been recommended in the governor's original submission. The chancellor was stunned. He was happy to report to his board that one of their priorities, not initially accepted by the governor, had been funded. Privately, he was unnerved and wanted to know how I pulled that off. I told him how it happened, but I also reminded him that what I did was consistent with his board's recommendation to the governor.

It would not be the last time we received special support from the legislature because of our unique mission. Our trustees were right: the state did not know how to fund us, and by any measure, we were never supported in an equitable manner when compared to the traditional institutions. We always received significantly lower operating support, and further, our capital funding was nonexistent. Besides, our total appropriation was so small that no other public institutions ever perceived us as a threat.

My belief in mission differentiation is genuine. In most states, there is a large, public flagship university and a group of other institutions that aspire to similar stature. Too often, American higher education is driven by a quest for status and prestige as opposed to service and quality. In New Jersey, that was not the case. The three public research universities and the nine state colleges were all distinct, each with a clearly defined niche. There was only room in New Jersey for one comprehensive public research university, and everyone agreed that it was Rutgers. We were all committed to creating a differentiated set of public institutions that, when taken together, created a broad range of high-quality public options to satisfy the higher education needs of the state.

Like most states, New Jersey developed an enrollment-driven funding formula, but it failed because the state could never afford to fund it. Formulas only work when the various institutions are templates of each other. If the institutions are truly differentiated by mission, their costs are differentiated as well. Formulas can't adapt. For the last forty years, New Jersey has failed to find a rational basis for funding higher education. Consequently, the state's support for its public institutions varies wildly, with no coherent rationale for the differences.

When I came to the state, New Jersey had a funding policy goal that provided 70 percent of each institution's operating costs through state appropriations. The remaining 30 percent was made up of tuition. It would keep the institutions adequately funded while guaranteeing that tuition remained affordable. Unfortunately, it never happened. State appropriations for higher education continued to decline after Governor Kean left office. State support today is around 20 percent, and tuition at its public institutions is among the highest in the country.

I understood from the beginning that it was unlikely that appropriations would ever adequately support the high-quality, pioneering institution we were committed to building. Though it was unfair, we knew we were on our own in generating the necessary resources beyond our meager appropriation. That's why our advocacy work in securing and maintaining resources from state government was so crucial.

Cary Edwards would be appointed attorney general by Governor Kean, followed by an unsuccessful run for governor. He also served in later years as chair of the New Jersey Commission on Investigation, a waste and fraud-fighting agency. He became a lifelong advocate for the institution and received an honorary degree from Thomas Edison. He also became a dear and trusted friend. The nursing school he helped fund grew to become the largest school of nursing in the state. In 2010, shortly before he succumbed to cancer, the board of trustees renamed our school of nursing in his honor.

While all of this was going on, I turned my attention to the housing allowance. Solving this problem was uncomfortable because while it was an important policy issue, it was also self-serving. In navigating the Kean administration to identify whom I needed to speak with, I ended up in the office of Chris Daggett. One of the hallmarks of the Kean adminis-tration was the quality and talent of the people he recruited. Chris was young, energetic, and had a doctorate in education from the University of Massachusetts. Though a lot of his work and experience was in public finance, he served as Kean's acting chief of staff for educational policy.

I made the case to Chris that Thomas Edison was the only public insti-tution without a house or housing allowance for its president. He was sympathetic and acknowledged the inequity. While others were skeptical of the legitimacy of our model, he appreciated the value of our work. Fol-lowing the meeting, the chancellor and the state treasurer were informed that the provision of a housing allowance for Thomas Edison was approved. I often chuckled about the disconnect between how pundits, academics, and policy wonks *think* policy is made and what *really* happens.

Chapter Twelve

It was the best of times, it was the worst of times.

—*Charles Dickens*

The major goals the board and I discussed upon my arrival were achieved by the end of the fiscal year. Governor Kean signed the Appropriations Act funding our new nursing program, we established an amicable and mutually respectful relationship with the chancellor and BHE staff, and we were no longer the only school in the state whose president didn't have a housing allowance.

I was inaugurated as the third president of Thomas Edison State College on my birthday, July 9, 1983. I was thirty-seven years old, the same age as my good friends Jim Fisher and Buzz Shaw were when they were appointed to their first presidencies. I was overjoyed to celebrate my inauguration and birthday with many of my friends and mentors, including Jim, Buzz, Paul Wisdom, King Cheek, Fred Humphries, and Morris Keeton. Delores's extended family came as well as my close friends from as far back as elementary school, Clarke Williams, Linda Locke, Rodney and Andrita Hammond, and Jurnice Sellars, my secretary from Morgan.

My mother, father, and brother came from California; Uncle Doc and Aunt Bert came from Mississippi; my Uncle Ralph and Aunt Evie came from Philadelphia, along with my cousin Janice and her son, Evan, who is the same age as Shayla. It would be the last time we would all be together.

It was heartrending delivering my inaugural address seeing my mother in the audience, knowing how sick she was. When your father is a mortician, you learn that for every celebration in life, loss is lurking quietly in the shadows. A year later, on my birthday, Uncle Ralph died from pancreatic cancer; two years later, I lost my mother; and in 1988, I lost Uncle Doc. Life and loss are inextricably intertwined, and there are no words to describe how it feels when you lose the people most important to you.

Uncle Doc once told me that life is not a spectator sport; you need to get in the game, do the best you can, and leave things better than you found them. I have always taken his advice and lived my life with a deep sense of urgency and desire to do just that. I am grateful for the time I had with my family, and I love them very much. They always did the best they could and gave me everything they had to give.

As my first year in office drew to a close, things were going well. The new team was in place, we were building the new nursing program, and we had survived the state's fiscal crisis of the moment. The solution was in part due to an increase in the state income tax; the top rate went from 3 percent to 3.5 percent. (The top rate is now 9 percent. Ahh, for the good old days.)

But all honeymoons must come to an end. The first hiccup occurred when we instituted annual evaluations and performance reviews for all staff. The nonmanagerial employees were represented by two unions, the statewide Communications Workers of America (CWA) and the American Federation of Teachers (AFT).

The local unit of our AFT objected to annual evaluations for staff members on multiyear contracts. They contended that the only purpose of performance reviews was associated with contract renewals, and since people in the middle of multiyear contracts were not being considered for renewal, the evaluations were inappropriate. The purpose of annual performance reviews is to provide evaluative feedback to reward positive performance and where necessary identify areas for improvement. It is an essential accountability tool that applies to everyone, including the president. Our differences were irreconcilable, so the union filed a grievance. The grievance was denied at the local level and again at the state level. We were free to implement the practice, but the union's tone was unnecessarily contentious.

During the contract renewal period the following year, we had another dispute with a staff member who was not performing satisfactorily. His supervisor responded by providing feedback and guidance to elicit improvement while documenting deficiencies as they occurred. When she performed his evaluation, she concluded that his work was unsatisfactory and recommended that his contract not be renewed. His file, along with the nonrenewal recommendation, went to the vice president for academic affairs, who concurred, and the matter was referred to me for a decision. The file was thorough, and the recommendation was well supported. Accordingly, he was notified that his contract would not be renewed when it expired at the end of the fiscal year. Everything was done by the book. The problem was that this individual was president of the union. All hell broke loose.

Between my uncle Robert's work with the union in Detroit and my father, who greatly benefitted from the organizing work of A. Philip Randolph, founder of the Brotherhood of Sleeping Car Porters Union, I am not antiunion. However, this was not a debate about the value of unions. This was about the standards of performance required of all members of our professional community regardless of their office. It was not that he wasn't capable of doing the work, but he seemed to feel entitled not to. The lines were drawn, and the war began.

One of the most attractive features of belonging to a union is job security. If the college could get rid of the union president, then "no one was safe." I was not naive. I knew that the union's reaction would be severe, and it was. We had numerous grievances filed against us as well as a multicount unfair labor practice charge. They asserted that his dismissal was retaliation for his union activity, which is protected by law. However, any reading of his personnel file and the quality of his supervisor's documentation made it obvious that this was not the case.

We were attacked legally, politically, and personally. The college was picketed, and I was vilified. My doctoral dissertation was examined for any impropriety, plagiarism, or lack of attribution. My resume was scoured for any evidence of padding or exaggeration. I received more than one verbal threat from Marco Lacatena, president of the statewide AFT. He pledged to defeat and punish me for attempting to take down one of his leaders. He wanted to use me as an example, lest the other college presidents think they could get away with something like this.

I knew that we could win the battle and lose the war. This conflict could disrupt the campus in such a way that I wouldn't be able to put it back together and continue as president. While I understood the consequences, I also knew I wouldn't want to be president of an institution where we couldn't employ appropriate professional judgment, especially in a case where the evidence was so clear. Unless we were all prepared to be held to the same standards of professionalism and accountability, none of the things we wanted to build would be possible.

The legal and procedural fights went on for about a year and half, and we prevailed at every level. The grievances and the unfair labor charges were all found to be without merit as were the court appeals. The personal attack on me was so extreme that it offended the members of our own local union. Union members began expressing their support for me and their disapproval of the unfair nature of the attacks.

When the dust cleared, the employee in question was gone, and I was still standing. Jerry Middlemiss was overwhelmingly elected as the new president of the AFT. He was independent, fearless, and equally committed to the success of the college as well as the protection of his members. Our small and skillful staff possessed a missionary zeal for the college's work that stemmed from those who viewed themselves as part of a movement, and they understood that I was committed to their welfare.

Lacatena believed that the relationship between a union president and a college president should be adversarial. He was infuriated to learn that the relationship between Jerry and me was not. He filed an unfair labor practice charge against me and Middlemiss, the president of his own union local! That was unwise of him, but it was great for me because it united me, Middlemiss, and our local union together against him and the statewide AFT council.

From then on, I enjoyed a collegial, mutually supportive, and respectful relationship with our two local unions. One of the plaques that occupies a prominent place on my wall is a statement of appreciation from my local AFT chapter. My battle with Lacatena led to an invitation from the other state college presidents to assume a broader role in statewide negotiations between the colleges and the AFT.

New Jersey has a particularly odd arrangement for collective bargaining. Even though the employees of the nine state colleges work for their respective institutions under their boards of trustees, the governor is the employer of record for the sole purpose of conducting collective bargaining negotiations with our unions. That places these institutions in a peculiar situation in that the governor negotiates our employees' contracts.

For years we unsuccessfully fought for the autonomy to bargain with our unions. The union, of course, opposed that. They understood that they had more leverage over elected officials than they would over college and university boards of trustees. Since we couldn't bargain directly, most of the presidents tried to gain more influence over the negotiating process managed by the governor's office. This was not just a matter of reasonable management principles, but it had very real practical effect. The governor negotiated a contract with our unions and then handed the bill over to us to pay.

Governor Corzine, amid the state's continuing fiscal crisis, imposed the largest cut in public higher education among all fifty states, while at the same time granting the AFT a 34 percent increase in salaries over the four years of the contract. This forced the colleges to make double-digit tuition increases and staff retrenchments to pay for the governor's commitment. These same politicians then chastised the public institutions for tuition increases that they themselves had caused. Politicians often make decisions that drive up costs and create inefficiencies and then criticize the administrations and trustees for the consequences of what they did as a way of avoiding accountability for their actions.

The state college presidents were successful in joining the governor's negotiating team, but many of the presidents were reluctant to subject themselves to Lacatena's wrath and abuse. He was profane and could be intimidating, particularly to some of our more genteel colleagues. After what I went through, they all knew I wasn't afraid of him, so I was asked to chair the team. Over time, through our work with the governor's office, we were able to regain some of the reasonable management prerogatives given away at previous negotiations. The turnover among the college presidents became beneficial as some of the timid presidents were replaced with those who were more assertive.

During my time in the sausage factory, I got an insider's view as to how these agreements were made. We were eventually able to restore a more appropriate balance between the political influence of the AFT and the legitimate interests of the presidents and the trustees, ensuring that the institutions served the public and the students over the self-interest of certain bargaining groups. We've made a lot of progress since those days in both tone and outcomes. It still makes no sense to me why the president and trustees of an institution aren't allowed to bargain and negotiate with their own employees. This irrational process only survives because of the perverse political culture of New Jersey.

The strange artifact of history and culture that created the collective bargaining structure also kept the colleges and universities smothered by an insufferable state bureaucracy. When the legislation that created the BHE was passed, it explicitly stated that the governance of the nine state colleges was the responsibility of their respective autonomous boards of trustees. Even though this was set forth in law, the state agencies never let go.

Early in my tenure, our payroll was processed by the state, and we could not add a position unless the state budget office approved it. It didn't matter whether the president or board of trustees authorized the action. If a vacancy occurred, the college was required to petition the Vacancy Review Committee in the New Jersey Department of Personnel for the authority to refill the position. When Arnold Fletcher retired, I was required to justify why a college needed a chief academic officer. We lived in the worst of worlds. While we were responsible and accountable for the conduct of the institution, the authority to affect the institution's performance was vested in well-intentioned but unaccountable people in the state bureaucracy.

In my experience in recent history, the state has only had two governors who were genuinely committed to higher education. The first was Governor Richard Hughes, who created the Department of Higher Education, the community college system, three new state colleges, and the greatest expansion of higher education in the state's history. The second was Governor Thomas H. Kean.

The impediments imposed by the state bureaucracy on higher education were a topic of concern of the New Jersey Board of Higher Education under Governor Kean's predecessor, Brendan Byrne. During Byrne's administration, the BHE created the Commission on the Future of State Colleges. The fundamental conclusion of the commission was twofold: first, that the institutions would not be able to fulfill their obligation to the public under the crushing weight of the current bureaucratic conditions; and second, that the colleges needed the autonomy and authority envisioned by the enabling legislation that created the BHE. Unfortunately, the state was unlikely to do that. Instead, the commission suggested the creation of a state college system with a chief executive officer and a centralized administration similar to SUNY, the logic being that if the state wouldn't give the institutions' authority, it might give it to a state system. Because of its proximity to New York, New Jersey often looks across the river for example. Some of the presidents familiar with the City University of New York (CUNY) as well as SUNY thought this was a good idea. But many of us who had worked in state systems hated it.

In a meeting Governor Kean called to discuss the matter, we expressed our objections. He understood and thought that if the institutions believed their trustee boards should have autonomy, then that was what should be done. While some of us thought it could be achieved by executive action on his part given the wording of the current statute, he was convinced that if it were to survive beyond him, it should be done by changing the legislation. Most of us enthusiastically embraced the idea, but we also knew there would be serious opposition from the faculty union as well as the state bureaucracy itself. There was also a faction in the legislature who didn't believe the trustees and the management would be efficient stewards of the public resources, but there was no question in my mind that this was the right course of action.

There was an influx of dynamic new leadership at some of our institutions around this time: Vera Farris at Stockton, Arnie Speert at William Paterson College, and Herman James at what was then Glassboro State College. We had the benefit of two strong veteran presidents, Bill Maxwell, president of Jersey City State College, and Harold Eickhoff, president of Trenton State College. Harold, Bill, and I were tasked with developing and coordinating a strategy to have the bill drafted and guided through the legislature.

Jersey City and the county in which it resides have had a long-standing reputation as one of the most corrupt political entities in the United States, but Jersey City State College was an island of integrity in a sea of shady practices. Bill grew up in Jersey City, was a student at the university, and went on to become dean, provost, and president. He passionately loved his city and the people and students who came from there. He envisioned what would become New Jersey City University, an institution for people who loved cities and who wanted to use them as learning laboratories for educational enlightenment and personal empowerment. He was fearlessly principled and witty and had an endearing personality.

Harold Eickhoff was quiet, thoughtful, introspective, and determined, and I was the brazen kid from Chicago. The three of us brought a great deal of knowledge and experience in navigating political systems to get things done. I think that's why our colleagues deferred to us in leading this effort. To be sure, all nine of us were united in our commitment and actively participated with local legislators and spheres of influence in advocating for our common purpose. We also had the active support of Governor Kean and particularly his chief education aide, Rick Mills. Rick was the governor's point person and our liaison. We also regularly worked with Jean Bogle in the governor's counsel's office. In the legislature, both the senate and assembly were controlled by Democrats, and Kean was a Republican, so it was imperative that we had bipartisan support for this to be successful.

Bill was a member of the Commission on the Future of State Colleges and an early supporter of the notion of a SUNY- or CUNY-type system, but in the deliberations and debate that followed, he became a committed advocate for state college autonomy. Where applicable, we took advantage of those aspects of the commission report that set forth the kind of authority and autonomy the trustees should have, much of it already stated in previous legislation. We then had our respective staffs delineate the specific operations and business practices that would need to be transferred from the state to the institutions and drafted unambiguous language conveying the assumption of this authority to the trustees.

Harold, Bill, and I took the results of all this work and met with the chair of the Assembly Education Committee, Joe Doria. Joe, a friend of Bill Maxwell's, worked at St. Peter's College. We had considerable discussion and some debate about the elements of the bill. I am not sure whether the final draft was written by Doria's staff in the legislature or by Kean's staff, but the resulting bill contained the best provisions possible at the time to pass through the legislature.

We deliberately left out the collective bargaining issue because we feared it might sink the entire bill. Mattie Feldman, a democratic senator in Bergen County, was the most visible and outspoken advocate for higher education in the state senate, and we spent considerable time going over it with him as well. The bill was introduced in the legislature, sponsored by Joe Doria in the assembly and Mattie Feldman in the senate.

The opposition from the AFT was immediate. Assembly Speaker Alan Karcher tended to oppose most of the initiatives personally identified with Kean. The nine state colleges and universities along with their trustees began a coordinated campaign to demonstrate the value of the bill to legislators. In private conversations, virtually all of them admitted that they understood why we wanted it and agreed that it was the right thing to do, but they had difficulty overcoming the opposition from the public employee unions.

I had one particularly memorable encounter with a larger-than-life, boisterous state senator from south Jersey. We had become good friends and could speak candidly with each other. The first words out of his mouth were, "Doc, I know you're here about that damn autonomy bill, so let me save you some time. I've read the bill, and it's a good idea, but I'm not gonna vote for it." When I asked him why, he said, "Because the unions are against it."

I tried to appeal to his service of the public interest but to no avail. He said, "The unions contribute to my campaign and get people to the polls on election day. What can you college presidents offer to compete with that?"

I shrugged my shoulders, laughed, and admitted, "Not much, just a good idea for the public interest," to which he smiled. I then advised him not to be so candid when others came to visit in search of his vote. I even gave him a couple of arguments he could use that were a bit more defensible. We departed on good terms, but I knew his vote was not obtainable.

I had much better luck with the powerful and influential senate president, John Lynch. Senator Lynch had a successful law practice, was former mayor of New Brunswick, and was instrumental in joining Johnson & Johnson and Rutgers University to start the urban revitalization of his city. He was a formidable political force, not only in his region of the state but far beyond. Several years earlier, he had prevailed in a contentious fight with the New Jersey Education Association, the state's powerful teachers' union. Unlike most members of the legislature, he was not intimidated by the AFT.

We met on several occasions to discuss the merits of the legislation, the benefit to the colleges, and the impact on the educational needs of the state. He understood the importance of getting this done and pledged his support. He also shared with Governor Kean, his willingness to work on getting the bill passed. I think Senator Lynch's support was a major turning point in achieving the bill's ultimate passage, but that achievement was going to have to wait awhile because Speaker Karcher's opposition in the assembly was hardening.

It was disappointing because the Speaker's resistance had nothing to do with the merits of the legislation or even the public interest. It was used as a pawn to oppose the initiatives of a Republican governor in deference to an influential political constituency. Even though the bill was sponsored by his fellow Democrat and committee chairman Joe Doria and favorably reported out of Doria's education committee, the Speaker refused to post the bill.

Our fortunes changed when, in the following midterm elections, Democrats lost control of the assembly and the Republicans gained a majority. This time around, Joe Doria's bill was introduced by Republican Assemblyman John Rocco. In the Democratic caucus, Karcher, who was then minority leader, called for a party line vote against the bill. It passed the assembly with only Republican votes. Even Joe Doria had to vote against his own bill. This is New Jersey politics!

Now it was the senate's turn. The original Democratic senate sponsor, Mattie Feldman, held firm and reintroduced the bill, and it was reported out of the Senate Education Committee for a vote. With Senator Feldman's leadership and the strong support of Democratic senate president Lynch, the bill passed the senate by one vote.

While I had worked in Maryland to achieve autonomy for Morgan from the state college system, helping to get the State College Autonomy Bill

passed in New Jersey was the single most important legislative victory of
my career. Harold Eickhoff and I, who were standing next to each other
in the senate chamber, hugged each other. Hugging is not unusual for me,
but it was totally out of character for Harold. Bill Maxwell was elated, too.
Marco Lacatena, who was in the room, was crestfallen. Sometimes justice
does prevail and the good guys win. At the time, Harold was chair of the
state college presidents' group, and I was vice chair, but all nine of us shared
in this victory.

Some of the presidents expressed a "be careful what you wish for" sentiment. Sometimes it is easier to hide behind the bureaucracy than to lead
and accept accountability for the conduct of your office, but for me, Harold Eickhoff, Bill Maxell, Herman James, Vera Farris, and Arnie Speert, it
was a door to a new future for our institutions and higher education in
New Jersey.

A month after the passage of the legislation, I assumed the chair of the
state colleges' presidents' group. Governor Kean signed this bipartisan legislation on my birthday in 1986 and gave each of us a pen used in the
signing. I have the front page of the bill with a picture of Governor Kean
with the state college presidents and board chairs, along with that pen,
framed in my office. None of the good things that followed for Thomas
Edison would have been possible had that bill not been passed.

When the original autonomy bill was blocked by Karcher, there was a
companion piece of legislation to abolish the Council of State Colleges and
create the New Jersey State College Governing Boards Association (GBA).
That bill passed. The Council of State Colleges was part of the Department
of Higher Education and comprised the presidents of the nine state colleges, one trustee from each institution, and the director of the Office of
State Colleges, who reported to the chancellor. The chancellor's office
exerted considerable control over the council, to the point where we were
told we couldn't meet without someone from his office in attendance. Not
that I agreed to that, of course. The GBA, later named the New Jersey Association of State Colleges and Universities (NJASCU), was independent of

the department and operated with a staff who were hired, paid for, and controlled by the institutions themselves.

The GBA recruited Dr. Darryl Greer as its first executive director. Darryl had been a government relations executive with the College Board in New York and had a great deal of legislative experience at the state and national level. He was brought to our attention and recommended by Bill Maxwell. While we interviewed several candidates, Darryl was our unanimous first choice. He also came with a strong recommendation from George Hanford, president of the College Board and a member of Thomas Edison's board of trustees.

There was a personal aspect of working with Darryl that proved to be a lot of fun. His academic credentials were impeccable, complete with a PhD from Stanford, but he had grown up as a Black kid in the streets of Gary, Indiana. Gary is a suburb of Chicago, at the tip of Lake Michigan across the Indiana border. It was home to several gigantic steel mills, which served as the central source of employment for the large African American community who lived there. While it wasn't the South Side of Chicago, it was similar but on a smaller scale. The other irony is that Darryl's uncle was Howard Gentry, the distinguished athletic director of Tennessee State University. We had a lot in common and became great friends.

Darryl worked closely with the presidents, the legislators, and their staffs in formulating the strategy and executing the tactics that eventually resulted in the passage of the autonomy bill. The presidents had great respect for Darryl. His innate ability to build consensus among the group when combined with his knowledge and experience in government resulted in thoughtful, strategic, and united educational policy work for the state for many years.

In spite of the legislation and the governor's support, the bureaucracy still couldn't let go, but with the intervention of the governor's office and his cabinet, they were forced to relinquish their hold on us. We were able to establish our own banking relationships, create our own payroll systems, and obtain control of the administrative apparatus of running an institution. We no longer needed the approval of the bureaucracy to execute the decisions we were always responsible for in theory but could never accomplish without the control of the machinery. All that changed after the signing of this bill.

Some of the opposition was downright comical. Thomas Edison conducted testing at various sites scattered throughout the state. On one occasion, we mailed admissions credentials and information for the students to take their exams at their registered location. When the test administrator arrived, none of the students were present, and we couldn't figure out what happened. All our mailing was sent to the state capitol post office. We found out that when the head of that operation saw several hundred letters marked first class, he decided, as a cost-saving measure, to change the postage to bulk rate. Unfortunately, that meant that the students' registration materials didn't show up until three weeks after the testing date. We were all livid, but this was the type of pre-autonomy madness inflicted on us regularly at multiple levels.

I immediately directed our administrative staff to create our own mailing capacity and establish postal relationships directly with the U.S. Postal Service. We stopped using the statehouse mail operations, acquired our own zip code, and proceeded with independent operations. The head of the statehouse mail operations was so enraged that he took his objections to the governor. I don't think he ever actually got to him, but I received some good-natured ribbing from some of Kean's staff about looking over my shoulder for the angry postmaster.

I was pleased about the way things were progressing and the opportunities that lay ahead, but no one was more overjoyed than the members of our board of trustees. The trustees had been frustrated by their inability to exercise their authority from the day the institution was founded, especially since it was outlined in statute. Despite the unorthodox structure in New Jersey to have the board of higher education select and appoint trustees, they had done an excellent job at Thomas Edison. Every member of this board was experienced, talented, and fully qualified to execute the enormous responsibility of trusteeship. They were also wonderful people, and I thoroughly enjoyed their company both individually and collectively.

The chair, Ellie Spiegel, had been a member of the original steering committee that recommended the creation of the college. There were many people involved in the formation of the institution, but none of them had more influence than Ellie. Vice chair of the board was Alan Ferguson, an executive from Prudential and chair of the presidential search committee that recommended me. George Hanford was the distinguished and long-serving president of the College Entrance Examination Board (the College Board). He was distinguished, highly regarded, and influential in the world of college admissions and assessment.

Patricia Danielson was an early graduate of Thomas Edison who went on to earn a master's degree from Princeton. Rita Novitt was an executive at Johnson & Johnson. Tom Seessel was an authority on housing policy, had been a housing expert in the Byrne administration, and was president of Structured Employment Economic Development Corporation (SEEDCO), a community-development intermediary created by the Ford Foundation. Bob Taylor was an executive at Bell Labs, Chris Yegen was a financial services executive, and H. Harvey Myers was an African American architect in Princeton.

George was as Harvard as you could get. He graduated from there and remained active with the alumni as an ongoing participant in the intellectual culture of the university for the remainder of his life. Harvard regularly held symposia and seminars at the faculty club. Because of George, I was invited to speak there at a faculty symposium. I was flattered and deeply honored, and when I saw the list of previous speakers, I was downright humbled.

It was a stereotypical Harvard affair. The faculty in attendance dined in a small, intimate room with dark wood paneling before retiring to a similarly appointed lounge. After George introduced me, I provided remarks about adult learning and prior learning assessment. When I finished, I joined the group reclining on the elegant leather furniture, accepted a glass of brandy, and engaged in thoughtful conversations for the next hour.

When we were done, one of the attendees thanked me for coming and told me that he learned a lot from my informative comments. I thanked him for his generous response. George agreed that things had gone well, and when I conveyed the kind message I had just received from his colleague, he said, "Do you know who that is?" When I said I did not, he told me it was David Riesman. My mouth fell open. David Riesman, author of *The Lonely Crowd*, is one of the most respected sociologists this country has ever produced. Some of his research had been considered by the Supreme Court in the *Brown vs. Board of Education* case that ended legal segregation. I looked around at my surroundings and thought once again, "This is a long way from the South Side of Chicago."

The relationship of a president and their board is unique, intimate, and often misunderstood. While the president is accountable *to* the board, they are also an extension *of* the board. The president is the tool by which the board ensures that the institution is led with integrity and effectively fulfills its mission. It is a relationship built upon mutual trust and confidence. If that trust is ever abrogated or that confidence ever lost, neither the presidency nor the institution can be successful. Boards have an enormous tolerance for bad news but no tolerance for surprises or deception. The board has an obligation to be engaged, thoughtful, and candid. The president is singularly accountable to the board for the condition, welfare, effectiveness, and success of the institution.

The board trusted me because I never asked them to. My responsibility as president was to set forth the options, justify my choices, and, most importantly, describe the expected outcomes and my accountability in achieving them. The objective and measurable assessment of an institution's performance and success in fulfilling its mission serves as the principal criterion for evaluating the effectiveness of its president. It is not about personalities or charisma; it is about execution and achievement. Having said that, personal relationships are vital. Trust and confidence are intangible; you know when you have it, and you know when you don't. If the president ever loses confidence in his or her board, they should leave. You can never win a confrontation with your board, whether you are right or not. Likewise, if the board loses confidence in their president, they should make a change.

Over the years, trustees would come and go, but we were always successful in identifying and attracting extraordinary people to take on this important responsibility. When recruiting trustees, we had three essential criteria. First, they needed an understanding of and a commitment to the unique mission of Thomas Edison. Second, they should have the experience, capacity, and qualifications to perform the role. And third, they should be prepared to commit their time, energy, reputation, and resources in advancing the institution's performance.

We also had an important but unwritten prerequisite: they had to be people we enjoyed being around and working with. Some people can be successful but toxic, ego driven, or agenda driven, which can disrupt and destroy the collegial culture necessary for a high-performing board. I had the privilege of being one of the few executives who looked forward to board meetings because we genuinely liked and respected each other and found joy in the work we did.

One of the early rookie mistakes I made as president was when I met with the CEO of Johnson & Johnson, shortly after coming to the college, and didn't think to notify Rita Novitt, my board member who was a senior executive at the company. The visit would have been far more productive if I had consulted Rita in advance and she had orchestrated the visit, not only with the CEO but with some of the other senior executives as well. When Rita found out that I had been there, she was not happy, and I had no satisfactory explanation. It was thoughtless, and I had made a mistake. Fortunately, Rita acknowledged my mea culpa and was forgiving.

Soon after, the two of us were having lunch in New Brunswick and ordered iced tea to drink. The server asked whether we wanted a regular or a Long Island iced tea. Neither of us had ever heard of a Long Island iced tea and thought we would try them. We proceeded with our conversation and small talk and each ordered another one. After the second, we ordered a third. About halfway through, it occurred to both of us that we were tipsy. We called the server over and asked what was in them, and when she told us, we both erupted in laughter. After drinking a couple cups of coffee, we wondered what kind of afternoons we were going to have back at the office.

I wish I had time to talk about the many extraordinary trustees who enriched my life and the work we did at the college. Maybe that's another story, but I do want to note two that we lost. The first was Carol Nerlino, who was a graduate of Thomas Edison and an executive in the financial services world. Carol was knowledgeable, magnetic, and fun-loving. She was the kind of graduate every college president wants to have representing their institution. She served with distinction on the board and eventually became its chair.

During her tenure, we established an important relationship with the University of South Africa (UNISA). UNISA was an adult-serving institution founded in 1946, had over 120,000 students, and was a pioneer in what today is called distance education. Following the postapartheid reconstruction of the country, UNISA and Thomas Edison formed a collaboration. We wanted to learn more about their use of technology-supported learning, and they wanted to learn more about prior learning assessment. After a lot of staff work between the two institutions, I was invited to Pretoria by the CEO of the university for a signing ceremony. Their board would be present, and I thought it would be fitting for the chair of our board to be there as well. It was an extraordinary visit with all the trappings of a treaty signing between two countries.

Shortly after returning from South Africa, Carol was diagnosed with cancer, and we lost her not long after. It was a devastating loss to the board, the institution, her family, and the many people whose lives she had touched. In honor of her memory, we named one of our conference rooms the Nerlino Suite and had her portrait commissioned to display on the wall.

The second trustee we lost was an extraordinary renaissance man, Fred Abbate. I wish I could say that I had the foresight to recruit Fred, but he was brought to my attention by Larry Marcus, head of the state college section of the BHE. At the time, Fred was an executive with Atlantic Electric Company in south Jersey. He would go on to become CEO of the state's utility association, representing the industry in Trenton with state government. Fred was nothing like the typical "lobbyist" you meet in Trenton. He had a PhD in philosophy and authored several books and pamphlets. He was invited by a British university to lecture on Shakespeare, and he wrote and produced a play that was performed at the Blackstone Theater in Chicago. He was brilliant but exceptionally modest. He never talked about his achievements or diverse interests, and you would not have known about them had you not discovered them from other people. He also had a great sense of humor, a quick mind and wit, and one of the kindest hearts you'd ever encounter. He had a generosity of spirit and was just an all-around exceptional person. He was diagnosed with a rare, degenerative brain disorder. This affliction was particularly insidious because it attacked this wonderful man at the point of his greatest gift, his brilliant mind. The course of the disease was rapid, and we lost him in 2017.

When I arrived at the college, we had no advocacy organization to raise money and to support giving. We incorporated the Thomas Edison State College Foundation as a 501(c)3 organization, and the first chair was trustee Chris Yegen. It was complicated recruiting that initial foundation board for two reasons. First, this was a young, obscure, experimental institution, and second, we knew that the initial foundation board would establish the peerage for all of those who would follow. The people of great means, stature, and influence we needed to find were not going to join a board unless they were joining colleagues of similar standing.

We had a compelling case to make, but people are reluctant to give to public institutions, especially in a place like New Jersey, where the private colleges draw a great deal of the philanthropy. People frequently asked, "Why should I give to a public college that is supported by taxpayer money?" Our task was to make the case for why an investment in this distinct institution went beyond an investment in a public school. We had the benefit of our unique story as the only college or university in the state and one of a few in the country that exclusively served self-directed adults.

We were fortunate in recruiting a number of respected leaders of great prominence early on. They were Ed Booher, retired chairman and CEO of McGraw Hill publishing company; Richard Gillespie, founder of a distinguished and significant advertising agency in the area; Robert Hillier, noted architect in his own right, whose father has a major Dow Jones facility bearing his name; Nicholas Carnivale, a highly regarded insurance executive in Princeton and former president of the Nassau Club; Jim Carnes, CEO of Sarnoff Laboratories and leader of the consortium that created high-definition television; and Clarence Lockett, corporate controller of Johnson & Johnson.

With that nucleus, we were able to build and maintain a distinguished board and began to solicit private giving. We respected the foundation's autonomy and formally requested its support as we would any other foundation. The purpose of this foundation was to promote private giving and stimulate advocacy and relationship building with external sources of support. We wanted foundation investments in the university to serve as our venture capital fund, in which to make discreet investments for new initiatives and to support innovation. Any funds we requested from the foundation were for one-time expenditures or to start initiatives that would become self-sustaining. We never asked the foundation to support anything normally funded from the college's operating budget. Building a board who would be tirelessly committed to their stewardship of the foundation's resources while also lending their reputations, talent, attention, and resources to this institution was the goal, and we succeeded.

Raising money from alumni was a challenge. At traditional colleges and universities, students had a shared campus experience, they graduated in cohorts, and there was an expectation to contribute to their alma mater. We didn't have a long-standing tradition of alumni giving, but our graduates had an enormous sense of gratitude to this institution that made it possible for them to achieve a lifelong objective.

Because our students were midcareer adults, they had assets and relationships available to them that took graduates of traditional colleges years to develop. Our alumni association comprised about ten volunteers who organized on their own to form an alumni body. Given that our graduates were all over the world, with no "homecoming" game to attend, we knew this alumni structure would not be viable.

We persuaded our small, vestigial alumni group to disband and formed an alumni affairs office that had the capacity to maintain contacts and relationships with our entire alumni base. We eliminated the dues structure the informal group had put together and extended membership to everyone who earned a Thomas Edison degree. We slowly built a donor base that accumulated and accelerated over the years; however, it was an area of some disappointment because we never realized the potential in giving I thought we had.

We did have some notable successes, however. One of our graduates is Gary Heavin, founder of the Curves Fitness chain. Gary is a successful entrepreneur with a fascinating story. In his youth, he was traumatized when his mother suffered a heart attack and died in his presence. He founded the profitable Curves Fitness chain to create a business that advanced the health of women.

We first met at Gary's commencement ceremony. This was one of those rare moments when two strangers develop instant rapport. While we are two very different people, there was, at our core, a common sense of shared values around which to build a relationship. Gary Heavin is a man of deep faith, and he believes in giving as not only a matter of principle but also as an extension of his religious beliefs. In 2004, Gary and Diane Heavin made a two-million-dollar gift to the college's foundation, which stands to this date as the largest monetary gift the institution has ever received. There was no quid pro quo involved, but out of appreciation for his generosity, the board of trustees named our school of social and behavioral arts the Heavin School of Arts and Sciences.

In 2013, the Martinson Family Foundation donated a $450,000 three-year grant to support a new multimedia technology studio to enhance our online courses. We received two other important nonmonetary gifts. John Martinson, head of Edison Ventures Capital Fund, had accumulated the largest collection of Thomas Edison memorabilia owned by any private individual. John was a supporter of the college and a regular donor. He appreciated our dedication to innovation and accountability in achieving tangible learning outcomes for our students and measurable progress for our institution. In 2013, he donated more than 1,500 pieces from his collection, which included framed advertisements and promotional materials, signage, patents, artwork, and several products invented by Thomas Edison, including phonographs, mimeographs, an Ediphone, light bulbs, fans, and several appliances.

When George Washington left his home in Virginia and rode north to assume his presidency, he stopped in Trenton to receive the greetings of an adoring crowd. That scene was captured in a brilliant oil painting by N. C. Wyeth. The enormous painting adorned the wall of a large bank building in downtown Trenton for many years. The bank that owned the painting was acquired several times through a series of acquisitions until finally it came into the possession of Wells Fargo Bank. Following the acquisition of the painting and the bank that owned it, Wells Fargo closed the branch where the painting was housed.

There were concerns raised by the preservationist community in Trenton about keeping this famous portrait from leaving town. Wells Fargo has an illustrious history of its own and has kept many mementos in its museum. There was some discussion that the Wyeth painting would be relocated there. The historical society and other preservationists organized to keep that from happening. We volunteered to house this national treasure and pledged to keep it in the city in perpetuity. In 2013, the bank agreed to move the portrait to the Kelsey Building Complex on an indefinite loan, with the assurances that the bank had no intention of reclaiming it. In 2019, the bank completed the transfer by deeding the portrait to the university with an appraised value of $4 million dollars.

Chapter Thirteen

A college is a garden where people grow.

—*George A. Pruitt*

Governor Kean provided the leadership for the last higher education capital facilities bond issue that New Jersey would have for almost thirty years, but perhaps his most effective contribution to higher education aside from the autonomy legislation was his Challenge Grant initiative. Previous administrations provided modest but incremental funding increases in response to normal inflationary costs, but Kean's approach replaced those increases with Challenge Grants.

The Challenge Grant initiative had two major policy objectives: to foster mission differentiation among the state's senior public institutions and to make substantial progress in achieving institutional excellence when benchmarked against aspirational peers and validated against objective measures by appropriate third-party experts.

For the three public research universities, the mission differentiation was clearly in place. The ambition for Rutgers was to be a "world-class public research university." Its aspirational peers were places like the University of Michigan and the University of California, Berkeley. For NJIT, the aspirational institutions included MIT and the California Institute of Technology, and for UMDNJ, the great medical educational centers of the nation. Each of these institutions was challenged to identify what steps they would take in this direction if given a significant investment to achieve them.

With the exception of Thomas Edison State College, mission differentiation among the other state colleges was less obvious. Herman James's vision for Glassboro State College was for it to become the regional university specifically designed to respond to the needs of southern New Jersey. Most of the higher education assets of the state were concentrated in the north, and Glassboro State College was the only public institution in south-central New Jersey. Stockton College's location in the environmentally sensitive New Jersey Pine Barrens and proximity to the Atlantic Ocean supported Vera Farris's view that it could become an important center of environmental research and education. New Jersey City University, embracing its urban commitment, pursued a significant cooperative education initiative, turning the city into a learning laboratory. Ramapo College of New Jersey, under President Bob Scott's leadership, exploited its proximity to New York to focus on international education. Montclair State College invested heavily in the fine and performing arts.

Harold Eickhoff had a bold and transformative vision for Trenton State College. Harold wanted to turn this former teachers' college into a highly selective residential scholarly community attracting the nation's most gifted high school graduates and providing them with a powerful faculty committed to quality undergraduate teaching. He identified the College of William and Mary, the second oldest institution of higher learning in America and one of the country's finest, as an aspirant institution. Harold's vision was scoffed at by many and ridiculed by the chancellor and the staff of the BHE. It certainly seemed like a heavy lift given the state of public funding and the magnitude of the metamorphosis he proposed.

Kean's Challenge Grants were indeed challenging to acquire. The evaluation process to qualify was rigorous and competitive. It was also risky for the presidents because attaining these grants was a very public declaration of what the institution and its president would be held accountable for. Not surprisingly, the most effective presidents had the biggest visions. It was a lot of pressure, and not all presidents are self-confident enough to embrace it, but for several of these institutions, the Challenge Grant initiative was transformative.

Herman James was able to solicit a $100 million dollar gift to the institution by the industrialist Henry Rowan, which was at the time the largest single gift given to a public college or university in the country. Today Rowan University is a living testimonial to James's vision.

What is today Stockton University became a major center attracting environmentalists from all over the country to engage in cutting-edge research. The street entering the university is named after President Farris in recognition of her foresight and leadership.

Harold Eickhoff continued the transformation of Trenton State College, even changing its name to The College of New Jersey (TCNJ). This was controversial as many people objected to the removal of the word *Trenton* from the name, symbolizing a distancing of the college from its roots in the state capital even though the school had resided in Ewing Township for many years. Another point of controversy was the reaction of nearby Princeton University, which when founded in 1746 was called The College of New Jersey. Some history-conscious Princetonians were not pleased by the name change despite the fact that the university had long since abandoned using that moniker.

At the point of his retirement, after serving as president for nineteen years, Eickhoff had laid a solid foundation for his new vision. Fortunately, he was succeeded in the presidency by R. Barbara Gitenstein, a dynamic and visionary leader in her own right who fell in love with the school's mission and Harold's vision. Harold Eickhoff and I were good friends, and it was gratifying to watch Barbara Gitenstein, who became a close friend as well, build and create through her eighteen-year presidency the institution Eickhoff dreamed of. When Gitenstein retired in 2017, TCNJ's selectivity and four-year graduation rate compared favorably to William and Mary. It was a remarkable evolution and achievement.

When I was a student at the University of Illinois, I participated in early research about computer-assisted learning. The university paid students to participate in psychological experiments as research subjects. The experiment I took part in was fortunately benign, unlike some others at the time. I sat in front of a computer screen and answered questions based on information I was provided. I later learned that I was participating in an experiment to test a system called PLATO that would be marketed to educational organizations by the Control Data Corporation as a teaching tool to "forever change education." Of course, it didn't, but it did provide me with an early preview of my future, though I had no idea of that at the time.

At Thomas Edison, we wanted to use emerging technology to overcome barriers of time and place to revolutionize access to a high-quality education for working adults. We saw how the British Open University in cooperation with the British Broadcasting Corporation (BBC) and funded by an enormous investment from the British government created telecourses of extraordinary quality. We were able to offer courses using the videos produced for the British Open University through our membership in the International University Consortium. By the mid-1980s, people began to experiment with computers and apply them to teaching and learning. This emerging technology was ideally suited for our institution.

I always organized the staffing structure of the institution to accommodate a person's strengths rather than whatever boilerplate educational and work experiences they had listed on their resume. Don't get me wrong; that stuff is important, but I never had the inkling to hold someone back because they didn't have a certain credential. It was more important to me to assemble intelligent, curious people who were driven by their passion for our mission.

We were fortunate to have three knowledgeable and technology-savvy people, who together would transform not only our ability to deliver an excellent educational experience to our students but whose work would influence the future of technology-supported education around the world.

Drew Hopkins, a guitar-playing history major, who was the administrative assistant to the director of institutional research, possessed an intuitive understanding of and gift for computers. While he was intrigued by the technology and its potential, his colleague Jim Brossoie, an avid photographer, was especially skilled in understanding software systems. Whereas Drew and Jim were technologists, Bill Seaton, the executive assistant to the vice president for academic affairs, was the visionary who figured out how to apply this technology to education.

In 1982, Thomas Edison State College did not have any computers. All the complexities of our work were done manually with the assistance of IBM Selectric typewriters. Our first foray into automation was with a WANG word processing system. Drew Hopkins, Jim Brossoie, and David Oakley made modifications to the WANG system to accommodate our needs, which enabled it to exceed its performance specifications. The WANG Corporation found out and sent a representative to study the improvements they made and ultimately hired away Dave Oakley.

Our provost, Jerry Ice, and I recognized both the opportunity and talent we had in Bill, Drew, and Jim and sought funding in our Challenge Grant application for them to establish the Computer Assisted Lifelong Learning network, or, as it was affectionately known to us, CALL. CALL was the new and innovative platform Bill envisioned for serving our adult learners. The CALL network evolved into DIAL—Directed Independent Adult Learning. This was the beginning of online technology-supported course creation and delivery.

In DIAL's early days, talented faculty—many of whom were senior, experienced scholars from across the country—learned of our work and wanted to experiment and play in our sandbox. While some faculty can be threatened by the idea that they might be replaced by technology, there have always been the adventurous pioneering few who are eager to embrace new possibilities. We shared a commitment to rigorous evaluation in this new approach, and we never sacrificed quality for innovation.

Like most movements, we had assembled a group of missionaries ready to change the face of higher education. Every major initiative at the university was driven by the passion and ideas of our educational entrepreneurs. We invested in them, turned them loose, and got out of their way.

Jerry Middlemiss wrote his dissertation on postcareer NFL football players. On discovering that most of them never finished college, he launched an initiative that at its peak saw over twenty-five active NFL players enrolled at Thomas Edison completing their degrees. We liked to joke that we had the best football team of any college in America.

Howard Bueschel had a passion for flying and built our aviation program, attracting a large number of airline pilots. Delores Brown Hall was the competent founding dean of our school of nursing, but it was Susan O'Brien who built the nursing school into one of the largest in the state.

Louis Martini led the development of our military and veteran education programs into one of the largest and most respected in the nation. He was a three-term president of the Council of College and Military Educators (CCME) and was honored with the title of president emeritus of CCME at the end of his tenure. He was also inducted into the International Adult and Continuing Education Hall of Fame in 2020.

Janet Eickhoff came to the college as a summer intern and for almost twenty-five years worked her way up through various positions in the organization. She eventually founded our Corporate Partnerships Office, which established collaborative relationships with a number of major companies, including McDonald's, UPS, and JetBlue. These companies provided tuition assistance for their employees to attend the university.

It was Bill Seaton, supported by Drew Hopkins and Jim Brossoie, who became one of the pillars of distance education in the United States. Drew, Jim, and Bill worked together for over thirty years until their respective retirements, evolving and refining technology-supported learning.

By the early '90s, we had made great progress. As far as we can tell, Thomas Edison State University was the first accredited institution in the country to offer a complete degree program online. I have always hated the term *distance education*. It proves my point that while all institutions

claim to be student centered, their history, culture, and traditions are concentrated on the faculty. If you assume that learning is of, for, and about
the student, then how can it occur at a distance? The term *distance* assumes
that learning has to occur where the faculty member is and not where the
student is.

We learned some valuable lessons about how to use technology to produce successful learning outcomes. It is not an effective tool for all people,
but it *is* especially suited for self-directed, mature adults who have the discipline and drive to complete the work in a timely manner.

We also learned that the key to an excellent technology-delivered course
is in the quality of the course design. Traditional college and university
faculty are not typically taught *how* to teach. They are educated in their
discipline with the hope that they can figure out how to transfer that
knowledge to their students. We understood this early on and focused on
recruiting some of the finest course designers in the world. We were able
to pair the content knowledge of the faculty with the expertise of the course
designers, who understood how to make the course engaging and inter-
active, while building assessment strategies to document the learning
outcomes.

The faculty member's principal value is to serve as a subject matter
expert and work in conjunction with the course designer to populate the
content of the course. Once the course is complete, the subject matter
expert's role in course development is done. Students are then *mentored*
through the course by subject matter experts who usually had nothing to
do with the development of the course itself. Most colleges and universities don't do this, and the difference in the effectiveness and quality of their
technology-supported courses is usually apparent.

This approach requires a radically different relationship between the
student, the faculty, and the institution. Course designers, if they are good,
construct the experience around the learning style of the student, not the
teaching style of the faculty. I don't know if Bill Seaton originated this, but
he would often contrast the role of faculty to mentor with the phrase

"instead of being the 'sage' on the 'stage' they are 'guides on the side.'" This combination of expert course design populated with scholarly content and guided by a skillful mentor created extraordinarily high-quality outcomes, as was validated by third parties. For instance, for many years our accounting graduates achieved the highest pass rate on the certified accountant exam of any college or university in New Jersey.

We had to vigorously oppose the perception that we were an "online school" as our capacity, competence, and reputation in this area increased. Online classes were only one of the many options we offered, but they certainly don't define who we are. We developed a menu of learning options and pathways to a degree for our students. These included prior learning assessment, online courses, independent study, military education, corporate training, portfolio assessment, testing, and the opportunity to transfer credits from other accredited institutions to satisfy our graduation requirements. It is misleading and inaccurate to define the institution by just one of the many arrows in our quiver.

As an undergraduate, I took a lot of large group lecture courses, but no one would call the University of Illinois a "large group lecture institution." The press and others liked to call us an online school because it was shorthand and easy for them to understand, but it did us a great disservice. Being labeled an online school destroys our differentiation. This became more important when the "for-profit" online schools began to flood the market. We always took painstaking measures in our branding and marketing to express that we were an accredited state institution created exclusively to provide flexible, high-quality collegiate learning opportunities for self-directed adults. Various methodologies to achieve this mission will come and go, but it doesn't change who we are.

During my onboarding at Thomas Edison and my introduction to Trenton and New Jersey, I met many interesting people whose impact both personally and professionally would have lasting consequences. One was Chris Daggett, Governor Kean's staff member who resolved the housing allowance issue. He went on to a successful career in finance, became a trustee at Thomas Edison, a candidate for governor, and president of the Geraldine R. Dodge Foundation.

I met John S. Watson in 1983, and until his untimely death in 1996, his friendship and colleagueship would be one of the most important and valued relationships I would ever have. We developed an instant rapport. He was principled, honest, and unpretentious with a gift for solving challenging political issues with ingenuity and common sense. Growing up in Camden and serving in the merchant marines made him a force to be reckoned with; however, he was affable, compassionate, and thoughtful in his efforts to promote change for people without a voice. He had a successful career in insurance, but his innate desire to help people thrusted him into a distinguished political career. He never aspired to power or influence but gained respect with his integrity and adherence to values.

He was the first African American freeholder in Mercer County and the first in the state elected freeholder president. He was elected and served the New Jersey State Assembly for twelve years after serving eleven years on the county level. He became the country's first African American state legislator to chair an appropriations committee.

Throughout his legislative career, John used his position to advocate for the institution in substantial ways. He worked with Cary Edwards from the legislative side to secure the funding for our school of nursing. He also sponsored the legislation that dedicated the state-owned Kelsey Building Complex to the exclusive use and control of the college.

His legacy includes many good public service works that continue with the work of his children. His daughter, Bonnie Watson Coleman, is the first African American congresswoman from New Jersey. Prior to her election as representative for New Jersey's Twelfth Congressional District, she served eight consecutive terms in the New Jersey General Assembly in the seat previously held by her father and shattered racial and gender barriers to become the first Black woman to serve as majority leader and as the chair of the New Jersey Democratic State Committee.

His three sons—William A. Watson, John S. Watson Jr., and Aaron (Tim) Watson—also followed in their father's footsteps with distinguished public service careers of their own. Bonnie and Tim are also graduates of Thomas Edison.

Another amazing person in my life was Mary G. Roebling. The Roebling family and the company they founded were influential in the industrial revolution of the country and the economy of the Trenton area. The John A. Roebling's Sons Company invented the steel I beam and the wire cable that made suspension bridges possible. Steel from the Trenton-based company was used to make the North Sea Mine Barrage in World War I and the Golden Gate Bridge in California. A famous sign on a bridge over the Delaware River as you enter Trenton states, "Trenton Makes, the World Takes," in reference to Trenton's industrial past.

Mary Roebling was from Philadelphia and married Siegfried Roebling. The marriage was cut short by Siegfried's death. Mary's inheritance from her husband included a significant ownership interest in what later became National State Bank, headquartered in Trenton.

Mary was a feminist before people knew what feminism was. She was one of the early women admitted to the prestigious and conservative Union League of Philadelphia, helped cofound the Women's Bank of Denver, became chairperson and CEO of National State Bank, was the first female governor of the American Stock Exchange, and was the founding president of the Army War College Foundation.

She had been on a first-name basis with several presidents of the United States and was a devoted supporter of the U.S. military. I believe her involvement with the military started in World War II at the request of President Roosevelt, and it never wavered. I met her early upon my arrival in Trenton. I was warned that the first thing she would inquire about was where I did my banking. Before our first meeting, I made sure to open my bank account with National State Bank. We got along famously from the very beginning and developed a mutual respect and affection for each other that I found both improbable and enjoyable.

Mary used to play bridge and hold court at the Trenton Country Club, which had a beautiful facility and golf course near downtown Trenton. When I was organizing and recruiting members for the Thomas Edison State College Foundation Board, I asked Mary for her assistance. She declined to join herself, but she graciously volunteered John Connelly, president and CEO of the bank at the time.

She also offered me use of her membership at the country club whenever I needed a place to entertain. A year or so later, she suggested that I become a member of the club. I thought it was a good idea too, because we didn't have suitable facilities to entertain guests and donors, and to conduct advocacy on behalf of the institution. The foundation board members concurred and agreed to fund my membership as well as appropriate entertainment expenses. Mary sponsored my application for membership in the club.

Shortly thereafter I received a call from Adrienne Hayling, a good friend, who informed me that I had caused quite a stir among the social circles in the area. Adrienne and her husband, Les, a well-respected dentist, were longtime residents and members of the African American community in Trenton. When I inquired as to the nature of the gossip, she told me that in the long history of the Trenton Country Club, they had never admitted anyone of color, and their bigotry had extended to Jews as well. My consideration, therefore, raised a lot of eyebrows.

I was surprised. To me, it was a nice place to entertain. I had forgotten that country clubs are not just recreational facilities but are often exclusive cultural organizations as well. I was deeply conflicted. I had never had "country club values," and I found the racism and bigotry represented by many of these organizations offensive, something I had spent my entire life fighting. I don't mind controversies if they are associated with something I value, but this didn't qualify. Part of me wanted to withdraw my candidacy, but the other part of me wanted to confront the matter. Besides, I had not applied, I had been nominated, so I decided to play it out.

A couple of weeks later, I received my invitation to join and promptly called and requested to meet with the president and chair of the membership committee. They accepted my invitation, and the three of us had lunch. I came prepared to the meeting having reviewed the club's bylaws and legal documents for any evidence of discriminatory language and could find none; nevertheless, I expressed my concern about the club's history, reputation, and lack of diversity. They acknowledged that while my understanding of the club's history was accurate, those practices had long since ceased. They were delighted I accepted and hoped that my membership would encourage other people of color to follow. Of course, whenever I used the club for entertaining, the staff never had to ask for my membership number. They all knew who the Black member was.

Not long after that, the state built a large office building near the capital complex and named it in Mary Roebling's honor. A date was set for the dedication, and Governor Kean presided over the ceremony. Mary invited me as her guest and escort for the dedication and the private lunch she hosted afterward at the Trenton Country Club. She suggested that I meet her there, along with two of her closest friends, since the site was just a block from my office. I arrived slightly early and was shocked to see Mary walking up with her two friends, Walter Annenberg and Richard Nixon.

Mary told me that she and Nixon had been friends for many years and that he was a frequent guest at parties hosted at her home in downtown Trenton, adjacent to National Bank's building. We took our seats at the table reserved for the four of us and after the ribbon cutting, we accompanied Mary to the country club for lunch. I am rarely at a loss for words, but listening to the casual banter among these three friends was riveting. By coincidence, the dedication took place on an anniversary of Nixon's pardon by Gerald Ford, a fact that the press made prominent mention of in their coverage of the event.

While I am a Vietnam-era person, I did not support the war and did everything I could to legally avoid the draft, but I am not antimilitary. Several of my friends were drafted, and my close friend Clarke Williams joined the marines and saw active duty and combat. During the entirety of his service, I worried about his welfare and hoped that he would return safely. I never blamed the military for that war. I was troubled when some antiwar activists with whom I shared great sympathy attacked the men and women who served. I appreciated the military conceptually and had great admiration for "The Greatest Generation" and their heroic sacrifice in winning World War II.

Mary's love of the military ran deep. She requested that I spend a day with two of her colleagues visiting Fort Dix, an army training base outside of Trenton. I was curious about the request, but of course, anything for Mary. Our host provided the three of us with an extensive, private tour of the base, where we observed the trainees being put through their paces. I heard stories that basic training was grueling and unpleasant, but those sentiments were from draftees who didn't want to be there. By now the draft had been abolished, and what I was observing was an all-volunteer force who embraced the experience with determination and enthusiasm. When I looked into the faces of these young men and women, I saw a sense of pride and commitment in learning their chosen craft. At the end of the day, when they marched in parade before the reviewing stand, I had my hand over my heart and a lump in my throat with admiration and respect for the sense of duty they demonstrated in service to their country.

Mary Roebling's invitation that day was guided by her hope that the college would support the work of the military at Fort Dix, McGuire Air Force Base, and Lakehurst Naval Air Station, the site of the historic Hindenburg disaster. This was the beginning of an organized initiative by the college called the Military Degree Completion Program to help active-duty service members combine their military training with their academic studies to earn a degree.

Several years later, we received an invitation from the Department of Defense to join a select group of institutions from around the country in a pilot program to explore options for active-duty service members to complete their college education. Up until that time, the military provided incentives to persuade people to enlist by promising them attractive benefits when they completed their service. Training and force readiness are the single largest expenditure in the military's budget. This incentive structure encouraged people to *leave* the military after the government had made a huge investment to train them. Someone in Washington figured out that the country could get a better return on their training investment if the incentives offered were directed toward *retaining* service members instead. Veterans' benefits would support them when they left the service, but wouldn't it be better to give them the option of earning a college degree while they were still on active duty?

This was a great idea, but there were major impediments in making it happen. Military occupations are demanding, with long shifts occurring in remote locations around the world. We were invited to participate because we had an infrastructure already in place that would accommodate the mobility of our armed forces. What we needed now was to design the delivery mechanisms to reach them. It was a challenge for us, but challenges are frequently the source of innovation. We had already migrated our video courses from bulky cassettes to small video discs that could be played on a laptop computer. With the explosion of the internet and wireless communications, we could connect mentors with students and instructional materials anywhere our military students had access to a laptop and the internet. That was not a problem for our students who were on bases, but when the Gulf War hit, some of our students were deployed to remote areas of Iraq and Afghanistan without internet service.

Our creative course development staff along with a technology company from Princeton were able to bundle the content and create a simulated internet environment embedded in a thumb drive and later a computer chip that could be used in the battlefield communications equipment soldiers were deployed with. This technology was especially useful for our students on submarines.

Submariners were sometimes underwater for six months at a time. Students could complete coursework on the vessel and when they returned to land, hit a button on a computer, upload their materials to the college, and download materials for their next deployment. During the height of the Gulf War, we had over six thousand active-duty military enrolled in the college with four thousand serving in theater in Iraq, Afghanistan, and deployed on ships in the Persian Gulf.

Many of the military services kept comparative data on enrolled students, and Thomas Edison consistently held the highest course-completion rate in the navy college program of any college or university in the country. Many other colleges and universities flooded the market behind the pioneering group who participated in the pilot program, but we were proud of our innovative approach that proved to be so successful for our servicemen and women.

We also kept our pricing competitive, but for us, this was not a profitable undertaking. Our margins were low and barely covered our costs, but it was consistent with our mission, service to our country, and we were honored to do it. Unfortunately, we lost twenty-two students who made the ultimate sacrifice in service to our country.

My involvement with the military continued in other ways as well. I participated in and chaired some evaluation teams for the U.S. Department of Education who determined whether senior military colleges met the statutory criteria for awarding graduate degrees. I conducted evaluations of the U.S. Army War College at Carlisle Barracks, Pennsylvania; the Marine Corps University in Quantico, Virginia; the National Defense University at Fort McNair, Washington, DC; the Defense Language Institute Foreign Language Center in Monterey, California; and the Air Force Test Pilot School at Edwards Air Force Base, California. These institutions had to meet three criteria: that the level of academic work was comparable to the work done by traditional colleges and universities, that the institutions met the standards of recognition for their regional accrediting body, and finally, that the manner of instruction respected and honored traditional definitions of academic freedom and intellectual inquiry.

At the War College, I sat at General Omar Bradley's desk and read letters written by Generals Grant and Sherman. At Fort McNair, I stood at the site where the Lincoln assassination conspirators were hanged, but my most memorable trip was to Edwards Air Force Base. I saw the movie *The Right Stuff*, read the book the movie was based on, and had the unique opportunity to meet General Charles "Chuck" Yeager, one of America's most famous pilots and the first man to break the sound barrier. I also got to spend considerable time with this legendary pilot when we awarded him an honorary degree.

When I went to Edwards Air Force Base, I flew to Los Angeles, rented a car, and drove for what seemed like forever through the California desert. In the movie, they made a point about Edwards's location out in the middle of nowhere. They did not exaggerate. As we approached the base headquarters building, I recognized the aircraft mounted in front as a replica of the plane General Yeager was flying that stalled, caught fire, and burned him while he ejected and parachuted to safety. The base commander frowned and said they had been thinking about replacing that plane because people kept reminding them of that flight. From their point of view, it represented a failure, not something to commemorate. I understood and appreciated the comment.

I saw the dry lake bed that was used as a backup landing site for the space shuttle, and although they had to shoehorn me in, I had my photograph taken sitting in the cockpit of an F16. Fortunately, they did not take pictures of the struggle it took to get me out.

These schools represented some of the highest-quality education offered anywhere in the world. The week I visited the Army War College, Colin Powell had just left after lecturing the students, and the head of the Chinese armed forces had been there the week before. Most of the students at the War College were colonels who had graduated from West Point or Annapolis in engineering or technology on track to become future flag officers. One of my colleagues asked them how well their undergraduate education prepared them for graduate school and their careers in the military. Every one of them expressed a desire for greater exposure in the liberal arts. Their training in the military had given them war-fighting skills, but the principal tenets of leadership and effectiveness in the various geographies in which they had to function were dependent on them understanding things like history, religion, sociology, and anthropology—things they needed to understand to collaborate with the leadership, opinion leaders, and people they were trying to defend.

The more contact and experience I had with the military at all levels, the greater respect and regard I had for those who selflessly served our country. The Vietnam-era stereotypes of the military I experienced have been thoroughly expunged from the military of today.

One of the highlights of our commencement ceremony every year was when we called for the acknowledgment of our graduates who were veterans or active-duty members of our armed forces. It is not lost on me how privileged I was to have so many exciting experiences. I visited countless military bases, flew in military aircraft, went on refueling missions, and toured a host of naval vessels from submarines to aircraft carriers. One of my favorite mementos is a photograph of me sitting in the captain's chair of the USS *Enterprise*, our country's first nuclear-powered aircraft carrier. A special treat for such a big *Star Trek* fan.

For some time, I had been struggling with the idea of establishing the college's public service portfolio. Regardless of institutional mission, all colleges and universities have an acknowledged obligation to foster learning research and public service. At the time, we had no institutional vehicle for developing and delivering our public service agenda.

The idea for a public policy institute was inspired by Dr. Badi Foster's work at the Aetna Institute for the Aetna Insurance Company. Dr. Foster's team provided crucial research and information for the leadership of Aetna on public policy issues. They did not participate in the creation of the new policies, but they did compile the information from various experts for the executives who made the policies. For instance, following sweeping changes in the federal tax code in 1986 under President Reagan, they provided seminars to define the realities of a new tax environment for the leadership to consider. They coordinated multiple groups of researchers, assembling tax experts, lawyers, accountants, and even staff members from the congressional committees that drafted the bills, to provide information.

I thought that there was a demand for a public policy institute that would produce hands-on, real-world policy advice and information to governments, nonprofits, and community-based organizations in real time while they were faced with a problem. I did not want to construct another think tank. I have always respected the work of the important policy research and academic think tanks, but they conduct public policy autopsies. When the events have concluded, experts provide books and analysis about what happened and why. This work is valuable and instructive, but it is of little use to the practitioner in the trenches struggling with a complex problem, without guidance or outside assistance.

I asked Feather O'Connor, the New Jersey state treasurer what kind of assistance the state had available in considering the impact of federal tax changes on state and local revenues. I asked her if she thought it would be useful if Thomas Edison provided that capacity and made it available to her office as well as local governments and nonprofits that didn't have the resources of a Fortune 500 company. She responded that it would be valuable and welcome.

I had several more conversations with her about the kind of expertise we would have to assemble and the structure of such an organization that the college would create. I foresaw an organization within our institution staffed by a small core group of public policy experts who would recruit external consultants and practitioners and deploy them to support decision makers to resolve issues with specific solutions. The core group would be permanent, full-time staff and receive ongoing support and funding from the college. The peripheral experts would come and go depending on the work and resources available to support it.

Before we could stand up the organization, the Kean administration ended, and my first potential client departed for other work. However, in the spirit of that old saying "when one door closes, another one opens," the city of Trenton was in the process of changing administrations. Douglas Palmer, a spirited and personable county freeholder had just been elected the city's first African American mayor. Not long after Mayor Palmer took office, Bill Watson, my close friend and the mayor's chief of staff, contacted me. He had an idea for a collaboration between the city and the college to provide policy research and guidance to support decision-making by the new administration. I was amused. I had the idea and even the structure; now it looked like I had found our first client.

Bill and I had lunch with his colleague John Thurber. They had worked together previously at the New Jersey Public Advocate's Office. They shared with me that they were going to receive a small grant that would support some assistance in the policy arena for the city. They were hoping that the college could serve as fiscal agent and custodian of the grant and that we would further support this initiative. I am not sure they realized at the time how eager I was to get started.

Because of my confidence in Bill, I was prepared to hire John immediately with the understanding that he would be an employee of and wholly accountable to the college. Additionally, while the grant funding would be useful, it was not sufficient to support the kind of broader policy agenda we wanted to build. I pledged to provide the support to supplement the grant and to continue funding for the program out of college resources when the grant expired.

We agreed that the name of the new entity at Thomas Edison would be the Trenton Office of Policy Studies (TOPS). John would have a collaborative working relationship with the mayor's staff and cabinet, but he was not to participate in any political activity beyond his policy research and advice. We shook hands, and that's how our public policy portfolio began to take shape.

The vision we had for this institute was that of a tent with a broad range of clients and initiatives under its roof. One of the first initiatives we undertook stemmed from a request of State Senate Appropriations Committee chair Robert Littell. Bob's mother had been in a hospital and received a complicated multipage bill. Bob could not make sense of it. If he was having this problem as a sophisticated businessperson with a finance background, he could only imagine the plight of less-experienced consumers.

He approached me and Saul Fenster, president of the New Jersey Institute of Technology, to discuss a collaboration between the two institutions to simplify billing, medical records, and payment processes between patients, providers, and insurance companies. He sponsored a million-dollar appropriation with $750,000 for NJIT to work on the technology issues and $250,000 for Thomas Edison to work through the policy and regulatory environments. The name of this initiative, jointly managed by the two institutions, was the Healthcare Information Network Technology (HINT) project.

For HINT to be successful, we had to get consensus from providers, payers, and consumers to agree to a common set of standards, definitions, and protocols. It was a challenging diplomatic task to negotiate. These were groups that did not typically agree. NJIT created the technology platform. Our technology would have allowed a patient to go into a doctor's office and, with a swipe of a card, display all their medical information to be updated instantly by the doctor following treatment. Instantaneously, the physician's billing would be uploaded to the insurance company; the insurance company's payment would be transferred to the provider or the patient as appropriate. The technology and the policy work were successful, and this system could have been implemented, saving literally billions of dollars in costs and time with great efficiency.

What we produced was phenomenal. We successfully created common standards that all the insurance companies, hospitals, physicians' offices, and medical records agreed to for billing and medical claims. We also created common standards for patient medical information stored in a "smart card" similar to today's ATM banking card. Unfortunately, all this good work was blocked by privacy advocates who worried about too much personal information stored in one place and subject to piracy. Like the CAEL box, it was an idea too far ahead of its time. There were many more projects, some grant supported, some College funded, but all under the general umbrella and portfolio of the institute.

By 1995, TOPS had evolved into the Institute for Public Policy, a broader-based public policy organization. In 1996, I hired John Thurber as vice president for public affairs. After Mayor Palmer's first term, Bill Watson left his position as the mayor's chief of staff, and I was able to persuade him to accept the position as executive director of the institute. Bill was widely known and highly regarded among the state's mayors as well as officials in state government. His appointment as the institute's executive gave it instant credibility and gravitas among the state's many city officials. The following year, the institute was rededicated and named for Bill's father, John S. Watson. It was altogether fitting and proper that the college's principal public service vehicle be named in his honor.

When Palmer became mayor, he wanted to provide a resource for policy advice to a group of mayors from the urban cities, which at the time was called the Distressed Cities program. During the administration of Governor James McGreevey, and with the support of the legislature, the state provided an appropriation to support the institute's work with the organization formed by this group of thirty-two mayors from urban cities around New Jersey, now called the New Jersey Urban Mayors Association. It would prove to be the Watson Institute's most important client. The collaboration was extensive, statewide, and highly productive.

At pivotal moments in the university's development, we were somehow always able to attract exceptional talent to provide the stewardship for an important new initiative just when we needed it. I can think of no better example of this than when Bill recruited Joseph Youngblood II. He attended Florida A&M University, an HBCU in Tallahassee, as an undergraduate and went on to earn a law degree from the University of Iowa and a PhD from the University of Pennsylvania. With a powerful intellect, sharp analytical mind, and a passion for social justice and rational public policy development, he established the Watson Institute as a major force of influence in the state. He recruited a highly regarded core of resident public policy experts and practitioners to execute the college's public service mission.

We received a request from the mayors to partner with them in building the capacity of professionals working in the administrations of our urban centers. Many cities have residency requirements mandating that employees of the city be residents, and while there is an obvious logic to this requirement, it has the effect of limiting the talent pool available to mayors in recruiting and retaining people to take on some of the most demanding and consequential jobs that society has to offer. The mayors' request was simple: they wanted to work with us to develop academic programs and tailor them to respond to the unique requirements of professionals working in our cities.

In response to this request, the college developed several graduate programs with content specifically relevant to the needs of people working in city governments. Under Dr. Youngblood's leadership as vice provost and dean, these uniquely designed and structured programs were grouped together to create the John S. Watson School of Public Service, one of the first schools of its kind in the country. The institute continued its important public policy work under the umbrella of the school that shared its name.

At the time I left office, the John S. Watson Institute for Public Policy was composed of seven integrated policy centers and initiatives that informed and supported the work of the Institute:

Center for the Urban Environment
Center for the Positive Development of Urban Children
Center for Health Policy Development
New Jersey Urban Mayors Policy Center
Center for Education Policy and Practice Initiatives
Center for Civic Engagement and Leadership Development
Technical Assistance and Support Service Center

I am proud of all our work, but I must confess that the W. Cary Edwards School of Nursing and the John S. Watson School of Public Service, with its amazing public policy institute, will always have a special place in my heart.

Chapter Fourteen

Searching for candles in dark places.

—*George A. Pruitt*

The college was growing rapidly, expanding and developing into an exemplar in its field; however, we were not without loss and tragedy. It began with the loss of Jim Humphries, the college's director of administrative services, who had been with us since the beginning. He was a lovable man with a kind disposition. He had a long, successful career in state government before he joined the college, so it was no surprise when he informed us of his plans to retire.

We threw a well-attended retirement party. His wife arrived alone, late and visibly shaken. She stopped by on her way to the hospital to let us know that Jim got sick while getting ready for the party and was rushed to the emergency room. He passed shortly thereafter. His loss was shocking to us all. Days later, all of us who had been at his retirement party were attending his funeral.

In 1994, Tom Eklund, a member of our advising staff, and Tom Streckewald, our gifted director of institutional research, were returning home from a card game at Drew's house when they were struck and killed by a drunk driver. I was in Chicago at the time, and I'll never forget the phone call I received from Rich Hansen informing me that two of my colleagues had been killed. They were both married with young children. While the loss was horrendous, the circumstances surrounding their death made the tragedy unfathomable.

Our institution had a strong sense of community and common purpose, and the camaraderie among us magnified the personal sense of loss we all felt. At the time of his death, Tom Streckewald was chair of the board of the Princeton Regional Chamber of Commerce. We joined with them in sponsoring the Streckewald Memorial Golf Tournament to raise funds for a scholarship endowment in Tom's memory. The college's foundation took over this event in subsequent years, and the Streckwald Memorial Scholarship Fund, when I left office, was our second largest endowment.

In January 1996, Natale Caliendo, our vice president for public affairs, was walking home on the edge of a snow-covered street, when he was struck and killed by a pickup truck. Nat's loss was another blow to our tight-knit community and deeply personal as well. Nat's death kicked off what I call my "country western" year. During my time in Nashville, I developed a deep respect for country music, especially the earthy and witty quality of the lyrics. Sad country songs, in my judgment, were a specialized genre of the blues. A good, sad country song always had certain major elements. If you were a guy, you drank too much, lost your girl, lost your job, and your dog died.

At the end of 1994, my twenty-plus-year marriage failed. The circumstances are personal and not relevant to this story. I do want to say, however, that it was not the classic dramatic breakup. Delores is a wonderful woman, great mother, and excellent teacher. I would like to believe that we are both decent and honorable people, but we were unable to sustain our marriage. We are both devoted to our daughter, Shayla, and we are good parents. Emotionally, the failure of the marriage was the most painful thing that I had ever experienced, and I am pretty sure it was the same for Delores.

It triggered a depression on my part that was a struggle to navigate and manage. Work was the tonic for the despair I felt, and I threw myself into it. I also had a twenty-nine-foot cabin cruiser that proved to be an invaluable sanctuary. I spent a lot of time on that boat on the Delaware River, the Chesapeake Bay, and up and down the Jersey Shore.

My inner office staff was extraordinary—particularly my secretary, Anne. When I was in the office alone, I struggled greatly, and Anne protected me from the public when I wasn't able to face them. We had both experienced tragedies in our personal life. She lost her husband to mesothelioma.

I had some training in psychology, and I had an intellectual understanding of depression, but experiencing it firsthand made me understand what a powerful malady it is. Normally, your instincts work to protect you, but with depression, they sell you out completely. When you need to be around people, it makes you want to be alone. When you need to sleep, it keeps you awake; when you need to be awake, it makes you want to sleep. When you need to exercise, it makes you want to go to bed. I felt like I was living in a well, and I hated it. The good news is that I was committed to fighting my way out, and by the end of 1995, I did.

Then, in the beginning of 1996, we tragically lost Nat. Many people from the college drove up to attend his wake and service in Peekskill, New York. I attended the wake the night before, and the next morning, when I walked into the funeral home, I was told that I had an urgent phone call. It was my cousin Janice, calling to tell me that my father had died. I felt like I had been punched in the stomach. I'd come here to bury my friend; now I was leaving his service to bury my father.

Bill Watson accompanied me back to Trenton, where I got on a plane, flew to Los Angeles, and buried my dad. Approximately six months later, John Watson, who had become like an older brother to me, succumbed to cancer. In August, a budding new relationship crashed and burned, and in November, after a two-year separation, my divorce was finalized. I was really glad that I didn't have a dog.

GOVERNORS, BOOKS, AND BUREAUCRACY

Tom Kean was the best governor I ever saw. Jim Florio, a former congressman, lost his first bid for the governorship to Tom Kean by the smallest margin in the history of the state. Governor Kean won reelection by what is to this day the largest plurality in the state's history, capturing 70 percent of the vote. I have talked about him a lot, because in an era when politics is broken, it is comforting to know that statesmanlike political leadership, though hard to find, is still possible. At times he has found my compliments embarrassing, but I have also had some fun at his expense. I had the opportunity to introduce him when he was addressing the annual meeting of the American Council on Education in San Francisco. I expressed my sentiment that he was the best governor I ever had the pleasure of working with, but added, "Governor, lest you get bigheaded over my accolades, you need to understand my background. I left Illinois, and Governor Kerner went to prison. I left Maryland, and Governor Mandel went to prison. I left Tennessee, and Governor Blanton went to prison. All you have to do is stay out of the slammer to be at the top of my list."

Fortunately, he has a great sense of humor. After he completed his term as governor of New Jersey, he served with distinction as president of Drew University. Following the 9/11 attacks, he was named by President Bush to head the National Commission on Terrorist Attacks upon the United States, which culminated with the release of the 9/11 Commission Report. He served as chair of the Robert Wood Johnson Foundation and the Carnegie Corporation and continues his public service to this day. He's still the best governor I have ever seen.

In the gubernatorial election following Kean's second term, the Republicans nominated a conservative, Jim Courter. Florio ran again and defeated Courter, winning the election with a decisive majority. The Democrats also captured both houses of the state legislature.

Florio was a dedicated public servant and genuine policy wonk. He became most widely known for the dramatic restructuring of the state's income tax code. The Florio tax increase was aggressive. It doubled the top rate of the state income tax from 3.5 to 7 percent. That year 50 percent of all new tax revenues generated by the states came from New Jersey. This was a more progressive way of funding government and in theory would have brought relief to the state's beleaguered property taxpayers. It was supported by some smart people that I greatly respected.

However, the biggest mistake the supporters made was misdiagnosing the problem. They assumed that the problem was on the revenue side when, in fact, it was on the expense side of the balance sheet. The massive redundancy and overlap in layers of local government were bankrupting the state. The governor knew that this would be controversial and took advantage of his majority in both legislative houses to push through these dramatic tax increases very early in his administration.

The outrage from the public was immediate and ferocious. Because the tax package was passed so quickly, it contained missteps that a more prolonged discussion would have identified and corrected. It also expanded the tax to many items that were previously exempt. Perhaps the most visible sign of outrage was in response to the new tax levied on toilet paper. Instigated by a popular radio talk show, protesters began bombarding the entrance of the statehouse with rolls of toilet paper. In the following midterm elections, the governor's party was decimated as the Republicans attained substantial majorities in both houses of the legislature.

One prominent political figure who almost got caught up in the backlash was former New York Knicks star, Princeton graduate, and U.S. Senator, Bill Bradley. Senator Bradley and Governor Kean were two of the most popular elected officials ever to serve in the state, one Democrat, one Republican, both revered and having more in common than their different parties would suggest.

As Senator Bradley faced reelection, there was little doubt that he would retain his seat. Christine Todd Whitman, an undiscovered but competent candidate from an important political family, ran as his opponent. Conventional wisdom suggested that even if she conducted a respectable campaign, she would have no real chance of winning. Surprisingly, she was able to take advantage of the public's anger with Florio and tactically hang it around Bradley's neck. In her debates and advertising, she attempted to maneuver Bradley to a position of having to defend Florio, even though he wasn't on the ballot. He couldn't throw his governor under the bus, but neither did he want to get blamed for something he wasn't involved with. Whitman's strategy was effective, and the poll numbers began to show an ever-tightening race.

In the end, Bradley was reelected by a smaller margin than anyone expected when the campaign began. Whitman leveraged the success and name recognition she achieved in the Bradley campaign in securing the Republican nomination to oppose Florio in the gubernatorial election. It was a hard-fought campaign, but in January 1994, Christine Todd Whitman, a moderate centrist Republican, was inaugurated as the first female Governor of New Jersey.

I had great respect for Governor Florio. I have never participated in partisan politics and have always believed that once the election is over, all New Jerseyans have but one governor. Regardless of the party of the governor, I believe public college presidents have an obligation to public service.

Florio was never motivated by the pursuit of wealth or personal gain. He was conservative and prudent in his personal habits, and I admired his commitment to public service. He established a commission to seek ways to increase efficiencies and reduce waste through an examination of the state's practices. To support this work, I loaned him the services of Mike Scheiring, vice president for administration and finance at Thomas Edison.

Governor Florio's centerpiece initiative focused on increasing taxes and expanding government. Governor Whitman's platform aimed to reduce taxes and shrink government. The morning of Governor Whitman's first budget address, she called a meeting of all the college and university presidents to announce her intention to abolish the New Jersey Public Advocate's Office and the New Jersey Department of Higher Education.

Ted Hollander retired from the chancellorship at the end of Governor Kean's term. His successor, Ed Goldberg, lacked Hollander's deft touch in balancing the influence of the coordinating board with the respect of the autonomy of the institutions. Ed was full of initiatives but overmanaged the system and alienated most of the presidents. He and I got along fine, but that was not the case elsewhere, so when Governor Whitman made her announcement, the move was universally cheered.

While the BHE had become bureaucratic, burdensome, intrusive, and often overreaching, there were important and necessary functions for licensure, new program approval, and broad policy coordination that were still needed. The governor created a task force of a small number of presidents to plan for the post-BHE reconstruction and asked me to serve as a member of the group.

The task force report recommended the formation of two new organizations, the New Jersey Presidents' Council and the Commission on Higher Education. The commission was composed of lay citizens appointed by the governor and staffed by an executive director. It also included a president from each of the public research universities, one president who represented all of the state colleges, and one president for each of the sectors: the nonprofit independent institutions and the community colleges.

The New Jersey Presidents' Council comprised the presidents of all fifty-four senior public and private institutions and community colleges. The presidents' council was charged with promoting voluntary, interinstitutional cooperation and reviewing new program initiatives from individual colleges and universities against three criteria contained in statute.

Critics of the new structure thought the presidents would engage in mutual back-scratching, which would thwart their ability to execute this function with sufficient rigor. While I guess it was a fair concern, they misunderstood the nature of academics operating at this level. The academic program review was thorough, rigorous, and sometimes merciless. If an institution wanted to offer a program that exceeded its mission, the presidents' council would make a recommendation, but the final determination would be made by the commission.

During its early years, the presidents' council was quite effective. We generated voluntary standards to promote transfer credit between institutions, especially for community college graduates going on to baccalaureate-degree-granting institutions. We created and funded online databases that would allow students to determine how their credits would be accepted and applied at their preferred institution. This was one of the first systems of its kind in the country, and unlike other states where it was imposed by legislators, we did it voluntarily.

The other significant achievement was in the creation of New Jersey Edge Net, a wholly owned subsidiarity of the presidents' council that devised a specialized and robust technology network to support the requirements of sophisticated research and data-processing assets available to all the colleges and universities in New Jersey. It also developed opportunities for consortia-purchasing of telecommunications that achieved both efficiencies and cost savings. Most of the business of the presidents' council was conducted by a smaller executive committee made up of representatives of the various institutional sectors. I was pleased to have been selected by my colleagues to serve first as a member of the executive committee, later as an officer, and finally as chair. In any profession, perhaps the most meaningful acknowledgments you can receive are those from your peers.

As drawn up on paper, the presidents' council functioned exactly as conceived. The Commission on Higher Education, however, was often disappointing. While the members of the commission were experienced, competent, and successful people in their respective fields, the executive leadership they had was often weak, and the commission floundered in understanding its role and executing a thoughtful strategy. They did not effectively engage the institutions and their presidents, disaggregated higher education into constituent communities (i.e., faculty members, students, alumni, and so on), and failed to construct a statewide plan with support from the institutional leadership whose commitment was necessary to execute the plan.

Others complained that the commission didn't have sufficient authority to keep the institutions in line and hold them accountable. That wasn't true. The failure was not in structure but in leadership. Years later, Governor Chris Christie would abolish the commission and replace it with the position of secretary of higher education, investing in the new secretary the authority and responsibility previously granted the commission.

In Governor Whitman's budget address, where she announced the elimination of these two cabinet departments, she also proposed a 3 percent cut across the board in state income taxes. It was a reasonable response to her platform of shrinking government and cutting taxes. However, she faced one major problem. The state was broke, and cutting taxes would exacerbate its condition. The obvious question was, "How could the state be broke in the wake of the largest tax increase in the country?" The answer went back to the voracious appetite of the huge blob of municipalities and school systems.

Alan Karcher provided a compelling discussion of this issue in his book, *New Jersey's Multiple Municipal Madness.* It was published in October 1998, after Karcher retired from public life. I lightly chided the former Speaker that while he had been the leader of the assembly, he never raised any of these issues but waited until he was safely no longer accountable in government before he documented the structural absurdity that had so long afflicted the state. No politician is prepared to take on this issue.

The enormous tax revenues generated by the Florio initiative were immediately sucked up by the blob. It did stabilize property tax increases for a year or two, but then the pressure for increases resumed, only this time on a much larger basis. The normal inflationary increases in the cost of government still existed, but the size of these incremental costs were considerably more because the base was so much larger. A 5 percent increase in the cost of a small municipal budget is a lot less in dollars than a 5 percent increase in a large municipal budget, yet the size of the New Jersey economy was fairly constant. As a result, the fiscal condition of the state Governor Whitman inherited was, to say the least, stressed.

To make matters worse, the structure of the New Jersey budget provided that 75 percent of state revenues supported municipal aid, K–12 school aid,

and debt service. Only 25 percent was left to fund all the remaining services of state government, including higher education. While the spirit of
cutting taxes was understandable, the state's coffers couldn't afford it.

The sizeable contribution necessary to fund the public employee pension funds presented another major fiscal challenge. Not only did the state
have multiple school systems and municipalities; it had elected officials
that simultaneously held multiple offices. A mayor of Newark was also a
state senator. A mayor of Hamilton Township also served as a county freeholder and state assemblyman, accumulating pension credits from three
different elected offices at the same time.

While the nature of the benefits received by public employees was comparable to their counterparts in other states in the region, the sheer number of them per capita was without precedent. When Governor Whitman
took office, the state pension was adequately funded, but she was faced
with the choice of making the pension payment or supporting the operating budget. She couldn't do both. Fortunately, she had the benefit of a
robust stock market. Her treasurer, a creative and experienced financial
whiz, devised a plan to restructure the financing of the pension system.
As a result, the state didn't make the payments to the system *or* lower the
benefits to employees and retirees.

It was a very controversial move at the time, but it set the precedent for
the next three governors to withhold or drastically reduce payments to
the pension fund as well. Things were manageable when the economy
and the stock market were up, but as the country's economy waxed and
waned, the lack of contributions to the pension system put it on a course
to insolvency. Today New Jersey has one of the highest unfunded pension
liabilities of any state in the nation.

Governor Whitman's first budget was passed, balanced, and included
the tax cut and the elimination of the two cabinet departments. Within
her first year, I received a phone call from David Kehler, a well-known public policy authority from her administration. He had the idea that Thomas
Edison should take responsibility for the New Jersey State Library.

The New Jersey State Library is one of the oldest state libraries in the United States. It enjoys an extraordinary reputation and possesses an incredible collection of books, periodicals, and rich treasure of historical, pre-Revolutionary War publications. It has also suffered from sustained reductions in state support.

While I was curious about Dave's proposal, my initial reaction was skepticism. Even the best of people who work in the Department of the Treasury rarely support ideas that require increased state spending, but I respected Dave and I wanted to hear him out. His proposal was fairly simple. The New Jersey State Library would become a part of the college. The state librarian would be responsible and accountable to the institution's president, and the library's appropriation and resources would be managed by the college. I told him I had a lot of questions, but I wanted to discuss it with my cabinet and get back to him.

At the time, the New Jersey State Library was a part of the New Jersey Department of Education, an enormous state bureaucracy responsible for the funding and regulation of New Jersey's public schools. I called Leo Klagholz, the commissioner of education, who was an experienced and capable educator, to discuss the conversation I'd had with Kehler. I knew Klagholz well, and I didn't want to be a part of any plotting by Treasury involving another cabinet department without full disclosure and transparency.

I was surprised when Leo enthusiastically agreed that it was a great idea, though he did not know about it. He had been concerned for years about the neglect shown to the state library by the bureaucracy of his department. He thought that it had not fared well when competing for resources with programs that would always have a higher priority. He further noted that while the Department of Education knew how to regulate, its culture did not lend itself to running such an institution.

With his blessing, I began to explore the idea more seriously. The discussions led to the creation of a working group with representatives from all the affected parties. It soon became clear to me that there were promising

synergies between the two institutions. Although our students had access
to library resources, the college did not have its own library. Symbolically
and logistically, an old and established library would benefit a young
institution. Conceptually, there were common threads in the missions of
both institutions. Both served independent, self-directed learners, shared
a common interest in using emerging technologies to remove access barriers to learning, and made high-quality educational resources broadly
available to the public at low cost. The more discussions we had, the more
possibilities we saw.

The library was eager to get out from under the smothering weight of
the state bureaucracy. They were still afflicted by all the oppressive over-
regulation the college had escaped with the passage of the Autonomy Bill,
but most importantly, they were excited for the opportunity to advocate
for increased resources, state funding, grants, and private giving to support their work.

As part of the executive branch, the state librarian was obligated to support the governor's budget proposal even if it entailed cuts to library
funding. Colleges and universities are routinely expected to advocate for
increased resources. While it had to be done carefully, governors expected
that college presidents would make the case for increased support of their
institutions.

My major reservation was that the state would allocate the responsibility for the library without the funds to support it. This arrangement
would never work if the state saw this as an opportunity to offload its costs
onto the college. In all of our discussions, I made it very clear that I would
never use any tuition revenues paid by students or appropriations intended
for the college to support the state library. Funds from the federal government made up the majority of its resources.

One of the challenges we faced concerned the locus of regulatory
authority over the library community. There were both federal and state
laws that required the promulgation of regulations governing the management of all libraries. The state's regulatory authority had been vested in

the New Jersey Board of Education. Since the library would disengage from the department, the question arose as to what body would be given that responsibility under this new structure. In the enabling legislation that made the state library an affiliate of the college, the authority to promulgate state regulations was granted to the Thomas Edison State College Board of Trustees. I don't know of any other college or university trustee board that has the authority and responsibility to promulgate statewide regulations that carry the force of law.

As the treasurer, the commissioner of education, the governor's office, and the college began to pursue this transition, we all thought it was prudent that we cohabitate for a while before we got married. For the first several years of this arrangement, we operated through a memorandum of understanding (MOU) between the college and the state, which could be canceled by either party with ninety days' notice.

I had to learn a lot about libraries in a very short period. I was struck by the difference in how libraries have changed since I was a student. In high school and college, my impression of librarians was not favorable. They seemed to prefer the company of books over people. When we assumed responsibility for the library, Jack Livingston had recently come out of retirement to become acting state librarian. He invited me to join him on a Sunday afternoon at the Monmouth County Public Library, where he used to work, for their weekly jazz concert. The idea that a library would host such an event was disorienting to me to say the least. What I found when I got there was amazing. The music was playing, the facility was full of people of all ages, reading, engaged in conversation, and listening to the great performance provided by local musicians, some of whom I found out were also librarians. It was cool to see a place of books and learning transformed into such a vibrant community center.

One thing I love about New Jerseyans is that they love books, they love to read, and they love libraries. New Jersey is home to two NFL football teams, for a while an NBA basketball team, racetracks, and of course the casinos in Atlantic City. I'm pleased to report that the attendance at the state's libraries on an annual basis exceeds that of all the sports venues and Atlantic City gambling and entertainment combined.

We operated the state library under the MOU for several years. It was thoroughly tested, and no unforeseen impediments arose. As the years went by in the Whitman administration, we had to decide whether we wanted to make this arrangement permanent. If we were going to do so, the MOU would need to be codified in statute. The affection New Jersey citizens had for their libraries was useful in our advocacy efforts. We received bipartisan support from the legislature to make the arrangement permanent.

As we worked with our colleagues in the legislature to set the MOU in statute, we ran across an unexpected hindrance. Before we proceeded, I had a meeting with the governor where she pointed to the success of the Thomas Edison/New Jersey State Library initiative as an accomplishment she hoped would survive her term. She asked her general counsel and me if the two of us could get that finalized before she left office. We agreed and worked together to draft the bill.

Assemblyman Leonard Lance, future U.S. congressman and enthusiastic library advocate, came forward to sponsor the bill in the assembly. Senator Peter Inverso, a local and well-respected banker, volunteered to sponsor the bill in the state senate. It was legislation without opposition, without cost, and without controversy, but for reasons I could not understand, the bill was not introduced. Generally, a governor's initiative is added to a list provided to legislative leadership. The legislators were waiting for this to appear on the list before introducing the bill. It turned out that the delay originated from two members of Governor Whitman's own staff, who didn't think it was a good idea. One of the staff members had been involved in revamping the secretary of state's office. She felt that the library should have been included in the secretary's "Art and Culture" portfolio. The library community objected. They saw themselves as an educational institution and not an art or cultural agency.

I was agnostic on these questions but could not understand why the governor's own people were impeding her initiatives. The other obstructionist, from the fiscal side of the bureaucracy, had no philosophical objection but had a million concerns and hypotheticals that *might* pose problems. When I identified the source of the bottleneck, I met with them to expedite the process. As the meeting proceeded, I felt like I was being interrogated and asked to justify why this should go forward. I finally lost my patience and told them both that we had been operating this arrangement for several years without issue or incident and that we had already demonstrated the efficacy of the proposal. I had no intention of continuing to justify and defend a decision made by their boss. If they thought it was a bad idea, they should take it up with the governor, as would I. The meeting did not end well. Shortly thereafter, I informed Assemblyman Lance about the altercation and my frustration with it, when I ran into him in the statehouse. He was infuriated and promised to look into it.

About a week later, I was invited to attend a meeting in the governor's counsel's conference room with the same two staff members I had met with before, only this time, Assemblyman Lance and Senator Inverso were there. The two staffers began the meeting by raising questions that had already been asked and answered multiple times. Finally, Assemblyman Lance lost his temper and told the staffer that the governor, the president of the college, he, and Senator Inverso supported the bill and that he expected the bill to be on the governor's bill list for the next week. If that was a problem, he would take it up with the governor personally. The meeting ended abruptly, and the staff member stormed out without speaking.

The next week, the bill was introduced, passed both houses unanimously, and was signed by the governor. The benefits to the library were immediate. They achieved increased giving and grant support in addition to their new ability to advocate for their own budget. We served as a coordinating body in partnership with the New Jersey Library Association and effectively advocated for local libraries as well. We were now able to attract expert talent because our library became an attractive place to work.

When Jack Livingston retired, we recruited Norma Blake. In 2008, Norma was selected as Librarian of the Year out of the tens of thousands of librarians at all levels in the United States. To my knowledge, we are the only college or university in the country that has responsibility for its state's state library. The pioneering innovation and progress that our collaboration achieved were greatly admired by the nation's other state libraries. It has been gratifying watching this experiment mature and succeed.

Chapter Fifteen

*To George, a college president who has demonstrated that nontraditional
and quality can be synonymous. With admiration, Hank*
—Henry "Hank" Spille

Those of us who take on the role of college president are usually motivated
by a calling to do so. This work is tireless and unrelenting but the most
gratifying to those who consider it a vocation. As such, leadership and service do not exist without the other. I have always felt that the responsibilities of the office went beyond the borders of the campus or the self-interest
of the institution. While the public regard for colleges and universities has
lost some of its luster, college presidents are still generally held in high
regard. The presidents and business leaders I have admired the most have
always utilized their capital to advance the public welfare.

During my tenure as president, I was invited or elected to serve on many
boards and advisory committees. This is not something that is done for
notoriety or to list on a resume. It is a duty that stems from personal values. The relationships made with other service-minded individuals is an
added benefit but also a necessary asset in leadership.

It was important to me to serve and support the community especially
in and around the Trenton area. I served on the board of Mercer Medical
Center, the largest of the hospitals in Trenton at the time; the board of the
Economic Development Corporation of Trenton; the Trenton Savings
Bank; Sun National Bank; and Greater Trenton, Inc. The college served
as the anchor institution for what I affectionately called the "State Street
Block Club." This was a small but committed group of business owners in

and around the campus and the state capitol complex, who raised money for and funded several downtown beautification projects, including lightscaping and tree planting.

Governor McGreevey asked me to serve on a small advisory group that he called his "higher education cabinet." The New Jersey Board of Higher Education appointed the Commission on Higher Education for Southern New Jersey, which I was asked to chair. I also served on the New Jersey State Planning Commission, New Jersey Capital Region Convention and Visitors Bureau and the American Cancer Society, New Jersey Division. I was elected chairman of the board of the Mercer Regional Chamber of Commerce and served on the board of Choose New Jersey, a statewide organization comprising the CEOs of the largest corporations and economic influencers in the state.

On a national level, in addition to my service on the CAEL board, I was elected to the boards of the American Council on Education (ACE), the American Association of State Colleges and Universities (AASCU), and the Council on Higher Education Accreditation (CHEA).

It's fairly unusual for a sitting president to be asked to serve as a university trustee, and I would largely advise against it. A university can only have one president at a time, and having another president as a trustee has the potential to complicate things. However, I served on the boards of two universities, Rider University in Lawrenceville, New Jersey, and the Union Institute and University in Cincinnati, Ohio, where I completed my doctoral work. I joined the Rider board at the request of its then president, Bart Luedeke. I was reluctant to do it, but Bart persuaded me that my contribution would be useful. At both schools, I was always careful to stay in my role as trustee and to defer to the president on matters of executive leadership and management.

Much of the service work I was involved in specifically regarding higher education was related to accreditation. Accreditation in American higher education began as a voluntary process among peers to enhance the quality of academic work. It had no intersection with government until the passage of the GI Bill following World War II. The government wanted to make sure that veterans' educational benefits were used at institutions with appropriate standards of quality. Accordingly, schools that served former military who received veterans' benefits required accreditation.

Additionally, in the first federal higher education act, under President Lyndon Johnson, the government created massive student financial aid programs (Title IV) and required that these funds could only be used at accredited schools. The structure of institutional accountability at the time was known as the "triad." The states were responsible for institutional licensure and consumer protection; the U.S. Office of Education was responsible for compliance, oversight, and regulations governing the use of federal funds; and the accrediting agencies continued their traditional role as the overseers of academic quality. It was a rational and reasonable structure to protect students and consumers and provide for the appropriate stewardship of taxpayers' money. Unfortunately, the structure was never fully deployed.

Many of the states to this day never established mechanisms for state licensure and consumer protection. The Office of Education was never provided the resources to exercise its oversight of federal funds and student financial aid. Both the states and the federal government walked away from their obligations and punted to the accreditors. Unfortunately, this lack of state licensure allowed unscrupulous people to set up a cottage industry of diploma mills and fraudulent operations masquerading as schools, colleges, and universities.

One day, I received a call from a gentleman who wanted to speak to me about his recently acquired doctoral degree from Thomas Edison College. I told him that he must have been mistaken because we (at the time) did not offer any doctoral programs. He said he knew that and identified himself as Allen Ezell, an FBI agent who was pursuing and prosecuting proprietors of fraudulent diploma mills. He informed me that his work had led to the successful indictment and conviction of George Cook Lyon, who in addition to being "president of Thomas Edison College" had a long ecclesiastical title as head of a bogus church. He ran both enterprises out of a post office box in West Benton, Arkansas.

Agent Ezell, a member of an FBI antifraud task force, wanted my assistance with their project, Operation DipScam. Many of these diploma mills used language similar to, and masqueraded as, legitimate adult-serving colleges and universities. Not only were there fraudulent "schools"; there were also spurious "accrediting agencies" that some of these outfits would cite as their accreditors to suggest legitimacy. He thought I could be useful in helping him identify triggers that would make these illegal operations easier to identify.

David Stewart and Henry "Hank" Spille, of the American Council on Education, authored an excellent book on the subject, *Diploma Mills: Degrees of Fraud*. Hank signed my copy of the book with the inscription, "To George, A college president who has demonstrated that nontraditional and quality can be synonymous. With admiration, Hank."

The second part of the triad was the U.S. Department of Education (USDOE). Ronald Reagan attempted to abolish the department because he believed it represented an inappropriate federal intrusion into education, which had always been left to the states. While Congress never allowed him to do it, the new organization was starved of funding. It never received the resources or personnel to carry out its oversight and compliance obligations, especially for student financial aid.

In the '60s and '70s, the department's grant programs and forgivable loans represented the bedrock of student financial aid. Under Reagan, the grant programs were reduced, and a shift occurred placing a greater reliance on loans made by banks and guaranteed by the federal government. By the late '80s and early '90s, student loan defaults on federally guaranteed debt had grown into the billions. The public and the Congress became alarmed and wanted answers.

Responsibility for the supervision and oversight that allowed this crisis rationally belonged to the states and to the USDOE. Naturally, the finger pointing began. Both the states and the federal government had an easy scapegoat in the accreditors.

The structure of accreditation of American higher education is complicated. Most of what people think of as accreditation for traditional degree-granting colleges and universities is vested in the seven regional accrediting bodies. Embedded within traditional colleges and universities are also specialized accreditors for programs within certain disciplines (e.g., the American Psychological Association provides specialized accreditation for programs in psychology). There are also specialized accreditors in chemistry, business, education, nursing, libraries, and so on.

The proprietary schools that accredit institutions providing technical, vocational, and occupational training reside outside the realm of traditional colleges and universities. These schools are profit-making businesses that exist to train and educate people for particular jobs. Most of them are honest and of reasonable quality. If their graduates are not found to be qualified for the occupations their students pursue, or if the employers that hire their graduates are not satisfied, these schools would not stay in business very long.

For the purpose of receiving Title IV federal funds, an institution must be accredited by an agency recognized by the U.S. secretary of education. At the time of the guaranteed student loan default scandal, there were over eighty accrediting bodies recognized by the secretary. They accredited cosmetology, truck driving, secretarial, chiropractic, and mortuary schools and a host of other trades and occupations. Indeed, my father was a 1946 graduate of the Worsham School of Mortuary Science in Chicago. It still exists today and from what I can tell has an excellent reputation, though I do not intend this as a commercial.

I remember viewing a presentation that reported over 90 percent of guaranteed student loan defaults derived from 3 percent of the schools and 90 percent of that 3 percent were from proprietary schools. The majority of those proprietary schools were involved in cosmetology education. That is not to say that there were no problems in this regard from traditional higher education, but the numbers and dollar amounts were very small when compared to the profit-making institutions.

Sometime around 1989, the George H. W. Bush administration inquired as to my interest in joining the National Advisory Committee on Accreditation and Institutional Eligibility, an advisory committee to the secretary of education, which evaluated accrediting agencies for their compliance with the department's eligibility criteria for recognition. This committee had an essential role in the nation's quality assurance machinery, and the impact of its work was widespread and consequential.

I had no idea as to how my name had come to the administration's attention. Under most administrations, the recruitment and appointment process is managed from the White House, even though the committee is advisory to the secretary. This inquiry could have come from my work with CAEL, ACE, or AASCU. I also knew that Governor Kean and President Bush were friends and that their staffs often collaborated. In fact, Governor Kean introduced me to President Bush during his presidency at a State Chamber of Commerce event in Washington, DC. Again, I have never been involved in partisanship, so when I am asked to serve my country, I feel obligated to do so unless there is some reason why I can't. I was flattered, honored, and accepted the appointment.

Reagan's low regard for the department carried over to the Bush administration. The department was demoralized, understaffed, and underfunded. The National Advisory Committee comprised an interesting collection of people. The chair of the committee was a gentleman I respected and held in high regard, but there was also a collection of characters from the other end of the spectrum.

Consistently and predictably applying the department's regulations in evaluating compliance by the accrediting agencies was the primary function of the committee. It was sometimes difficult to maintain our discipline around this function. The committee's discussions were often wide ranging on topics that had nothing to do with our statutory responsibility. Nor did we have much engagement with Secretary Lauro Cavazos Jr.

Examining the accreditor's role in the guaranteed student loan default scandal was a significant focus of our work. We heard testimony from the accrediting agencies, the department staff, and other experts who expressed a variety of opinions as to why the crisis occurred, who was to blame, and what was needed to respond to the problem. It followed the usual pattern: the department staff and the states blamed each other, and both of them blamed the accreditors.

We also heard case studies highlighting a series of bad practices and outright fraud on the part of many proprietary institutions. The accrediting agencies themselves were often branches of their respective industry's trade associations, and instead of focusing on accountability for the bad actors in their midst, they closed ranks to defend the industry. The Council on Postsecondary Accreditation (COPA), the organization that collectively represented the accrediting agencies at the time, continually presented microdata suggesting that the crisis was overblown and exaggerated. This position had no credibility in the face of billions of dollars in taxpayer losses and damning examples of malevolent behavior by some of the schools' owners.

Some recruiters were paid on commission for the number of enrollments procured and preyed on uninformed students to sign up for loans. These students, some of whom didn't speak English, incurred debt they did not understand. Many of these students were unqualified for the programs, and others took advantage of easy money to borrow to support their living expenses without any intention of doing the academic work. Others wanted the job training but had skills deficiencies too great to overcome.

It is important to note that the swindlers made up a very small percentage of the proprietary schools, but there were enough of them to generate billions of dollars in loan defaults. Fortunately, once engaged, corrective actions by the department staff and pressure from the broader accrediting community resulted in significant reforms that dramatically reduced the default rate.

This enraged Congress, and they got involved. Senator Sam Nunn of Georgia's committee held hearings on the matter. They were greatly disturbed by the mutual finger pointing and lack of ownership by the elements of the triad. If the groups who were supposed to fix it weren't going to, the senator decided he would. His frustration was understandable, but as is often the case, Congress showed up to close the barn door after the horse was gone.

In the subsequent reauthorization of the Higher Education Act and in response to Senator Nunn's influence, two important reforms were made. First, separation and independence between the accrediting agencies from the trade associations were required. Also, the accrediting bodies eligible for recognition by the secretary were limited to those agencies that served as gatekeepers for federal funds. This meant that the committee's time was released to focus on the accrediting agencies that served a federal purpose. The responsibility that was and should have remained with the Department of Education was placed on the accreditors, making them liable for holding institutions accountable for the compliance, management, and administration of rules governing federal funds. For the first time in American history, quality in higher education was no longer defined by its academic programs. It was now defined by institutional compliance with federal rules.

While well intentioned, it was a bad decision, and the adverse consequences are still in effect today. A college can have a great faculty and an outstanding academic program but have weaknesses in the financial aid and business office jeopardizing its accreditation. At the same time, another institution can have a critically weak academic program but have great compliance departments that will mask the deficits of its academics. Traditional accreditation and the peer review process at its heart, a tested and proven mechanism for quality assurance, are ill suited to function as a compliance agent for the Department of Education's many complex rules.

Anytime you separate accountability from the entity holding the authority and responsibility for it, you encourage a bad outcome. The rule-making authority remained with the government but had to be enforced by the accreditors. Compliance is essential, and the accreditors have a responsibility to ensure that college administrators are competent stewards of the taxpayers' dollars, but this change in the law compromised the accreditor's autonomy from the federal government. This stood as a distraction from their principal role of ensuring academic quality and satisfactory educational outcomes.

In the middle of this work, the committee became preoccupied by an issue outside of the scope of its mandate and mission. The Middle States Association of Colleges and Schools, which accredits colleges and universities in New York, New Jersey, Pennsylvania, Delaware, Maryland, and the District of Columbia, decided to adopt a standard by which it would evaluate its member institutions related to their commitment to achieving diversity among their students, faculty, and leadership. The federal regulations were silent and permissive on the subject. Simply stated, it was up to the commission and its members to determine whether they wanted to do this, and it was clearly outside of the committee's and secretary's authority to intervene on the subject. Unfortunately, the word *diversity* signified a red flag to many members of the committee, the department, and conservative supporters of the Bush administration.

As president of an institution accredited by the Middle States Association of Colleges and Schools, I recused myself from the deliberations and vote, but one of my colleagues from Dallas made a comment that was so outrageous that I could not restrain myself. She passionately declared that this "diversity stuff" was a communist assault on American values. By this time, the Soviet Union had fallen, and communism was in retreat around the world. I could not help but remark, "They aren't even talking about communism in Russia anymore, so why are you so afraid of it in Dallas, and what does any of that have to do with diversity anyway?" There was a lot of laughter in the room followed by my apology for violating my recusal. There was a strong sentiment among the committee to punish the Middle States Association of Colleges and Schools for adding the standard on diversity, but fortunately, there was no legal mechanism to do so.

Lamar Alexander replaced Secretary Cavazos when he left his position. After Alexander completed his term as governor, he became president of the University of Tennessee. His appointment as secretary of education was great for the department and good for the country. He had a solid relationship with President Bush, and he deeply cared about education at all levels. He also brought the perspective of both a governor and university president to the office.

The members he appointed to the committee brought qualifications and experience that were better suited to its responsibilities. The reforms, initiatives, and quality of dialogue Alexander introduced were interesting and exciting but were cut short when President Bush did not win the election for a second term. I think Alexander would have been one of the best secretary's had he had a longer term.

> Carol, we're not in Chicago anymore.
> —George A. Pruitt

While there were disagreements, I had respect for President Bush, but I was thrilled by the election of President Clinton. Also victorious in that election was Carol Moseley Braun, who became the first African American and the first woman to represent Illinois in the U.S. Senate. Carol and I were friends and classmates at Martha Ruggles Elementary School in Chicago.

After she was sworn in, I reached out to extend my congratulations on her historic victory, and she invited me to Washington for lunch. I had our eighth-grade class picture framed and took it to her as a gift. We had a great time together catching up, reminiscing, and speculating about the fate of some of our classmates. She took me to lunch in the Senate dining room, where we ate in the presence of her senatorial colleagues from both sides of the aisle. I distinctly remember seeing Senator Claiborne Pell from Rhode Island, the father of the Pell Grant, Senator Edward Kennedy, and many other members of that very select club.

After lunch, Carol took me down to the Senate floor, and I couldn't help but reflect on the hallowed ground on which I found myself. I mused about the great historical figures and monumental debates that had taken place where I was now standing, and I turned to Carol and laughingly said, "This is a long way to come for two Black kids from Seventy-Ninth Street in Chicago." I was very proud of her. Given our respective circumstances, it had been an improbable journey for us both.

It was winter, and when I walked down the steps of the capitol, I was struck by the beautiful moonlight reflecting off the dome. On the way back to my hotel, I passed the White House and chuckled, because for the first time in my life, the president of the United States was younger than me. The words from President Kennedy's inaugural address "the torch has been passed to a new generation of Americans" came to mind, quickly followed by Alan Shepard's prayer, "Please God, don't let me f-ck up." Someone of my generation was in the White House, and I had a schoolmate in the U.S. Senate. I personally felt that it was our generation's turn, and I really hoped that we wouldn't f-ck it up.

I assumed that my term as a member of the National Advisory Committee would conclude with the party transition of the administration. During the presidential transition, I received more than one call inquiring about my interest in joining the Clinton administration. As with the advisory committee, I had no idea how I came to their attention. President Clinton gained a lifelong fan after I met him at that AAHE meeting, and though I was flattered, I had no interest in leaving Thomas Edison or working for the federal government. I was happy, however, when I learned that I had been reappointed to what is now called the National Advisory Committee on Institutional Quality and Integrity (NACIQI).

While I could make no sense of the rationale for the membership of the previous committee, each of the appointees under the Clinton Administration was an able, experienced person of great stature and gravitas.

The staff of the Department of Education was also reinvigorated under the direction of Secretary of Education Richard Riley. Riley was deeply and personally committed to education and, like Alexander, had gubernatorial experience.

I had the privilege of sitting next to Secretary Riley at dinner one evening. The richness of his experience and perspective made for an enlightening conversation. The quality of the staff he surrounded himself with was also impressive. The eight years of the Clinton administration were the most enjoyable of the twenty years I served on this committee.

There was, however, one accrediting agency I found particularly exasperating, and that was the American Bar Association (ABA). The association's delegation included the ABA's executive director, members of their board, and was chaired by the chief justice of a state supreme court. While I understand that judges are accustomed to deference, they succeeded in alienating just about everybody on the staff and committee with the patronizing and indifferent manner in which they addressed us. They were dismissive of the committee's authority, which identified several areas of noncompliance with the recognition criteria, and they were unresponsive to the committee's and department's deadlines and reporting requirements. They acted as if somehow none of the regulations, requirements, or time frames required of the other accrediting bodies applied to them.

When you are before a group who has control or authority over something you need, it's best to be mindful of whose house you're in. These proceedings weren't taking place in a courtroom. They were in our house, and the manner in which they responded to us was disrespectful. Three of us took particular exception to their conduct: Tom Salmon, former governor of Vermont and president of the University of Vermont at the time; David Adamany, the distinguished president of Wayne State University in Michigan and later Temple University in Philadelphia; and of course, me.

There were several areas of substantive concern that went beyond the delegation's affect. The regulations required that the ABA take corrective actions within a time frame required by the committee. They failed to comply and cited their meeting calendar didn't accommodate the committee's request. I couldn't help but wonder how the judges in the delegation would have responded if the subject of one of their court orders had not complied because it inconvenienced them.

The ABA adopted accreditation standards that appeared to be more concerned with protecting the economic interest of the guild than promoting quality assurance in legal education. This was a problem. They prescribed student-to-faculty ratios for law schools to maintain and even included language that had the effect of propping up the salaries of the faculty. Because the bar association in most states controlled the eligibility for licensure, it had effectively created a monopoly for itself.

I took particular issue with the low pass rates of law school graduates taking state bar exams. Law schools are highly selective and very expensive. One would expect that the graduates of an ABA-accredited law school would have little difficulty passing their state's threshold licensing test. Graduates of accredited medical schools and dental schools have pass rates in the high nineties. The bar exam pass rates for law school graduates was around 70 percent at the time. A 30 percent failure rate raised significant questions about the quality of legal education. I was reminded that John F. Kennedy Jr., who graduated from Harvard Law School, finally passed the bar exam on his third attempt. The success rate on third-party exams is a legitimate and important factor in determining the quality of professional education and the competency of the accrediting agency involved.

Adamany and Salmon, both attorneys and members of the bar, and I pushed these points aggressively with the ABA delegation and clearly made them uncomfortable. In fact, we were later told that following the hearing, they complained to the secretary's office about the grilling they received. Several years later, under a different administration and on a different topic, another colleague and I would lead the charge in the ABA's defense.

Work on NACIQI was exhausting but important. I enjoyed the fellowship that existed among members of the committee, and I had great respect for the department's staff assigned to work with us. Those years went by quickly, and when President Clinton was succeeded by the second President Bush, I figured again that my service on the committee was about to conclude.

Sometime in the period between the November election and President George W. Bush's inauguration, I received a repeat of the two earlier inquiries. I was again approached about whether I would like to join the Bush administration in the Department of Education, which like the earlier overture I respectfully declined, and was then asked if I would accept reappointment to membership on the NACIQI, which I did.

Richard Riley's successor as secretary of education was Rod Paige, elected chair of the Board of Education of the Houston Public Schools and a former football coach we'd competed against at Tennessee State. He was the first African American secretary of education. Just as it had previously, the committee composition changed dramatically under Secretary Paige and the Bush administration. The Clinton appointees had no political agenda. They were principally concerned about quality assurance and fairly applied the recognition criteria. Many of the new committee members appointed by the Bush administration brought with them a politically conservative point of view.

During Secretary Paige's short tenure, "No Child Left Behind," a much-heralded bipartisan piece of legislation was passed by Congress and signed into law. This act, championed by Senator Kennedy and supported by his Republican colleagues and President Bush, was one of the last examples of truly bipartisan legislation enacted for quite some time. After it passed, Secretary Paige left to pursue other opportunities, and Margaret Spellings succeeded him.

There is an old saying, "The more things change, the more they stay the same." I was reminded of this when my old friends at the ABA came before the NACIQI again for the renewal of their recognition. This time, the character, style, and demeanor of the group were considerably different, and I was happy to see it. The temperament and composition of the NACIQI had changed as well, but it still retained several distinguished members. One of them was Larry DeNardis, former Republican member of Congress and president of the University of New Haven in Connecticut. We had a lot in common and became good friends.

On this occasion, the ABA was under attack by the secretary's staff for including a standard on "diversity" among its criteria for ABA accreditation. It was a throwback to the attacks on the Middle States Association of Colleges and Schools during the first Bush administration, but the attack on diversity was now orchestrated from the highest levels of government and not the committee itself. This time I wasn't recused.

Normally a member of the committee's staff reviews the agency's petition, evaluates its submission, and reports any deficiencies and recommendations for corrective action to the committee. The committee is free to accept, reject, or modify the staff recommendation in making its recommendation to the secretary. This time, the committee's staff member assigned to the ABA had his report confiscated. It was then rewritten in the secretary's office. He was provided a report he had not authored or agreed with and was asked to present it as his own.

The committee is normally assigned legal counsel by a member of the department's legal staff; however, on this occasion, the general counsel of the department replaced the committee's counsel. The ABA was being set up. The secretary's recognition criteria were blatantly distorted to make a political statement. This was wrong, and I was enraged. The staff member assigned to read the substitute report considered resigning rather than comply. Larry DeNardis was just as concerned as I was.

The ABA, as an organization comprising lawyers, was well equipped to defend itself. I believe they were preparing for litigation to contest what they assumed was a preordained outcome. When it was the ABA's turn on the agenda, the committee staffer read the report he was given, not the one he authored. The agency made its presentation, and the committee began its deliberation. While the setup included the staff, it apparently had not been widely vetted among the committee members, and after a vigorous debate led by DeNardis and me, the committee voted overwhelmingly not to accept the staff recommendation and to recommend renewal of recognition by the secretary. The department's senior staff who engineered the attack were shocked. The ABA, while surprised, was elated. I never asked if my contrarian disposition, implemented this time around in their defense, changed their mind about me.

While the committee's recommendation to the secretary is not binding, the American Bar Association would have undoubtedly sued the secretary if their recognition was threatened. The affirmative vote by the committee would have made legal defense of the secretary's position more difficult. Justice does not always prevail, particularly in partisan Washington, but Larry and I both felt that we had done our duty and served the public interest well.

When the Bush administration ended and the Obama administration took office, I felt that after twenty years on the committee, under five secretaries of education and three presidents of both parties, I had done enough. To my knowledge, I was the only member of the committee reappointed when the administrations changed parties. I let the staff know I was not interested in serving another term on the committee. I did perform one final act of service for the department before I left. As the Obama administration took office, Arne Duncan was appointed secretary of education, and new legislation passed that changed the composition of the committee once again, allowing for Congress to appoint some members in addition to the administration's appointees. I was asked to conduct the orientation and training session for the new committee. It had been an extraordinary run; I learned a lot, and I assume, because they kept inviting me back, I did a good job.

Chapter Sixteen

Jazz washes away the dust of everyday life.

—*Art Blakey*

In October 1997, I was on an assignment with the Kellogg National Fellowship Program (KNFP), one of the premier leadership development programs in the country. The Kellogg Foundation conducted most of its work through grants to providers, but a few programs, including the KNFP, were run directly by the foundation itself, staffed by members of their leadership teams.

Every year, the foundation cast a broad net to identify and recruit individuals who had demonstrated leadership ability and, more importantly, potential for future growth. Each class consisted of about forty Kellogg Fellows and a small group of advisers to mentor them. The class term of three years included a series of residential seminars, an individualized professional growth plan, and an international experience. In addition to serving as an adviser to two of these classes (cohort 12 and cohort 15), I served on the screening and selection panel for two other classes. The foundation invested about $250,000 in each of the Kellogg Fellows. It was an extraordinary opportunity and privilege for the fellows, and it provided a powerfully enriching experience for those of us serving as advisers.

On October 10, after spending a week in Nebraska with our class studying rural leadership issues, I was tired and anxious to get home. While I waited in line to check in for my flight out of Omaha, the woman in front of me turned around and said my name. I immediately recognized her face, but her name escaped me. She said, "Pam Moffett," and I immediately remembered the adorable sophomore I had worked with at Hirsch High School's program office.

I had not seen her since graduating in 1964, and here we found ourselves together again in an airport in Omaha, Nebraska, thirty-three years later. She worked for ABC Radio and was returning home to Dallas from a business trip. We discovered we were on the same flight, since I had to change planes in Dallas. When we reached the ticket counter, we asked the agent if we could sit together. When she pulled up our record, she laughed and told us we had already been assigned seats next to each other. We sat in front of the gate waiting to board and got so carried away talking that we almost missed the flight.

After we caught up on our past, we began to talk about our present. Like everyone else who had gone through a painful divorce, I was now "a relationship expert." Pam was involved with someone, and after hearing about her situation over a few inflight cocktails, I advised her to leave the guy and go be happy. I was seeing someone at the time, and my advice had no self-serving intention. The two of us becoming involved didn't cross my mind. After the flight, we went our separate ways and spoke occasionally on the phone.

That winter, the tumultuous relationship I was in finally came to a merciful end. I thought about Pam and wondered how her relationship was going. On New Year's Eve, I picked up the phone and called her office, not expecting her to answer. I was pleasantly surprised when she did. After dispensing with the appropriate small talk, I told her about my situation and asked about hers. She told me that hers was falling apart as well.

Christine Todd Whitman had been reelected as governor, and her inauguration was a couple of weeks away. I invited Pam to fly up to accompany me. We had a great time at the inauguration and began spending more time on the phone, flying back and forth to visit, and had the occasional rendezvous in cities where one of us traveled for business. In May 1998, I proposed, she said yes, and we were married on October 10, 1998, a year to the day of our reunion at the airport in Omaha.

Pam and I grew up in the same neighborhood in the South Side. As a product of a single-parent household, she was thrilled when she received several full scholarships to attend college after graduation. Unfortunately, her mother didn't share her enthusiasm and wouldn't allow her to accept them. Instead, she took her downtown, got her a job, and told her to get college out of her head.

Pam wasn't going to let her mother or anyone else squash her dreams and talent. While writing an article for the high school newspaper, she met Smokey Robinson and the Miracles and, most importantly, Claudette Robinson, the group's female lead, who became a dear and lifelong friend and mentor. She also met Marvin Tarplin, the Miracle's gifted guitarist. It was the beginning of a close, personal relationship and professional collaboration. Smokey and Marvin are both members of the Rock and Roll Hall of Fame, and Claudette was the first female artist ever signed by Motown Records.

Pam became an accomplished lyricist, writing songs and collaborating with Smokey Robinson, Marvin Tarplin, and other legends, such as The Supremes, Eugene Record of The Chi-Lites, and Curtis Mayfield of The Impressions. Her song "Baby Come Close," written for Smokey Robinson, was sampled by the artist Ne-Yo for his duet with Jennifer Hudson, entitled "Leaving Tonight." In 2007, the album *Because of You*, featuring "Leaving Tonight," won a Grammy Award.

Having never gotten over her desire to further her education, she took advantage of the opportunities provided by Thomas Edison to earn her baccalaureate degree in 2010. She went on to earn a master's degree from Rutgers University in 2012 and a doctorate from the University of Pennsylvania in 2016. Pam has led a fascinating life, which she writes about in her own book. Nothing I can say here will compare to hearing her story in her own words.

After she moved to New Jersey, Pam took a job at Dow Jones with Wall Street Journal Radio. Her office was in World Financial One, directly across the street from the south tower of the World Trade Center. I was in

my office, the morning of September 11, 2001, when Anne came in to tell
me Pam was on the phone and sounded distressed. She told me there had
been some kind of explosion at the top of the World Trade Center. She tear-
fully described the scene: chaos on the streets below, fire at the top of
the building, and debris everywhere, including human body parts on the
streets beneath her window. I immediately turned on the television in
my office and looked on in horror at the devastation. The broadcaster
announced that a plane had crashed into the building, and like everyone
else at the time, I assumed it was an accident involving a noncommercial
aircraft.

Pam told me she thought she should leave the building, but I urged her
to stay to put. I could see her building on the television, and it looked fine,
while everything around it was immersed in smoke, ash, and debris. From
what I could tell, she seemed safer inside. She agreed and said there was
an announcement for everyone to stay in the building.

As I continued to watch the scene unfold, the second plane exploded
into the south tower, and it appeared to me that the top of Pam's building
was now engulfed in flames. I immediately tried to call her back to tell her
to get out of the building, but I was unable to reach her. I was terrified. I
kept trying to call her office and cell phone with no luck. I hoped she had
ignored my earlier advice and evacuated the building. I watched in shock
as the buildings collapsed, completely engulfing Pam's building with that
awful gray cloud of dust. People held hands and jumped to their death to
avoid incineration by the fire while the world watched on national TV.

My anxiety for Pam's safety intensified over the next few hours. Finally,
she called. After the second plane hit, an evacuation was ordered for her
building. Although she had a grueling time getting out because of the
crush of people in the stairwells, she and her colleagues were able to successfully evacuate the building but didn't know where to go. By then, she
understood we were under attack and worried about the next target.
She was afraid to go toward Penn Station because of the Empire State
Building's proximity to it.

She and her colleague Bryan Mitchell decided to walk to his apartment in Brooklyn. They walked around lower Manhattan through Battery Park and up to the Brooklyn Bridge. They were getting ready to cross the bridge when she called me. Her voice was trembling. They were petrified to cross the bridge because they didn't know whether it would be attacked. Brian asked that I call his wife, who was on an airplane to Chicago, and let her know that he was OK. What I did not tell him was that, at the time, the news reported that several planes were unaccounted for. I called Bryan's wife and left a message on her cell phone. I was later relieved to find out that she had received my message and was safe.

Later, I received another call from Pam that they made it safely to Bryan's place, and though her feet were in bad shape walking that distance in heels, she was grateful she still had feet given what she had seen. Because the rail traffic had been shut down, there was no way for her to get home until the following day. I met her at the train station and accompanied her to the garage to get her car. The parking attendant told us many of the vehicles in the garage were unclaimed from the day before. It was a horrible ordeal for the nation, the city of New York, the people who survived it, and for the families and loved ones of those who didn't.

One Saturday, sometime later, we were running errands, and Pam asked me to take her back to her office to see if she could retrieve her computer and other personal belongings. I tried to talk her out of it, because the site had been roped off and the heap left by the collapsed buildings was still smoldering, but she insisted. I wanted to be supportive, so off we went. I was surprised that I found a parking space so close to the building and more surprised that we were able to get to the guard's station by the loading dock. Pam knew the guard, and he agreed to escort us to the twelfth floor, where she worked. It was probably a mistake. The building was still full of smoke, most of the windows were blown out, and the guard told us that there was fourteen feet of rubble in the lobby.

We were able to access Pam's office and retrieve her laptop, Rolodex, and a few other things we could carry, but we were required to take them to a decontamination site that was set up in the building. At Pam's desk, I peered through the cracks in the boarded-up windows and looked down upon the massive, glowering pile that had once been the World Trade Center. From what I could tell, some sort of confrontation was taking place between the firefighters who refused to leave and the police, who had orders to clear the site. Emotions were high as they had all lost colleagues and friends, some still entombed in the site. Nevertheless, given the smoke and debris, as subsequent events would prove, it was an unsafe place to be.

That was true for me and Pam as well. We thanked the security guard and put her belongings in the trunk of my car. We were deeply saddened by our trip and thought visiting a quiet bar to have a drink was in order. We saw a flier on the street advertising the appearance of Chuck Mangione at the Blue Note that evening. Pam and I both have a great appreciation and love for music, especially jazz. For us, ending what was a depressing day with Chuck Mangione helped take some of the sadness away.

We weren't dressed for it; in fact we looked terrible. We were both wearing the blue jeans and sweatshirts we had planned to wear to the grocery store, now smoke-filled. We didn't know if the Blue Note was open in light of the circumstances, so we called, and they told us that Mangione was in town. They didn't know if anyone would be there for the performance, and they weren't taking reservations, but they were going to open the doors to see what happened.

We were among the first people to arrive, and we were seated at a table directly in front of the stage. Mangione was walking around and engaged us in conversation. He was generous with his time and gave Pam a personalized autographed picture. People gradually came in off the street and filled up the place before showtime.

An attractive, well-dressed African American couple arrived and were seated next to us. They were visiting from out of town, had made reservations, and had dressed accordingly. Like reconnecting with Pam in the airport, I have experienced strange, improbable coincidences on several occasions in my life, and this turned out to be another one. The gentleman was seated next to Pam, and he was an executive at Gulf Oil from Pittsburgh; his wife seated next to me went to a neighboring high school in Chicago. I knew a lot of her classmates, and she knew a lot of mine. Her husband knew my cousin Percy, who had been an executive at Gulf as well. We enjoyed an engaging conversation with them before the show started.

Mangione did not disappoint. His performance was magnificent, and every time I play his music, I think about the evening we spent cheered by his exceptional talent. We exchanged information with the couple we chatted with, and the next day, when Pam was looking at the wife's business card, she laughed. Given the way the seats were arranged, and the noise in the place, she did not have much time to talk with her, but when we got home and she saw the card, she realized the two of them had double dated at *my* prom. Their boyfriends at the time were friends and classmates of mine. Serendipity.

The college's commencement ceremony was held a week or so later in early October. Even though our graduates receive their diplomas as they satisfy their degree requirements, they are invited to an annual fall ceremony to participate in the formal exercises complete with all the pomp and circumstance appropriate for their achievement.

One of our graduates, scheduled to march in the ceremony, was killed in the 9/11 attack on the Pentagon. His widow requested to attend the ceremony to receive her husband's diploma for their two young children. Of course, we did everything in our power to accommodate and honor her wishes. After all of the graduates commenced, I introduced the widow and invited her and their two children to the stage. The entire arena stood and applauded, with tears streaming down their faces. As I shook their hands and passed her the diploma, I couldn't stop weeping. I greatly admired her poise and courage. We hugged, and she whispered some comforting words to me. I was embarrassed but mused on the irony of her comforting me, which I shared with her, and we both found something to smile about in the moment. I presided at over thirty-five commencements during my tenure as president; none of them would be more emotional and moving than this one.

There was another aspect of New York's response to 9/11 that occurred outside of my role at the college. Tom Seessel was president and CEO of the Structured Employment and Economic Development Corporation (SEEDCO). Sometime after Tom left the Thomas Edison board, he asked me to join the SEEDCO board, where I served many years as vice chair and subsequently chair of the board.

SEEDCO was created by the Ford Foundation as an intermediary to promote economic development by fostering collaborative relationships between large, nonprofit anchor organizations and local grassroots community groups. The nonprofits were usually hospitals or colleges and universities. SEEDCO is a national organization headquartered in New York promoting economic development sites all over the country.

Its most successful collaborations include the East Baltimore community revitalization projects around the Johns Hopkins Medical Center; the community revitalization work anchored by Johnson C. Smith University in Charlotte, North Carolina; and much of the urban renewal in Jackson, Mississippi, in cooperation with Jackson State University. Perhaps SEEDCO's finest hour occurred after September 11, 2001, in lower Manhattan.

The Ford Foundation contacted SEEDCO and expressed some concern about the survivability of the small nonprofits in the area that were put at financial risk by the destruction. Many nonprofits are dependent on event fundraising, and after the attack, lower Manhattan was shut down. Our task was to identify and provide funding to organizations that could stay viable with a short-term infusion of cash. Ford understood that this was an emergency, and time was of the essence. They provided a substantial grant and empowered us to deploy the resources swiftly to save as many organizations as possible.

The SEEDCO staff did a heroic job, and our work soon gained the attention of the press. All of the sudden, we started receiving millions of dollars in grants and gifts from other foundations, corporations, and individuals to carry out the same function, only this time with small businesses in the area.

The United Way, the Red Cross, and the 9/11 Fund were the major providers of relief aid, but their procedures and bureaucracies did not allow them to move as quickly or nimbly as the situation demanded. With so many companies disrupted, a number of young Wall Street "MBA types" were temporarily out of work and available. The SEEDCO staff recruited some of them to volunteer to work for very little pay. We described the objectives for the program and the criteria they should use in making loans and grants. That was the extent of the bureaucracy and oversight. We gave them checkbooks, asked them to document their decisions, and unleashed them.

There was one business in particular that stands out in my mind. It was a quick-turnaround film-processing store dependent on camera-toting tourists who needed their film developed while they waited. Unfortunately, the ash cloud infiltrated the store and destroyed the photo-processing machine, but the tourists still came in droves to document the wreckage. With our help, the owner purchased new equipment and quickly reopened for business. He returned to profitability and paid back the money we loaned him. When the project concluded, we had distributed millions of dollars in assistance efficiently, quickly, and without a single instance of fraud or abuse. The program was incredibly successful, and I take great pride in walking around lower Manhattan today seeing all the thriving small businesses that wouldn't have survived without our assistance.

Tom Seessel was provided a grant to conduct a post-9/11 assessment of the philanthropic community's response to the events. He asked if Thomas Edison would serve as fiscal agent and recipient of the grant. When he completed his work, he invited me to join him to report to the heads of all the major foundations and philanthropic organizations in the city. I happily accepted and enjoyed an audience any nonprofit executive in the world would have traded places to engage with. It was gratifying to receive expressions of gratitude on behalf of Thomas Edison from this extraordinary collection of philanthropists for our support of Tom's work but also for SEEDCO's amazing contribution in rebuilding lower Manhattan after the 9/11 tragedy.

A RARE AND BEAUTIFUL PEARL

The October 2001 commencement was the most heartrending we ever had, but the 1987 ceremony was the most joyful and fun. That year, we awarded an honorary degree to the famed singer, actress, comedienne, and humanitarian Pearl Bailey. We invited Ms. Bailey to accept our highest honor because she was an adult learner who earned her degree later in life after having achieved honors and accolades for her extraordinary career.

Even though Pearl Bailey was famous, she was warm, unpretentious, and down-to-earth. She lived in New York, so we offered to send a limo for her. She declined and took Amtrak. We reserved the largest suite in the Princeton Hyatt, which had, among other amenities, a grand piano. Again, she declined and told me that she intended to take the train back to the city following the ceremony. I picked her up from the train station, and it was love at first sight. There are certain people who have naturally endearing personalities, and Pearl Bailey was one of them.

Until we outgrew it, our commencement ceremony was held at the beautiful War Memorial Auditorium on the banks of the Delaware River in downtown Trenton. It's a magnificent facility with amazing acoustics. After I conferred the degree on Ms. Bailey, she delivered one of the best commencement addresses I have ever heard. It was inspiring and witty and filled the auditorium with laughter and applause.

While our graduates always processed at commencement to "Pomp and Circumstance," our recessional, if appropriate, was accompanied by music associated with our honoree. For example, when we honored Chuck Yeager, we played "Off We Go into the Wild Blue Yonder."

Pearl starred in a long and successful revival on Broadway of the musical *Hello, Dolly!* As we stood to leave the stage, the band began playing the title song from the play. Pearl turned to me and asked, "Would anyone mind if I sang?" I laughed and replied, "Of course not, but the problem is, if you start singing, no one is going to leave." I then escorted her to the lectern, directed the rest of the platform party off the stage, and stood back while she led the entire assembly in a rousing rendition of the title song, "Hello, Dolly!" After appropriate time had passed, I offered her my arm to escort her off the stage, but instead she came into my arms, and we danced our way out of the auditorium to a standing ovation by the crowd. A few thousand people were singing, laughing, and applauding. The atmosphere was electric.

Pearl and I became good friends and stayed in touch until she died. She authored several books, including some for children, and sent autographed copies to me and Shayla. She also held the status of special ambassador to the United Nations. Pearl Bailey was an exceptional woman, and when she passed away in 1990, her loss was mourned by celebrities, public officials, and ordinary people all over the world who were blessed by the warmth of her light.

Another notable commencement was as far removed from the joy of Pearl Bailey as you can get. In 2011, we decided to hold a second commencement in the spring but were run out of town by a group of neo-Nazis. The fact that our campus brackets the New Jersey statehouse is both a blessing and a curse. On the positive side, the proximity allowed constant access to state officials and legislators. On the downside, we were at ground zero for every public demonstration or protest staged on the steps of the capitol.

On this unfortunate occasion, the American Nazi Party decided to have a rally in front of the statehouse on the same day of our commencement. Several other organizations announced counterdemonstrations held at the same time. We didn't know what would happen if our graduates and their guests arrived in the middle of all this. We had several discussions with the state police and other law enforcement agencies tasked with managing this potentially explosive event. At the end of the day, we were informed that the authorities could not guarantee the security of our staff, graduates, and guests. At the last minute, we were forced to relocate our ceremony to the Rutgers University New Brunswick campus about thirty miles north. Even though it was a logistical nightmare to relocate such a complicated event on such short notice, the Rutgers community welcomed us with open arms. Nature inflicted poetic justice on the Nazi group and their supporters that day in the form of torrential downpours. We, on the other hand, were tucked away in the comfortable accommodations provided by our host.

Chapter Seventeen

There is nothing so useless as doing efficiently that which should not be done at all.

—Peter Drucker

There were two things I never thought I'd see during my lifetime: the Chicago Cubs win the World Series and an African American elected president of the United States. I'll never forget the Election Day when I watched Barack Obama walk onto stage in Chicago and acknowledge the crowd waiting to celebrate his victory. I couldn't help but reflect on all of the bigotry, violence, and horror I had observed and experienced in my lifetime in both Mississippi and Chicago and the progress I lived through that culminated in the results of that evening. For me, it wasn't about the individual elected, though I certainly thought he was a thoughtful and elegant man, but his election represented a monumental leap forward in the pursuit of the American promise. I also thought that it was a watershed moment in the "politics as usual" of both political parties.

Initially, President Obama's election was widely celebrated and welcomed among my colleagues in the higher education community. That enthusiasm quickly tempered when the Department of Education issued a new set of rules it called its Program Integrity Regulations. There is a process in the federal government called negotiated rule making. Simply put, the government invites negotiators who are representatives of the areas affected by the rules to negotiate the regulations with the agency responsible for issuing and enforcing them. There is a sound logic behind this process because it allows the regulators the opportunity to understand the effects and consequences of the regulations from the sectors of which they have oversight. The objective is to reach agreement on the proposed regulations between the government and the negotiators, and in the past, in higher education, this usually happened.

The Obama administration was deeply concerned, with good reason, about the abuses it perceived perpetrated by profit-making colleges and universities. Historically, proprietary schools had done well in job training and occupational education. However, several large companies, like the University of Phoenix, Capella, Strayer, Kaplan, and a host of others, began offering traditional undergraduate college degrees that had previously been the exclusive purview of traditional nonprofit, public, and private colleges and universities.

The University of Phoenix was among the first and certainly best known of these institutions. When the University of Phoenix first began, it actively recruited adult students supported by tuition reimbursement from major corporations. John Sperling, the university's founder, understood that the idea of a profit-making university would be controversial and took great steps in its formative years to ensure the quality and integrity of its academic programs. He expected attacks from traditional higher education, and he wasn't disappointed.

When the Higher Learning Commission (HLC) extended regional accreditation to the university, it was greeted with much skepticism and concern. Later, other proprietary institutions followed Sperling's lead. These places were marketing machines, grew rapidly, and were enormously profitable. Somewhere along the way, the pursuit of profit began to overwhelm the concern for quality. Some proprietary institutions incentivized recruiters, and consumer protection scandals began to crop up. The TV show *60 Minutes* aired a scathing segment on the fraudulent practices some of these schools engaged in. As the number of these institutions increased, so did the examples of abuse. The failure of ITT Tech, Corinthian Colleges, and Argosy University, among others, created a national scandal, depriving thousands of students of an education and saddling them with billions of dollars of student debt with nothing to show for it.

The Obama administration aggressively set out to impose regulations that would hold these institutions accountable and protect the public and taxpayer interests. Most of the higher education community acknowledged and applauded the intent, but the specific means by which they chose to go about it were ill conceived. The remedies they proposed in many cases were more damaging than the maladies they were designed to cure.

I recall sitting in an ACE board meeting when Terry Hartle, ACE's well-respected vice president for government affairs, laid out the specifics of some of the proposed new rules to an astonished and disbelieving board. They were generally horrible, but we hoped the negotiated rule-making process would provide the usual opportunity for dialogue with the department staff in producing regulations that would support achieving outcomes we all agreed with without damaging the strongest system of higher education in the world.

Unfortunately, the negotiated rule-making process was a disaster. The negotiators from the department concluded that higher education was broken. They had the answer, we were the problem, and they were going to *fix* us. There were several negotiated rule-making committees impaneled, and unlike past years, many of them failed, unable to reach consensus.

The process is designed so that if the department can't achieve agreement, it is free to impose its original set of regulations. Several of these rules were especially troublesome. The fatal flaw in all of the proposals was that it assumed that American higher education was the province of eighteen-year-olds who graduated from high school, attended college full-time for four years, and graduated when they were twenty-two years old. That version of higher education has not existed since the '60s. Higher education now is larger, more diverse, and complicated, with many older students attending part-time. The Department of Education's approach of a one-size-fits-all template assumed a reality that no longer existed for most Americans and most institutions.

One of the regulations set forth was the federal College Scorecard that evaluated colleges based on their four-year graduation rate. That is a reasonable expectation for traditional institutions that only enroll first-time, full-time students out of high school, but what about an older student, working full-time, taking an ambitious two courses per semester? It would take this student ten years to achieve a baccalaureate degree assuming they stayed in school continuously in a 120-credit-hour baccalaureate program.

Most colleges have a mix of both full-time and part-time students. The more part-time students enrolled, the longer the average graduation rate would be. This is a function of the demographics of the student body, not the quality of the institution. Since most college students today are part-time, holding a school accountable for maintaining a four-year graduation rate is unreasonable.

Another regulation was the "credit-hour rule." The department decided that the number of credit hours a college can offer for a course was a function of the "seat time" a student sat in a classroom. For example, in a three-credit course, a student needed to spend three hours a week in a classroom seat. Credit hour is a measure of the quantity of content in the course, not the amount of time a student sits in a classroom.

When I was a student at the University of Illinois, I took a five-credit-hour chemistry course in quantitative analysis. There was a one-hour lecture on Monday, Wednesday, and Friday and two five-hour labs on Tuesday and Thursday. For this five-hour course, I was physically in class for thirteen hours a week. By the department's logic, that should have been a fifteen-credit course.

This rule did not take into account laboratory courses, practicums, internships, independent study, prior learning assessment, asynchronous online courses, research courses, and so on—an array of instructional methodologies where the actual time a student spent mastering materials should not and could not be a function of the credit hours assigned to the course. This was the first time in American higher education that the quantity of the academic content of a course was determined not by the faculties of universities but by the Department of Education in Washington. It made no sense.

Another rule barred all incentive compensation for university employees excluding athletic coaches. Proprietary schools sometimes paid commissions to their admissions counselors to incentivize them to recruit more students. This is a practice that encourages conflicts of interests and is generally prohibited by accrediting bodies and codes of ethics at most colleges and universities. A federal ban makes sense for deceptive recruiting practices, but this rule extended across the board. To authorize payment to a football coach for a winning season while denying an incentive to a Nobel Prize winner or a researcher who produces a breakthrough innovation or someone who secures a major grant from a foundation is a bizarre reversal and juxtaposition of academic values.

The department's rules on "state authorization" also generated issues because of the department's view that consumers were suffering from lax state oversight of online education. This rule required state licensure from institutions offering online courses in the state where the student resided, even if the institution had no physical presence in the state whatsoever. The practical effects of this rule would have been chaotic. If a student at a New Jersey institution had an internship in Washington and took an online course while there, then the New Jersey institution would need to seek licensure in Washington for the student to take the course.

Like many states, New Jersey institutions have students that reside in neighboring states and commute to campus. If a student who lives in Pennsylvania drives across the river to attend a college in New Jersey and takes an online course from that institution, the New Jersey school would need to seek licensure from Pennsylvania because the student lives there, even if the New Jersey school has no physical presence in Pennsylvania. While it makes sense and I have always been an advocate for state licensure and oversight of schools operating with a physical presence within its borders, it makes no sense for a state to regulate the activity of an institution that has no presence within that state.

Some institutions, when faced with the prospect of securing multistate licensure for a small number of students, stopped offering online courses altogether. Some schools attempted to secure licensure in all fifty states and were confronted by fees that exceeded a million dollars. One school's licensure application in Florida was thirty-six inches tall and required the résumés of each member of the school's faculty.

Some consequences of this approach were ridiculous. Berry College— a traditional, reputable private college in Georgia—had a billboard on a highway in Tennessee. It had no students in Tennessee, online or otherwise, but the state of Tennessee demanded that the *presence of the billboard* required the school to be licensed in Tennessee. Many states saw this federal rule as a revenue-generating opportunity from out-of-state institutions. The school in Georgia sued Tennessee, and the state backed off.

The effect of the department's proposed rules stifled the legitimate use of online education to overcome access barriers and reduce costs. Practically every objective study evaluating the value of online education has concluded that the quality of outcomes using this methodology is at least equal and sometimes greater than those achieved by traditional on-campus methods. The irony is that the proprietary schools targeted by the department's regulations were not affected at all. Because of their model, they were already licensed in every state in which they were doing business.

Because of the effect of this rule on adult-serving institutions, I became actively engaged with the department and Congress in an attempt to bring some reason to a regulatory regimen that had gone off the rails. I reached out to my colleagues at Empire State College, University of Maryland University College, Charter Oak College, Colorado State University, and Western Governors University to form a national coalition of public adult-serving institutions in an effort to stop these regulations and to work with the administration and Congress to develop a more thoughtful and rational framework.

I was disappointed by the unresponsiveness of the department's leadership and the Obama administration. They refused to budge even when confronted with overwhelming evidence that their approach would not achieve the reforms they sought and would in fact damage the high-quality public institutions the country needed.

Fortunately, there were two interventions that pulled us back from the brink. First, the cavalry in the form of a joint letter to the White House by the presidents of Columbia, Duke, Harvard, Johns Hopkins, Stanford, the University of California, University of Michigan, University of Pennsylvania, University of Virginia, and Yale finally captured the attention of the administration enough for them to reexamine the regulations. But the real solution was a face-saving fix produced by the regional higher education collaborative led by David Longanecker, who had served with Secretary Riley in the Clinton administration.

Most of the states belonged to a regional higher education compact, and the solution was simple: if a college or university was licensed by a state that was a member of a regional compact, then other states in other compacts would provide reciprocity in their recognition of state licensure. The eventual agreement was called the State Authorization Reciprocity Agreement (SARA).

My colleagues on the New Jersey Presidents' Council requested that I represent them in working with Rochelle Hendricks, New Jersey's first secretary of higher education, to negotiate New Jersey's participation in SARA. I gladly took on the responsibility and succeeded in affiliating New Jersey with a regional compact. SARA was formally launched at an event, and the keynote for the occasion was provided by former secretary Riley. The adversarial relationship between the Department of Education under Arne Duncan and the broader higher education community continued through the remainder of the Obama administration.

The final absurdity was a posting on the department's website that identified twenty-three four-year schools with low costs that led to high incomes. It was a classic illustration where good data entered into an algorithm can sometimes produce wacky results. I was curious to see the institutions highlighted for both their affordability and their quality as defined by the financial success of their alumni. I was dumbfounded by what I saw. The list included Columbia, Dartmouth, Harvard, MIT, Princeton, Stanford, Yale, and so on—the most expensive and selective colleges and universities in the United States! These institutions were identified because the department defined "low costs" by the out-of-pocket expense of the Pell Grant–eligible students. The institutions they identified were all wealthy with large endowments. Therefore, they all provided sufficient financial aid for low-income students. If you were lucky enough and smart enough to get in, they would fund your education, with little, if any, out-of-pocket costs.

These were the most difficult institutions in America to be admitted to. Princeton University, for example, admits about 7 percent of its applicants, and most people don't even apply unless they are at the top of their class. It makes absolutely no sense for the Department of Education to suggest to working-class families that the way to achieve an affordable education for their children is to get them admitted to Harvard, Princeton, or Yale. For the overwhelming majority of people in this country, that is a completely unreasonable expectation. You might as well tell parents to go buy lottery tickets as a higher education financing strategy.

The harm they inflicted in some cases was substantial. Another example is the Parent Plus Loan Program, which was supposed to provide financial assistance for lower-income working-class students. After forbidding the banks from participating in the guaranteed student loan program, the Department of Education became the lender. The eligibility criteria were changed in the fall, which resulted in tens of thousands of students across the country losing their eligibility for student loans just as they were about to start classes.

The almost 7 percent interest rates the government charged posed another limitation, at a time following the Great Recession when mortgage loan rates were between 3 and 4 percent. The student applied to the government, the government granted the loan, and the universities had no input on who received the money, yet the colleges were held accountable for the student's loan repayment. A large number of students who were forced to rely on this program had to drop out, many of whom attended HBCUs. Some of the smaller private schools were destabilized, and more than one had their accreditation threatened for financial reasons.

This was also a difficult period for the associations in Washington that represented higher education's interest with the administration and Congress. The American Council on Education, the national higher education umbrella organization, provided great leadership, particularly under the experienced hand of Terry Hartle, but the Washington higher education establishments that tried to speak with a unified voice found themselves fractured in opposing the Program Integrity Regulations because the department put pressure on AASCU to discourage them from joining ACE in opposing these rules. One of the reasons we formed this coalition of institutions was because we couldn't depend on our association to represent our interests. At least one of the members of our coalition dropped their membership to AASCU in protest.

In our discussions with the department, some of the issues we had within the higher education establishment were driven more by the political dysfunction in Washington than by the merits of the issues. The hostility shown by the Republican Congress to the Obama administration made it very difficult to have a thoughtful policy discussion about much of anything. The Democrats though, rightly concerned about the behavior of proprietary schools, went too far in attacking them, and the Republicans in Congress went too far in defending them.

Those of us in our coalition simply wanted rational oversight and accountability directed at protecting the quality of the academic experience *and* the interests of consumers and taxpayers. The Obama administration perceived that they were protecting the public from predatory practices by proprietary schools, and the Republicans in Congress viewed that they were protecting legitimate businesses from oppressive government overreach. From our point of view, the debate was about what made sense versus what didn't. I have always felt that you'll never get the right answer to the wrong question, and both parties in the government were arguing over the wrong question.

There were simple and rational solutions to the problem. The accreditors and others quietly went to work executing them, but the toxic battle between political philosophies and ideological zealots on both sides threatened to degrade American higher education.

President Obama challenged the nation to regain its position as number one in the world in higher education attainment. There is some debate about where we stand now, but there is general consensus that we are not in the top ten. The National Commission on Higher Education Attainment was chaired by Gordon Gee, who at the time was president of Ohio State University. I was asked to serve as one of the vice chairs. We had excellent staff support and received a lot of information about the current and future demands of our society and its workforce; however, the data were sobering.

The 1970s capped a period of two decades of expansion in higher education, but the consequence of the disinvestment that began in the 1980s has resulted in diminished capacity and increased costs. The implications of this for the country are damaging, yet higher education continues to bear the assault as politicians attack what they can't fund to avoid accountability for the cuts they've made.

The commission issued a report directed to the higher education community urging reform and innovation. I was pleased to see support for a renewed commitment to adult learning, technology-supported education, and prior learning assessment. I suggested a line in the document stating that "a significant impediment in achieving the president's important national goal was the conduct of his own Department of Education." While the entire commission applauded the sentiment, they all suggested that we delete it. I, of course, concurred. I knew the sentence was inflammatory when I suggested it and never expected it to be included in the document, but it felt good to say it.

My advocacy work on Capitol Hill gained the attention of the congressional leadership interested in education on both sides of the aisle. I enjoyed my conversations with Dr. Virginia Foxx, Republican of North Carolina and chair of the House Education Committee, and Congressman Robert "Bobby" Scott, Democrat of Virginia and ranking member of the House Committee on Education. They couldn't be more different. Chairwoman Foxx is White, Republican, and conservative while Ranking Member Scott is African American, Democratic, and progressive, yet in matters of higher education, there was much they had in common.

Dr. Foxx invited me to offer testimony before her committee regarding considerations for the reauthorization of the Higher Education Act. I genuinely believe that she values my opinion, advice, and recommendations. It was also not lost upon me that the optics of having an African American from Chicago provide testimony that would criticize the Obama administration's Department of Education had ancillary benefits for Republicans. Even though I am militantly independent and nonpartisan, I was acutely aware of the politics. I was not going to pick sides, I just wanted the government to do the right thing, but my remarks *were* critical because telling the truth required it.

I was not surprised that my testimony was well received by the chairwoman and her Republican colleagues. When I was finished with the questions from the majority, I prepared myself for the rebuttal from my "Democratic friends," including Chairman Scott and Congressman Holt, my good friend and representative from the Twelfth Congressional District of New Jersey. Normally, when a witness testifies before Congress criticizing the administration, members of the administration's party will defend them in their comments, so I prepared for a line of questioning in defense of the department's actions. To my delight, no such thing happened. It seems that the Democrats were just as frustrated with the

Department of Education as I was. Sometimes congressional testimony can be contentious, but that was not the case this time. I believe the hearing was useful, informative, nonadversarial, and nonpartisan. I left the Hill that day encouraged.

I was later invited back to the Hill to testify before the Senate Health Education Labor and Pensions Committee (HELP), chaired by my old acquaintance Senator Lamar Alexander. The ranking member of the committee was Democratic senator Patty Murray from Washington. Both Senators Alexander and Murray were collegial, and you could tell by the atmospherics and dynamics between the two that the stories I had heard about them working across the aisle in search of common ground were true. However, while not directed at me, this hearing was much more combative.

When Corinthian College, a large national proprietary school, failed, it was a disaster for both the students and the taxpayers who guaranteed their student loans. The chief executive officer from the Accrediting Council for Independent Colleges and Schools (ACICS), the agency that served as the accreditor for Corinthian and other proprietary schools, was also there providing testimony. This institution and its accreditor were the poster children for everything that had gone wrong with proprietary higher education, and the senators were not happy.

Part of me felt sorry for the pummeling this guy received, but it was probably deserved. Government has a difficult time limiting its outrage to the individual offender. It tends to paint with a broad brush, inflicting widespread collateral damage. While this institution and this accreditor had failed, the attacks were broadened to all of accreditation, which was not deserved or justified.

Again, I was invited to testify before the House Education Committee, and as before, it was a wide-ranging and constructive dialogue in exchange of views. I'm greatly appreciative to both Congresswoman Foxx and Congressman Scott and their staffs for the good work we were able to do together. I was reinforced in my belief that even in the dysfunction that is

Washington, DC, honorable people of goodwill from both sides of the aisle still have the capacity to come together in service to the public interest. The possibility that more of that can happen gives me hope for the future. I was forced to oppose the initiatives of a president I desperately wanted to support but couldn't. I cannot overstate my frustration and disappointment in the actions of this administration's Department of Education.

After my long service on the NACIQI, I looked forward to a well-earned and well-deserved break from accreditation work. My respite, however, was short-lived. In 2012, I received a call from my good friend and colleague President Bobby Gitenstein, who, at the time, chaired the Middle States Commission on Higher Education (MSCHE). I had been nominated to serve as a Middle States commissioner, and she was calling to encourage me to accept the position. I did. Accreditation is important work, I had a lot of experience, and after all, I was just going to be one of many commissioners, so it shouldn't be too taxing. At the end of my first year, when Bobby's term expired, I was elected chair of the commission. So much for the break.

Under Bobby's leadership, the commission faced two major challenges. First, it was undergoing a complete reconceptualization and de novo creation of its accrediting standards. Steve Sweeney, former president of the College of New Rochelle (no relation to the New Jersey state senator of the same name), led the Committee on Academic Standards in the development of the new criteria.

The second challenge was restructuring the legal and financial relationship between the Middle States Commission on Higher Education, which accredited colleges and universities, and the broader Middle States Association of Colleges and Schools (MSA), which included K–12 accreditation. Their budgets and funding were intertwined. Because of the peculiar structure of the organization, the parent association had control over our resources and often exercised that control in a way that we found inappropriate.

When the Higher Education Act was amended to require accrediting bodies recognized by the secretary to be "separate and independent" from any third party, that applied to us as well. There had been long-standing negotiations designed to protect the commission's autonomy and independence from intrusions by the larger association, but those discussions had not gone well.

Dr. Gitenstein, her competent and conscientious executive committee, and Dr. Elizabeth Sibolski, the commission's excellent CEO, had moved the ball to the five-yard line on both issues, but we still had considerable work to do to get across the goal. I was pleased that, during my tenure, we achieved appropriate separation and independence from the MSA as required by federal law and, in doing so, resolved the administrative issues between the two organizations. We were also able to adopt new accreditation standards that emphasized learning outcomes, effective board governance, financial accountability, and the quality of the student experience.

As chair, I was involved in several serious and consequential highly publicized accreditation actions. The most unfortunate involved the commission's action in revoking the accreditation of Sojourner Douglas College in Baltimore. Sojourner Douglas was a small, private institution that served adult learners, principally from underserved populations. It was founded when I was at Morgan, and I had great regard for its mission and its president.

Its finances were fragile but stable until it was hit by the Parent Plus Loan debacle. As a consequence, it suffered a sudden and unexpected loss in enrollment that financially destabilized the institution. It was then unable to demonstrate that it had sufficient resources to sustain the effectiveness of its academic offerings. This institution suffered largely because of events over which it had no control. It was a tragic day for the institution. This college was doing good work, and no one wanted to see it fail, but the commission was obligated to take action.

It was a sad day for me as well. I felt especially sympathetic for its president, who had dedicated his entire professional life to building this institution. Loss of accreditation created licensure problems with the state of

Maryland, and it also meant that students attending Sojourner Douglas were no longer eligible to receive federal financial aid. In an attempt to keep its doors open, the college brought a suit against the commission in federal court, and I spent several days in the courtroom and some time on the stand providing testimony in defense of the commission's actions. On the merits, it was not a difficult case to decide, and the commission's actions were sustained. While we won the case, no one took joy in the circumstances.

I am grateful to my colleagues for electing me to three terms as chair. I knew that the end of my presidency at Thomas Edison was approaching, and I declined consideration for a fourth term, though I remained a member of the commission.

After my term as chair concluded but while I was still on the commission, we issued a "show-cause" order as to why the eleven public colleges and universities of the University of Puerto Rico system should not have their accreditation withdrawn. The University of Puerto Rico is a large institution embedded in the economic and academic life of the island. Despite the generous public support for the institution, the revolving door and deeply politicized nature of the university's leadership have been a severe impediment in its ability to achieve its mission.

For many years, the MSA had expressed its concern about the stability and effectiveness of the university's governance and accountability practices. We also became concerned about the effect of the federal oversight board appointed to oversee the island's finances after it became insolvent. Following Hurricane Maria's devastation of the island in 2018, we put our examination on hold to allow time for the island and the university to rebuild and stabilize. After an appropriate time had passed, we resumed our engagement.

Without going into detail, the university's response to our request was unsatisfactory, which triggered a show-cause action. The commission put together a team to visit the university and to make recommendations to the commission as to its disposition of the show-cause order. I was asked to chair the team. It was an exhausting visit that occurred during Super Bowl weekend 2019.

We met with the governor of Puerto Rico, the new president of the university, the staff of the federal oversight committee, and the leadership of each of the eleven campuses. It was clear early on that the show-cause order caught the attention of pretty much everyone on the island. Loss of accreditation would have meant loss of federal funds and the closure of the university, triggering a catastrophe. The university's experienced new president enjoyed the confidence of a new board and new governor. They all understood the gravity of the situation, and we were encouraged by what we heard and optimistic that the calamity of loss of accreditation could be avoided.

I took the liberty and opportunity of having a discussion with the governor about how to break the island's vicious cycle of politicizing the university's governing board and administrative leadership. I made it clear to him that one of the commission's new standards was on governance and oversight and that we would no longer tolerate repetition of past behaviors. We came home, delivered our report and recommendations, and in June 2019, after receiving the required materials from the university, the show-cause order was lifted. However, my hope for the settlement of the broader political issues were crushed when the governor who had made us feel so hopeful was forced from office and resigned. I am indebted to the dedication, talent, and commitment that the team and commission staff demonstrated. The people of Puerto Rico without regard to party deserve better leadership, and I hope they get it.

When Gary Wirt, the commission's chair, was unable to appear before the NACIQI for the renewal of the commission's recognition by the secretary, I was asked to stand in as part of our delegation. After my long tenure on the NACIQI, it was interesting to sit on the other side of the table. I was thrilled to see that the chair was Art Kaiser, who was a member of the NACIQI when I had served. We had an invigorating discussion; the

MSA was well prepared for the review, and we received a reaffirming recommendation without conditions.

While I was a member of the MSCHE, I was also elected to the board of the Council on Higher Education Accreditation (CHEA). CHEA is a nongovernmental voluntary organization of colleges, universities, and accrediting agencies focused on quality assurance and high standards without the compliance emphasis of the NACIQI. My work with the quality assurance community began at Tennessee State and continued throughout my career. Access to and the affordability of higher education have always been important to me, but without an abiding and uncompromising commitment to quality, the academy has no value.

Chapter Eighteen

When they call the roll in the Senate, the Senators do not know whether to answer "Present" or "Not Guilty."

—Theodore Roosevelt

Governor Whitman resigned before the end of her second term to accept appointment as head of the Environmental Protection Agency in the George W. Bush administration. After another New Jersey political circus, we had four different chief executives in seven days. Finally, the former senator and mayor of Edison Jim McGreevey was sworn in as governor. Governor McGreevey resigned from office before the end of his term, and this time, Democrat Dick Codey became acting governor.

McGreevey assembled a small ad hoc group that he called his education cabinet. It included former governor Kean, NJCU president Carlos Hernandez, several others, and me. We did not meet often, but McGreevey enjoyed our public policy discussions. It was also nice to have that kind of personal access to the governor. In 2006, Jon Corzine, a wealthy former Goldman Sachs CEO, was elected governor. In five years, the state had six governors, seven if you include Codey's second round.

Many of us were encouraged by Governor Corzine's election. He had accumulated significant personal wealth from Wall Street and self-funded his campaign. As a consequence, he was not beholden to the various political bosses and organizations that entangled his predecessor and was free to lead and change the political culture of the state. He was public spirited and well intentioned; however, there is a huge difference between running a Wall Street firm and governing a state. He had never worked in state government before, and the skills he'd developed on Wall Street were not transferrable. This deficit was compounded by the inexperience of some of the people he appointed to key positions.

To his credit, he had a great understanding of the state's financial mess, and he immediately recognized the systemic structural problems created by what Karcher had described as "multiple municipal madness." He knew that it was unsustainable and had the courage to say so, complete with charts and graphs; however, like many of his predecessors, he avoided taking on the massive consolidation of local government and public education necessary to solve the problem. Instead, he focused on the state's huge debt, structural deficit, and strategies for dealing with the massive public pension liability. His signature initiative involved refinancing the debt and shifting the debt service to a series of steady long-term increases in highway tolls.

New Jersey's location on a much-traveled corridor between Washington, DC, and New York gave credence to his logic that the bulk of the toll increases would fall more heavily on out-of-state residents passing through than on New Jersey taxpayers. While true, this did not exempt New Jerseyans from their share of the tax burden, and they were not happy. Someone calculated that the tolls would increase by 800 percent over the life of this plan, and the chant "800 percent toll increase" became the tagline for the opposition. While it might have made sense in terms of the state's balance sheet, politically, it was a nonstarter.

Following Governor Corzine's election, he asked that I serve as cochair of his transition committee on higher education. At the time, I was also serving as chair of the New Jersey Presidents' Council. While transition committee reports rarely serve as action plans, they are important in directional tone setting for new administrations. We had a good committee who conscientiously went about their work. We delivered some thoughtful, good advice to the governor-elect as he began his term of office.

Unfortunately, Corzine proved to be quite a problem for higher education. His chief higher education policy adviser had been a staffer for the

Senate Education Committee, and while she was knowledgeable about federal programs and especially financial aid, it was apparent early on that she knew very little about higher education. It was one of the most turbulent times for higher education during the entirety of my presidency.

By the third year of the governor's term, he was in political trouble and suffering in the polls. Meanwhile, Chris Christie, the federal prosecutor for New Jersey, was making major headlines pursuing and convicting scores of New Jersey public officials. In one day, Christie indicted forty-seven people: forty public officials accused of corruption and seven rabbis accused of human organ trafficking. You know you're in a strange place where even the clergy are corrupt. By the time Christie announced his run for governor against Corzine, he had locked up over two hundred public officials.

As a consequence of self-funding, Corzine found himself disconnected from the support of political organizations he needed to get reelected. As the election approached, Corzine's popularity declined while Christie's ascended. Though Christie's odds appeared promising, he did not have a clear path to victory. My old friend from the Kean administration and former Thomas Edison trustee, Chris Daggett, announced that he was running for governor as an independent. You'd be hard-pressed to find someone more qualified for the job. His desire to run for governor stemmed from his frustration with the leadership choices offered to the public from both parties ever since the Kean years. He saw this election as his opportunity.

Chris is a good friend, and I tried to talk him out of it. We discussed it at length on several occasions, but I didn't see any possible way he could win. Nonetheless, he forged ahead and declared his candidacy, performing well in debates and public appearances. His policy positions were both thoughtful and popular, and his support in the polls grew. He performed better than anyone expected. As the election neared, his numbers never quite reached an electable threshold, and a lot his support broke for Christie.

Christie was frustrated by Daggett's campaign because it could have split the vote enough to enable Corzine's reelection. Nevertheless, Christie won. We met for the first time at a television studio where we were both scheduled for unrelated interviews. I, of course, knew who he was, but I was surprised that he knew me. We had a pleasant conversation, and he assured me that he was committed to supporting higher education and looked forward to working with me and the other college presidents in building a higher education agenda for the state.

Christie is talented, astute, and has an ebullient personality. He is a great debater and does not back away from conflict. I got the impression on many occasions that he actually enjoyed it. As he began to assemble his staff, I was pleased to see that he was obtaining advice from Governor Kean, Cary Edwards, and several others who had grown up in the Kean order. As usual, the new governor was immediately faced with a serious financial crisis. He reported that the state's fiscal condition was much worse than the Corzine administration indicated, and the state would be out of cash in ninety days. He announced an across-the-board freeze in state expenditures and new hiring along with a number of other severe austerity measures. In his press conferences, he repeatedly warned the public that his first budget would be painful and unavoidable given the severity of the fiscal crisis.

New governors of New Jersey are inaugurated in January and expected to produce their budget recommendations to the legislature for the fiscal year beginning July 1 in February. This inherent structural problem in New Jersey government puts every new administration in an unreasonable position; nevertheless, it's the way things have always been done. Every governor has been faced with the same challenge, but the Christie administration saw the state's fiscal condition as unprecedented.

The morning of Governor Christie's first budget address, I received a message from Rich Baggar, his chief of staff, who wanted to meet. I was surprised at the timing but thought nothing of it. I had known and worked with Baggar before when he served in the legislature. I walked next door to the statehouse, went to the governor's suite, and was shown in to meet with him. He told me that while it was not in the governor's formal address, the budget proposal to the legislature contained a provision to have Rutgers University absorb Thomas Edison. I think *merged* was the word he used but *absorbed* was more accurate. He wanted to give me advance notice so that I wouldn't be blindsided by the news. Needless to say, blindsided was exactly how I felt. It made no sense to me from a policy, political, or fiscal perspective. I was dumbfounded.

I left the governor's office and walked across the street to where the other public college presidents were gathering for lunch in advance of attending the address. When I shared the news, they were all stunned. No one could figure out why this made any sense. I went back across the street and saw Senator Tom Kean Jr., Governor Kean's son and the Republican minority leader. I told him about my meeting with Baggar. He shook his head and echoed that he was surprised and he didn't understand it either. He looked exasperated.

I sat in the gallery in the assembly chamber and listened as the governor laid out a gruesome fiscal picture and described proposals for massive cost cutting across the board. While I could hear his words, my mind had already left the building. I was trying to figure out how to stop this proposal and save the college that thousands of adult learners depended on for their education.

Fortunately, there were a number of members of the governor's staff that I had known for a long time and had access to. One of them was Wayne Hasenbalg, who was a deputy chief of staff and longtime close associate of Cary Edwards. I needed to find out why this was done and what was behind it before I could make a plan. There was nothing about Rutgers's mission or aspirations that would make this a desirable outcome for them. I spoke to Rutgers president Dick McCormick, and he confirmed my inclination that they were not behind this proposal. Like me, he had been contacted by the governor's office and informed quietly before the public announcement, but he was reluctant to risk offending the governor by opposing it.

While CEOs of large organizations are accountable and responsible for the decisions and actions of their staff, I was certain that Governor Christie was not the author or even aware of the decision his staff made to eliminate Thomas Edison. I was confident that the person behind this proposal was one of the governor's deputy chiefs of staff who managed the budget.

Tactically, I believed from the very beginning that while I needed to criticize the proposal, I should not criticize the governor. We needed to take the high ground and demonstrate that our opposition was rooted in defense of the public interest, not just the college's. Fortunately, I was able to elicit the support of some of the governor's closest advisers, people whose opinion he held in high regard. Among them was former governor Kean, Cary Edwards, and Bill Palatucci, the governor's close friend, law partner, and former member of the Kean administration. Robin Walton and I went on the road in search of allies to support our cause, and the result was gratifying. We were successful in enlisting State Senate President Steve Sweeney, Senate Majority Leader Tom Kean Jr., Assembly Speaker Sheila Oliver, Assembly Minority Leader Jon Bramnick, Senate Education Committee Chair Sandra Cunningham, and Assembly Higher Education Committee Chair Pamela Lampitt. We also received support from the entire Legislative Black Caucus. Even the former chancellor Ted Hollander issued a statement in support of Thomas Edison State College and in opposition to the "merger." I was pleased to discover that no one on either side of the aisle, in either house of the legislature, thought this was a good idea.

Dick McCormick had given me private assurances that they had not been an advocate of this initiative, but I knew that the leadership in his continuing education division were salivating over the prospects of acquiring our rich inventory of high-quality, adult-centered online courses. I thought it important to shore up Rutgers's commitment to either join us in opposing the proposal or at least stay on the sidelines. I requested a private meeting with President McCormick, Reverend William Howard (chair of the Rutgers board), and Reverend J. Stanley Justice (chair of the Thomas Edison State College board).

Former governor McGreevey made a commitment to the African American ministers in the state to place at least one of them on the trustee board of every public college and university. I was fortunate in recruiting Reverend Justice, who at the time was the well-respected and highly regarded pastor of a church in Trenton, and Reverend Howard had been appointed to the Rutgers board as part of this initiative. As a testament to their stature and reputation, both had been elected by their colleagues to chair their respective boards.

It was fortuitous for me. Reverend Justice and I had become close during his service on our board, and Reverend Howard was a personal friend. In fact, he had officiated our wedding when Pam and I got married. Despite our personal relationships, we set about our work in dispassionately reviewing the consequences of the merger proposal and concluded that it was not in the best interest of Rutgers, Thomas Edison, or the people of New Jersey. We also agreed that Rutgers would convey its lack of support to the governor's office. I was curious about how that would be done because Dick's temperament did not lend itself to opposition, especially with the governor. His concern was well founded.

The governor of New Jersey is constitutionally the most powerful governor in the United States, and Governor Christie by nature often didn't take opposition lightly. Chris Christie is a capable and complicated man, and while it is true that his style could be aggressive and combative, the press and the media oversimplified and sometimes caricatured him. In my experience, Christie didn't mind being presented with an opposing point of view as long as he did not perceive it as an attack; however, when provoked, he could be intense.

It is my understanding that when Rutgers's opposition was communicated to the governor's office, it was met with understanding and a request to withhold any public comment. When responding to inquiries as to Rutgers's stance, McCormick was put in the uncomfortable position of reporting that they were "studying the issue." I, on the other hand, was free to comment that we had completed our study and concluded that it was not a good idea. After a couple of weeks, I began to detect that the governor was distancing himself from the proposal. Both from within and outside of the administration, it seemed that efforts were underway to find a quiet and face-saving way to abandon the merger.

New Jersey has a long-standing tradition of last-minute drama before adopting a state budget. Usually the budget is agreed to after marathon negotiations between the governor and the legislature around midnight on June 30. Those of us observing this process never know the composition of the final document until the day of or sometimes several days after it is signed.

The campaign to save the college was a chess game involving multiple complex moves. Fortunately, over the years Robin and I had accumulated a repository of goodwill, high regard, and respect for our work, and we called on every bit of it, traveling hundreds of miles around the state to save our special institution. The recommendation in the governor's original budget eliminated Thomas Edison and its funding. I was relieved when I finally received word that Thomas Edison State College had survived the process, was still in the budget, and would live to fight another day.

Afterward, someone approached me on State Street and congratulated me on "beating Christie." I quickly corrected him. We didn't beat him; we changed his mind. I believe that the real reason we were targeted was part of an elaborate plan of Christie's budget staff to confiscate our substantial cash reserves. The proposal was never meant to be a merger. Rutgers is not capable of continuing our mission, and Thomas Edison State College would have been abolished while Rutgers took over our assets.

My relief that we had saved the college was tempered when I saw the actual budget document. We survived, but not unscathed. The budget that year imposed substantial cuts in state support in practically all areas. The appropriation for the state's public colleges and universities was cut by 12 percent, all except for Thomas Edison. We lost 66 percent of our state operating support. Again, I was stunned. I did not understand why we had received such inequitable treatment. There were some aspects of this that felt personal. I later learned from some of Christie's people that there was an element of truth to that, coming from the architect of the original merger proposal.

I was angry about the cuts, and I felt I was entitled to an explanation. I received one from a member of the governor's staff. I was told that the $3.4 million we lost represented the amount the state subsidized for the facilities we occupied. The rationale was that the state did not provide operating support for the facilities at other colleges, so we weren't entitled to these funds either.

I was livid for a couple of reasons. That statement wasn't true. It is true that the state provided support for two buildings it leased for our use, but the amount of those leases was approximately $1.7 million, not $3.4 million. Also, prior to 1988 every administrative and academic building including the land it occupied at a state college or university had been constructed with 100 percent state funding.

The state of New Jersey, other than these two leases, had not spent one penny in acquiring our facilities, let alone land for us. To suggest that somehow we were being unfairly advantaged when compared to the other schools that all had beautiful multimillion-dollar campuses was idiotic. What's more, the state budget people knew that the leases were $1.7 million not only because they paid the bill but also because they provided us with the figures for our audit report, so even if you accepted their logic, the amount of the cut should have been half of what it was. Fortunately, the college was growing, and we had sufficient tuition income to manage the loss in appropriated dollars, but I had no intention, as a matter of principle, of letting this go unanswered.

I went back to Rich Baggar to protest the injustice. His response was straightforward and honest. He told me the state was broke, and in dealing with the fiscal crisis, this budget contained a lot of things that would have been done differently if there was more time and information. They did the best they could under the circumstances, and it was going to take time to sort through it all. But the bottom line was that there was no money, so anything that required additional resources would need to be addressed later.

I wasn't happy, but I understood and accepted his response with one exception. If the state was taking our money to pay for the leases on our buildings, then at least they could give us the money and turn the leases back over to us so that we could control our own buildings like all the other colleges did. It was revenue neutral and did not require one penny of new state money. We wanted control of our own facilities and the money they took away from us to pay for them. He paused in reflection and said he would get back to me.

I continued to press Rich on the matter, which was easy to do given that he often had to walk by my office on State Street to get to his. I was not above buttonholing him on the sidewalk. Soon after, Baggar announced his departure from the governor's office to return to his job as an executive in a pharmaceutical company. I was invited to his going-away reception and even there pressed him on responding. He told me that he would have to take it up with the person in charge of this area, who also happened to be the original author of the merger proposal. I immediately understood the nature of the problem.

Rich left before solving the issue, but I took it up immediately with his successor, Kevin O'Dowd. O'Dowd had a more direct style. He listened to the case I made, looked at the figures I gave him and the audit reports, and said he would get back to me. Kevin followed up on several occasions with questions from his deputy chief of staff who was behind the whole thing.

Finally, in frustration, he asked if I would be willing to meet in person with him and the deputy chief of staff. I told him I would be delighted. The meeting occurred, and I was well prepared. The data was irrefutable. It turned out that the staffer didn't want the buildings under the college's control because he wanted them for state use. The whole premise of what I had been told was a lie. Kevin's face turned red with embarrassment. I was outraged, and it showed. When I walked out of the office, O'Dowd stopped me in the hallway and asked me to be patient. He told me he felt confident that the matter would be resolved.

True to his word, in the next budget, $1.7 million was transferred from the Department of Treasury to Thomas Edison State College, and we were able to negotiate a transfer of the leases from the state to the college. For the first time in the school's history, we had direct control of our buildings. We were no longer a tenant on our own campus. I still felt that the state owed us the difference between what we were cut and the reductions received by the other institutions, but acknowledging that the state was teetering on insolvency, I knew I had to save that fight for another day. Yet finally gaining control of our campus was a major step forward.

After the merger fight and before Rich departed, I got another call from him requesting a meeting. In light of the first call, I wondered if I should come "packing." His secretary laughed and said she didn't think so. Rich informed me that the governor planned to assemble a small but select group to assess the status of higher education in New Jersey to make recommendations to inform his higher education agenda. He further indicated that both Governors Whitman and Kean suggested that I be asked to participate as a member of the group. The commission would be chaired by former governor Kean. The other members were Robert Campbell, vice chairman at Johnson & Johnson and former chair of the board of the Robert Wood Johnson Foundation; John McGoldrick, chair of Zimmer Holdings, Inc., and retired executive vice president and general counsel at Bristol Myers Squibb; and Dr. Margaret (Peggi) Howard, retired vice president of Drew University and former senior policy adviser to Kean when he was governor. It was distinguished company to be in, and I looked forward to serving. I was told to expect a formal invitation from the governor to attend a press conference announcing the formation of the group and explaining its charge.

Part of Christie's campaign platform was to reinvigorate higher education, which had been largely neglected by every governor since Kean. The governor reinforced his commitment by attending the New Jersey

Presidents' Council to show his interest and support for higher education. We were initially assigned staff support out of the governor's office but ended up relying predominately on the work of Mike Klein, who at the time was executive director of the New Jersey Association of State Colleges and Universities. We expected that our report would be influential in shaping the direction of higher education. Each member of the commission took their assignments seriously and invested a great deal of time and energy into this project.

We provided data that clearly documented New Jersey's historic lack of support for higher education when compared with other states and set forth criteria for a new rational basis for funding the state's colleges and universities, which reinforced and respected the mission differentiation and diversity of our institutions. We urged the governor and the legislature to support a much-needed higher education bond issue to fund the construction and upgrading of facilities at our campuses. Whereas most states have annual capital budgets to support higher education, New Jersey had not had a higher education bond issue since 1988, putting us dead last in the fifty states for capital support. Finally, we recommended that the Robert Wood Johnson School of Medicine, a part of the University of Medicine and Dentistry in New Brunswick, be made a part of Rutgers University. This was the higher education merger that made sense and had long been coveted by Rutgers and especially President McCormick.

We recommended the appointment of another commission specifically to examine the complicated issue of medical education in the state and its relationship to New Jersey's hospital and health care institutions. Governor McGreevey appointed a similar commission chaired by former Merck CEO Roy Vagelos. That commission made some controversial recommendations concerning a major restructuring of higher education, but they never gained traction.

We issued our report on December 1, 2010. It was well received by the governor and applauded by the higher education community and the legislative leadership of both parties. The fifty-four members of the New Jersey Presidents' Council unanimously endorsed the commission's report and recommendations. It was one of the finest pieces of work I have ever been associated with, and the friendships I developed with the commission members have lasted to this day.

Our recommendation for increasing operating support from the state never happened because New Jersey was still broke. The committee who studied medical education reinforced our advice, but when the commission's recommendations were considered by the legislature, they were greatly modified. The University of Medicine and Dentistry was merged into Rutgers University. UMDNJ's two-year allopathic medical school and osteopathic medical school in South Jersey became parts of Rowan University. The final outcome had not been recommended by either of the commissions but instead was shaped by broader economic interests and the political forces in the state.

The final recommendation resulted in the $750 million Building Our Future Bond Act, which was passed by the legislature and approved by the voters. While we recommended that the bond issue trigger annual capital support for higher education, the state's fiscal condition and debt rating have kept that from happening. It took twenty-four years from the enactment of the 1988 bond issue to the passage of the Building Our Future Bond Act. I fear it may be another twenty-four years until the next one.

The Building Our Future Bond Act was another example of the voluntary interinstitutional cooperation we had through the New Jersey Presidents' Council. We started advocating for it during the McGreevey administration. The need was great, and all the state presidents came together to advance the initiative. That is not unusual. What was unique about this was the level of consensus among the presidents around the size of the bond issue, the allocation among sectors, and even the designation of individual projects by campus.

A driving force behind this project was the vigorous leadership of President Susan Cole of Montclair University. The diplomatic skills of President Bobby Gitenstein in her role as the great compromiser and the special contribution of John Petillo, who was CEO of UMDNJ at the time of the initial proposal, were instrumental in securing the unanimous support of the presidents' council.

The original proposal passed through the remainder of the McGreevey and Corzine administrations, and the presidents' determined advocacy kept the momentum building for over a decade toward the eventual successful bond issue recommended by the Kean Commission and implemented during the Christie administration. Democratic Senate President Steve Sweeney was also an important advocate in securing legislative approval, and the state's building and construction trade unions' support was helpful in winning the approval of the voters. We achieved a level of unanimity that I don't think would have been possible in any other state. I'm not sure it could happen again today in New Jersey either.

Chapter Nineteen

Not everything that is faced can be changed; but nothing can be changed until it is faced.

—James Baldwin

The year 2012 marked the end of our current five-year strategic plan. Many college and university long-range plans are generalized collections of platitudes and clichés that don't provide the institution with any specific direction or agenda for the future. You can't build anything without a plan, and every day, we worked on building an institution that did not yet exist.

I never worried about being fired. My biggest fear was that I would become seduced by inertia and routine. I had seen it happen to other presidents, and I didn't want it to happen to me. I frequently advise younger presidents to find a way to know when it's time to leave. I always thought an aggressive, aspirational, and transformative strategic plan was the perfect test to ensure we were still relevant. Good plans refresh old practices and purge obsolete and irrelevant operations, structures, and programs. They assure agility with response to contemporary conditions, effectively anticipating the institution's evolution.

The institution I led in 2012 was radically different than the one I found in 1982. Through each iteration, we actively planned for transformation. By assessing our strengths, we could determine how to build on them and grow. We made decisions about our future capacity and designed a plan to acquire additional facilities space within an economic model that provided financial stability and growth in a state that was not likely to offer adequate support.

I was proud of Thomas Edison State College in 2012, and I knew that thirty years was a remarkably long time to be president of a public college anywhere but especially in New Jersey. I had not felt any atrophy in my energy or enthusiasm for our work, and I didn't think that my faculties had deserted me yet.

I greatly admired President Theodore Hesburgh, who transformed Notre Dame with visionary leadership for thirty-five years. I felt that was a good target by which to call it a day, so I assembled the team for one last bold, ambitious, and aspirational five-year plan. I didn't want to coast across the finish line; I wanted the pedal on the floor.

Usually presidents don't give their teams five years' notice. You don't want to become a lame duck, and sometimes people will leave. I shared that this five-year plan would be my last with my cabinet and my office staff and told them I hoped they would stay with me until the end. I was aware of the risk I was asking of them. I remembered how I wanted to get out of Tennessee State before Fred Humphries left, and I could understand if my team felt the same way, but everyone agreed to see it through.

This final plan had three principal objectives: meet the state's criteria to achieve university status, receive approval to offer our first doctoral program (Doctor of Nursing Practice [DNP]), and execute a facilities master plan. We wanted to ensure excess capacity so that we would have enough room to accommodate our growth and expansion without acquiring additional brick-and-mortar overhead expenses.

There were other aspects of the plan that included strengthening our five academic schools, offering a master's program in cybersecurity and creating a plan for our second doctoral program, Doctor of Business Administration (DBA). We also wanted to ensure our technology infrastructure was current and achieve improvements in both the business-processing and course-development divisions. We were committed to doing all of these things without expecting any significant increase in our state appropriations. Finally, we had to prepare for and undergo a successful MSA reaffirmation of our accreditation. If we could get all of those things done, I could leave a strong, high-quality, financially secure institution wrapped in a bow for my successor.

In September 2012, I presented our new five-year plan to our board of trustees for their consideration and approval. One of the hallmarks of any good strategic plan is the delineation of specific and measurable outcomes by which the board can hold the institution and its president accountable. Many plans I've seen simply set forth the things that were going to happen anyway in the normal course of business whether you had a plan or not. In all of our plans, we took risk, and this was no exception. Good boards don't punish executives for pushing the envelope. It's better to overreach and fall short than just roll with operational inertia. I shared with the board that I expected to relinquish my presidency when this plan had run its course. After deliberation, the board adopted the plan, and we were off and running.

Acquiring university status and establishing the doctoral program were related. The DNP was a logical and reasonable next step for our school of nursing. The dean of our business school felt that, in building on the success of our MBA program, a DBA could be ready soon after the DNP, for which planning had begun much earlier. We petitioned the Office of the Secretary of Higher Education for university status and received approval in 2015. The DNP was authorized in 2016.

Acquiring and building out the elements of the facilities master plan would be more fluid given the constant jousting with state government. I often found myself in the position of explaining and justifying why a university that didn't have on-site classes and classrooms needed a physical campus. We still had all the management and professional support staff requirements of a traditional institution. We had about 350 full-time employees managing about 575 dispersed faculty mentors and the educational activity of 16,000 students.

Governor Byrnes's staff promised us the historic townhouses adjacent to the Kelsey Building as we grew, but we were forced to relitigate the matter with Governor Kean's staff. Luckily, they agreed to honor the prior

commitment. We secured the funds for the project before the Kean administration left office but lost the money when the Florio administration
came in. We were able to get it back later in the Florio administration but
didn't get the project completed until the middle of the Whitman administration. By the time the project was finished, we had already outgrown
the facility. We persuaded the state to lease a building for our use a block
away in a distressed community, but by the time the facility was made
ready and we were finally permitted to move in, we had outgrown that one
as well.

In the beginning of the McGreevey administration, we convinced the
state to construct a campus facilities master plan with us that anticipated
future growth. We agreed on spatial standards and some predictable funding to support the plan. Our capital requirements were modest and
doable in spite of the state's ongoing and continuous budgetary pressures.
We agreed that the state would erect a 35,000-square-foot building including a forty-car, in-building parking garage through a long-term lease/
purchase. This would be the first structure we had ever had built from the
ground up for our use. But nothing is ever easy.

We were originally approached by the city of Trenton to acquire the historic mansion of Ferdinand Roebling on West State Street and to incor-
porate its restoration into our new 35,000-square-foot facility. The mansion
was in severe disrepair and was in danger of collapsing. The city did not
have the resources to restore the historic property and thought we might
take it on as our new location. We were glad to cooperate because it supported my belief in preserving and restoring what is left of Trenton's rich
heritage.

Often the lack of cooperation between multiple government jurisdic-
tions in Trenton generated frustrating impediments. The city had given
development rights of the property to a local businessman. While the state
was willing to support the college in this effort, the city, the state, and
the developer could never come to agreement on the terms, conditions,
price, and financing. Eventually, the state chamber of commerce stepped

forward and agreed to restore and build on the property. Ironically, the same difficulties that prevented us from redeveloping the Roebling Mansion also blocked the state chamber's plans. Fortunately, the New Jersey League of Municipalities successfully implemented the project. I was happy that the preservation was going to take place regardless of who got it done. With that out of the way, we agreed on another site on the same street as our other state-leased building. Though it too was constructed in the same distressed area, we began to see the possibility for us to serve as anchor tenants in the revitalization of a blighted neighborhood.

Trenton, in addition to being the state capital, is also the county seat of Mercer County. I never understood why the city, the county, and the state had individually and collectively allowed Trenton to deteriorate as it had. Fortunately for us, John McCormac was Governor McGreevey's state treasurer. McCormac was a competent and visionary leader in his own right, and working with his office was refreshing. He and his chief of staff, Carol Erhlich, saw the potential for the state and the college to work together to invest in the city. The building we named Canal Banks would not have been possible without their support and cooperation.

The other part of the plan was the acquisition of the Kuser Mansion, one of the last remaining grand residences on the Delaware River side of West State Street, built by one of Trenton's most important families. It had been acquired by the state during the Florio administration to house the secretary of state's office although that didn't last long. The secretary of state moved back into the capitol building, leaving the mansion abandoned. With Treasurer McCormac's support, $300,000 was included in the governor's budget for the state to acquire the mansion for our use.

One advantage of being in a distressed city is that property is inexpensive, but once again nothing in state government moves in a straight line. Even though the funds had been appropriated and approved in the budget, Governor Corzine canceled the project when he took office. I was furious. No other college or university in the state had to deal with the impediments and obstacles inherent in doing business with state government like we did. It was beyond frustrating. We needed the space afforded by the Kuser Mansion, and we did not want to see another property boarded up on State Street. We raised the funds to acquire and renovate the property on our own. No one from the state had anything to do with it and had in fact done everything they could to get in the way.

Throughout my tenure in Trenton, there were always collaborations between business owners in the city trying to develop some momentum amid the fits and starts of state and local government. The only requirement necessary to hold public office is the ability to get more votes than your opponent. That's it. You don't have to have talent, vision, ability, or integrity. Just get one more vote than your opponent, and you have all the qualifications you need.

There was no better example of this than Trenton mayor Tony Mack. In a city of 85,000 people, he had been elected with about 7,000 votes. I have always been committed to the notion that a university has an obligation to the stewardship of the community in which it resides. As a corporate citizen, we don't get to choose who the mayors are, but we do need to work with them.

One of the positive things Mayor Mack did was to appoint an economic development advisory committee comprising important business leaders in the city. It was the right group of people to have around the table, and we did the best we could to support economic revitalization.

At one of its meetings, the discussion turned to the status of Glen Cairn Arms. Glen Cairn Arms was an abandoned, 1920s-era apartment complex at the foot of the Calhoun Street Bridge crossing the Delaware River from Trenton to Pennsylvania. For over twenty years, it sat boarded up and blighted, an eyesore at the capital's gateway. Various administrations had made attempts to find a developer by providing incentives to put the land to better use, all without success.

There are certain properties that private-sector investors avoid for various reasons. In this case, the building that occupied the entire 8/10-of-an-acre footprint of the land was contaminated with lead and asbestos with no vehicular access. The demolition and site remediation costs alone would be $1.5 million. No private investor would touch it. A public-sector entity would be its only hope.

We had a particular interest in that the structure was next door to the Kuser Mansion. By now, the higher education community was in active discussions with the legislature and administration about the higher education bond issue. I indicated that if the city would turn the property over to us, we would take responsibility for raising the $1.5 million to demolish the building and remediate the site. If we were successful in receiving support from the bond initiative, we would make the site the location of our new nursing education center. I was confident that we could find the $1.5 million. Even if we didn't get the bond support for the new building, simply landscaping the property would preserve it for future use and protect the value of the Kuser Mansion next door.

The city's housing and economic development director and the mayor were both overjoyed with this proposal. The mayor was desperate for a win for his administration, and he was particularly excited about achieving something that his predecessor had been unable to do.

Not long after we had secured our board's approval to proceed, I was called to a meeting in city hall with the business administrator. Rumors were circulating about a grand jury investigation of the mayor. The business administrator was a hardworking, conscientious gentleman doing his best to cope with the situation. He informed me that he could not give us the property and that we would need to purchase it for $300,000. I was taken aback. I explained to him that while I could justify spending the money to remediate a property that we owned, I didn't know how I could purchase a property that was appraised in negative numbers. As a public entity, I felt legally and ethically prohibited from buying something at a price that could not be justified by the property's appraised value.

By this time, the prospects of having a bond issue looked promising, and I advised the business administrator that there were an abundance of properties readily available to me at no cost. I literally had people stopping me on the street offering me their land just to get rid of the tax burden. I further reminded him that we had agreed to take this extraordinary burden on to support the city. I did not agree with his terms and left the meeting.

He called me afterward and candidly explained that they had a $300,000 budget problem and no other solution. I didn't want a multimillion-dollar project to fall through over $300,000. There were already complaints from a member of city council who didn't want us to move forward with the project because, as a state entity, we didn't pay property taxes. That logic was spurious to me in that the property had been vacant for over two decades with no prospects that it would ever generate a penny in tax revenues. I suggested that we pay the city $300,000 not as a purchase price but as a fee to mitigate any potential lost property tax revenue. The lawyers approved it, and we proceeded to start the paperwork.

The mayor was eager to announce his achievement and, against our advice, issued a public statement prior to consulting with city council. Because the property was owned by the city, the council would have to approve its transfer, but they were irate that the mayor had not consulted them. There was also a small but vocal group of community activists who were prepared to oppose anything the mayor supported.

The rest of the community looked on in disbelief as the opposition gained traction. We were feeling more confident that the bond act would pass, and so we had the architect sketch a rendering of what the building and site could look like. As I watched the rancor between the mayor and the city council increase, I privately met with each member of the council, showed them the renderings, and shared the appraisals of the property, the site report documenting the contamination, and the estimates we had received for the demolition and site remediation.

Six of the seven council members understood the value and importance of the project. Five of them pledged their support. One ignored the figures and the appraisal and insisted that we give the city more money. This councilmember couldn't wrap her head around the fact that the price paid was related to the property's value and not the price the buyer could afford to pay. We agreed to disagree. The remaining member who did not agree to support the project understood the value but opposed it solely because the mayor supported it, without regard to the benefits of the city or its residents.

The council held several hearings on the matter, and the support from the community overwhelmed the irrational rantings of the four or five people attacking me, the mayor, the business community, and anybody else who disagreed with them. At the end of the day, the council approved the project by a vote of five to two. Mayor Mack was later indicted, convicted, and sent to federal prison for bribery. It should not have been that complicated or taken that much time, but this is New Jersey.

The architect John Hatch, who designed Glen Cairn Hall, did a magnificent job. I asked him to design the new building reminiscent of the historic mansions that once graced West State Street. His creation exceeded all my expectations. Not only was it an energy-efficient, modern marvel complete with a ninety-five-car parking garage and green space; it perfectly complemented the historic elegance and beauty of the Kuser Mansion and the Kelsey Building Complex.

The Building our Future Bond Act enabled us to complete this project and to make an additional investment in restoring the Kuser Mansion. We named the nursing education center Glen Cairn Hall in recognition of the two former properties that had previously occupied the space. Hatch preserved the original entrance from the old building and incorporated it into the design on the first floor of the new building. We also asked Sally Lane, Trenton native and local historian, who served as our director of special projects, to complete a historical exhibition, which was displayed adjacent to the former entryway. Thomas Edison State University was now able to provide, with two of our most elegant facilities, a scenic and impressive entrance into the city and capitol complex from Route 29 and the Calhoun Street Bridge.

We were also able to acquire and renovate another historic building across the street from the Kelsey Building Complex to house the Center for Learning and Technology, our expert technology-supported course design staff. Pursuant to my recommendation, in 2018 the board of trustees named the center the W. J. Seaton Center for Learning and Technology, a fitting acknowledgment for our long-serving provost and one of the founders of distance education.

We had grown from a small, experimental college with three thousand students occupying four floors of a five-story building to one of the largest universities in the state with an elegant eight-building campus bracketing the historic New Jersey statehouse. We had also finally secured ownership and control over our entire campus and created excess capacity for future expansion with the lowest facility cost when compared to our revenues of any college or university in the state.

I had nothing to do with the design of the building, but I did make one minor personal request. I knew at the end of my presidency I had an emeritus appointment awaiting me that included an office in the building. I requested a balcony overlooking the Delaware River, if possible. I remember watching *Boston Legal*, with William Shatner, who played the character Denny Crane. At the end of every episode, Shatner's character and a colleague finished their workday by sharing a glass of scotch on the office balcony. I thought that might be something I'd like to do as well.

When I was shown the Emeritus Suite that had been designed for my use, I was blown away. It not only had the balcony I requested, but it was beautifully designed and appointed. I was reminded of Roger Sublett's words; it was certainly "a hospitable place for disciplined reflection." I couldn't be more pleased, grateful, and humbled than the following year when the board of trustees renamed and dedicated the building George A. Pruitt Hall.

In that we had planned for everything else, I also gave considerable thought to how to be a good former president. I knew that I was incapable of retirement in the traditional sense and that I wanted to keep working as long as I thought I had something to contribute and my health, both physical and otherwise, remained intact. I had witnessed other presidents successfully transition out of the role and still maintain usefulness to their institutions. I had also watched a few of my friends who didn't know how to let go become a pain in the sides of their successors by meddling in the affairs of the campus. I was committed to not doing that.

I spoke with a number of my friends who had successfully made that transition: Bill Maxwell, Herman James, Harold Shapiro at Princeton University, Jim Votruba at Northern Kentucky University, and Dick McCormick. They were relaxed, happy, fulfilled by their work, and content. I wanted to model after them. I also admired the "retirement" of my friend and mentor Jim Fisher. He was engaged and productive but had the luxury of only doing work that he wanted to do, turning down projects that he didn't.

I have always been grateful for the mentoring I received from Jim Fisher and Buzz Shaw and have learned a great deal from Fred Humphries. I have spent much of my career trying to pay it forward for the benefit of others coming behind me. There is nothing I enjoy more than the mentoring work I have informally engaged in with other presidents and higher education officers. I enjoyed my mentoring role in the Kellogg Foundation Fellowship Program and in AASCU's Millennium Leadership Initiative, in which I was charter sponsor, and I believed that I had something to contribute in this area.

I was also concerned about what I had observed as the deterioration of the leadership capacity in many who are now occupying the American college and university presidency. I wanted to identify proficient executives who had *it* and help develop them into effective leaders by offering a Senior Executive Higher Education master class. Since my days as a doctoral student, I have been intrigued by the attributes that differentiate effective presidents from others. In order to recognize an effective president when you see one, I developed the following definition: "An effective presidency occurs when an individual assumes office, creates and articulates a vision and coherent agenda for advancing the institution in fulfilling its mission, successfully executes that agenda, and achieves recognizable and measurable progress. After accomplishing these results, they leave under their own terms, usually after at least seven to ten years in office, with the institution in demonstrably better and stronger condition than when they arrived."

In 2017, the American Council on Education published a study indicating that the average tenure for a college or university president in the United States is six years. By this measure, the majority of college presidents are not effective. While the challenges of the office have increased, the capacity of those serving has not kept pace. As a result, turnover among presidents has increased with the attendant disruption and destabilization of continuity on our campuses. I believe from years of observation and consideration of research that effective presidents possess the following attributes: vision, emotional intelligence, willingness to provoke, intellectual talent, strong values, high standards, experience, excellent communication and interpersonal skills, and a demonstrated capacity to execute.

There are many leadership-development programs out there, and the libraries have been filled with books written by those who have studied leadership. However, there are few places where practitioners spend quality personal time with an experienced and tested president. I have accumulated over fifty years of leadership experience, thirty-five of them as president in the trenches in one of the most challenging political environments in the country. I've learned a lot, and my calling now is to transfer that knowledge and the lessons from that experience to those coming behind me. Consequently, as the end of my presidency neared, the board of trustees created the Center for Leadership and Governance as a platform for my post-presidency initiatives.

Leaving a "bow" on an institution is a tricky thing because the damn thing keeps moving. Near the end, we had some challenges. The legislature, in its infinite wisdom, decided that members of the National Guard should be able to attend public colleges and universities without paying tuition, which is a wonderful thing to do and a great headline to have during a campaign, but they conveniently forgot to provide any funding for their generosity. It's not an unusual thing for politicians to do. It's another case where they gave a benefit without paying for it. I've always felt that if it was important enough to do, it was important enough to pay for. But who cares about that?

Because we were the most military-friendly school in the state, we enjoyed the highest enrollment of guardsman among all of our colleague institutions. It was an immediate million-dollar loss in tuition revenues. It took some brilliant work by Robin Walton for the legislature to award us an appropriation to compensate us for our loss.

I accomplished my goal of finishing strong, with all of the major objectives outlined in the plan achieved: applications for new enrollment were up, the National Guard tuition waiver program was funded, and the prospects for additional new funding from the legislature was on the horizon. I finally felt that I had tied the bow on the box.

Harry S. Truman said, "I always remember an epitaph which is in the cemetery at Tombstone, Arizona. It says, 'Here lies Jack Williams. He done his damnedest.' I think that is the greatest epitaph a man can have—when he gives everything that is in him to do the job he has before him. That is all you can ask of him and that is what I have tried to do."

I have been fortunate and blessed with the people and opportunities that have crossed my path, and I have never taken any of it for granted. From childhood, I have always been impressed by how precious and finite life is. The purpose of life is the living of it, striving to leave things better than you found them. When you can, pay it forward.

On June 1, 2017, I sent the following letter to the board of trustees:

"To everything there is a season." On December 1st of this year, I will have had the privilege of serving as President of Thomas Edison State University for 35 years. The quality of our academic work is exemplary. We have extended our degree offerings to the doctoral level, and achieved University status. Our learner services are excellent and our financial condition is strong. We have successfully completed our capital master plan. For the first time, our facilities are both adequate and appropriate for the students and educators they support, and the campus we have built has changed the face of Trenton's capital district. We are nearing the end of the current strategic plan, and next year we will need to engage in the process of articulating the vision, strategies, and outcomes that will guide the future direction of the University.

For these reasons, I believe that this is an appropriate time for a transition to new leadership. Accordingly, it is my request and intention to relinquish the presidency of the University effective midnight, December 31, 2017, or whenever my successor can be identified and assume office; whichever is later.

Having the honor of serving this wonderful University as its President has been the single greatest privilege of my professional life. I have no words to express my appreciation to the Trustees, past and present, as well as to my colleagues who have joined in the work of transforming the lives of the extraordinary students we have been given the responsibility of serving. I am eternally grateful for the support, cooperation, assistance, and kindness I have received from so many along the way. Thank you from the bottom of my heart.

I have always my lived my life with a sense of urgency and purpose. I have committed myself to social justice and the self-empowerment of others, and my greatest joy has been the love I've shared with friends, family, and colleagues. Like President Truman, I take my hat off to Jack Williams; he done his damnedest, and so have I.

Acknowledgments

What do you do with the lessons and experiences of a lifetime? You pass them on in the hope that they are useful to those who follow, but for a story to be told, it should be worth telling. My good friend and predecessor Lorraine Matusak would always ask the "so what?" question. Why does it matter? There is no question that I have been blessed with an abundance of experiences—the good, the bad, and the ugly—and I hope that passing on what I have learned is useful and instructive, or at least, interesting. I'm particularly grateful to my friend Buzz Shaw and my cousin Beverly Guy-Shefthall, both noted authors, and my friend Jeremy Abbate, publishing director of Scientific American Worldview, who convinced me that this book might have value, and to my colleagues at Rutgers University Press for agreeing with them. I would also like to thank Fred Humphries, Barbara Murrell, and Sterlin Adams for fact-checking the description of our shared adventure at Tennessee State University.

I want to thank my wife, Pamela; my daughter, Shayla, and her partner, Ricardo; my grandsons, Landon and Rylan; and my brother, Joe, for their love and support. No one's odyssey is taken alone, and mine has been shaped, pushed, and influenced by countless others: my family, friends, colleagues, mentors, role models, and, even on occasion, adversaries. I have acknowledged many of these individuals throughout the book as their stories have interwoven with mine, but this story would have been very different without the mentorship of my dear friends James L. Fisher, Kenneth A. "Buzz" Shaw, and Paul Wisdom, who saw something in me before I saw it myself. I would also like to thank my oldest friends Eugene Adams, Andrita and Rodney Hammond, Linda Locke, John Townsend, Clarke Williams, and the Watsons: John S., Bonnie, Bill, Jay, and Tim, and their spouses and children, who adopted me into their family. Finally, I want to thank Melissa Maszczak for her energy, ability, and sharp pen, which made the writing of this book both possible and fun. To so many in my life, thank you for letting me love you, and for those who have, thank you for loving me back.

Index

Note: Numbers in *italics* denote photographs in the photo gallery that begins after page 106.

About the Authors

George A. Pruitt is president emeritus and board distinguished fellow at Thomas Edison State University. Identified as one of the country's most effective college presidents funded by the Exxon Education Foundation, he is the recipient of numerous awards, honors, and commendations (including six honorary degrees) and has consulted widely in higher education, business, and government. His stewardship and service led to his appointment in an advisory capacity to five secretaries of education under three U.S. presidents of both parties.

Melissa A. Maszczak serves as senior fellow and director of the Center for Leadership and Governance at Thomas Edison State University.